THE CASE FOR THE
CENTRAL POWERS

THE CASE FOR THE CENTRAL POWERS

AN IMPEACHMENT OF THE VERSAILLES VERDICT

BY

COUNT MAX MONTGELAS

CO-EDITOR OF THE GERMAN DOCUMENTS RELATING TO
THE OUTBREAK OF WAR (SO-CALLED
KAUTSKY DOCUMENTS)

TRANSLATED BY
CONSTANCE VESEY

NEW YORK
ALFRED · A · KNOPF
MCMXXV

Printed in Great Britain

PREFACE

THE German edition of this book was published in 1923 under the title of *Leitfaden Zur Kriegsschuldfrage*. It was intended, as the title indicates, to serve as a guide to the question of responsibility for the war of 1914–1918, and deals with all the evidence at the author's disposal at that time. It will be seen, however, that the conclusion he drew from this evidence, based chiefly on official documents, was that Germany and Austria-Hungary were less to blame than the Entente Powers, by whom they were formally condemned at Versailles. Consequently, the title given to the English translation may fairly be considered appropriate. It was, in fact, selected by the author himself from amongst those submitted to him.

It is no part of the translator's task to discuss the points raised ; it need therefore only be said here that few men are better qualified to present the case for the Central Powers than Count Max Montgelas, who was not only entrusted with the work of editing the German documents relating to the outbreak of the war, jointly with Kautsky and Professor Walther Schücking, but was a member of the Commission sent to Versailles by the German Government in 1919, specially to investigate the question of responsibility for the war. He was one of the four signatories to the memorandum, presented on May 29, 1919, in reply to the allegations made by the Commission appointed by the Allied and Associated Governments to report on the subject, and, in the absence of the other members of the German Commission, was jointly responsible, with Delbrück, for a further memorandum, replying to the Allied Note of June 16, 1919.

The Count was born in 1860 in St. Petersburg, where his father was the Bavarian Minister. He joined the army in 1879, served in the Boxer Expedition, and was military attaché in Peking from 1901 to 1902. In 1914 he commanded the 4th Bavarian Infantry Division, but he retired in 1915, and has devoted himself, since 1918, to careful study of the matters on which he writes, acting also as official adviser to the Reichstag Committee of Enquiry.

Care has been taken, in translating the work, to verify the quotations from official and other documents, and to give the English official translations wherever possible. The latter are chiefly taken from the collection of Diplomatic Documents relating to the outbreak of war published by the Foreign Office. An exception has been made in the case of the telegrams exchanged between the Tsar and the Emperor William, which are given in the original English in the German documents to which reference is made.

Where English translations exist of the various publications referred to in the footnotes, the titles are given in the bibliography appended to this translation.

THE TRANSLATOR.

CONTENTS

7

PART III

THE CRISIS

CONTENTS 9

PART IV

INCIDENTS OF THE CRISIS

PART V

APPENDICES

SUPPLEMENTS

PART I

THE INDICTMENT

1. The Versailles Verdict.

What Bismarck had said as to a terrible war, which would set Europe in flames from Moscow to the Pyrenees, and end in no one knowing why they had fought, came to pass in the second decade of the twentieth century. What could have brought about an international conflict which devastated extensive tracts of land, cut off many millions of men in the flower of their youth, and crippled the economic strength of our continent for generations to come?

One answer is that the world war was inevitable, because all the Great Powers, without exception, were saturated with Imperialism, only intent upon extending their power and securing it, by rival armaments on land, at sea, and in the air. War was bound to come, because the Governments had forgotten that peace alone can serve the true interests of nations, and the peoples failed to realize the economic solidarity of their countries.

This, no doubt, may explain some of the underlying causes of the great catastrophe, although to accept the world war as having been inevitable might savour too much of fatalism, and seems to take the influence of leading politicians into too little account. But there is no need to consider here how far such resignation is justifiable. Our object is to enquire into the justice of another answer—the one given at Versailles by accusers who set themselves up at the same time as judges, and this at a time when none of the belligerent Powers' archives had been published in full. Men who had not seen either their adversaries' or their allies' State records, and who carefully preserved strict secrecy as regards their own, maintained in Article 231 of the dictated Peace that the war had been imposed upon them by the aggression of Germany and her allies. And, stripped of its profuse verbiage, the gist of the ultimatum of June 16, 1919, which forced Germany to sign her political and moral death warrant, is simply as follows :

Of all the Powers, Germany was the only one prepared for a great war.

For decades past Germany had systematically prepared for an offensive war of conquest and subjugation, and had deliberately kindled this war in 1914, in order to acquire the upper hand in Europe, and achieve her aims of world supremacy.

The nations who opposed her were only bent on preserving their liberty.

2. THE POLITICAL AIMS OF THE GREAT POWERS.

On the many occasions when the world had been divided up in former days, Germany had been left out in the cold, and even in the re-partitions of the last few decades, she had come off very badly. In 1914 the German Empire had a population of sixty-seven million in the mother country, and a colonial population of only twelve million. The German people did not aspire to world supremacy, but only to a modest " place in the sun," an aim which was surely attainable without war, and without injuring the interests of other nations. The colonial agreement with England, which had already been drafted, and which would have done justice to Germany's legitimate and moderate demands, was actually to have been signed in August of the fatal year.

As against this, France, with her population of thirty-nine million, had succeeded, after 1871, in building up a powerful colonial Empire, with fifty-three million coloured subjects, from modest beginnings. That had only been possible thanks to Bismarck's moral and diplomatic support. The security afforded by the first German Chancellor's assurance that Germany would not attack her, no matter how many French troops were sent across the water, enabled the Republic to acquire Tunis, Annam, Tongking, Laos, and valuable territory in West Africa, as well as the island of Madagascar. The last ten years, however, had secured Morocco to the French, who were infringing one treaty after another, and it was in Morocco that the ball was to be set rolling which ended in world war, as will be shown later on.

The British Empire was still more powerful. There were only forty-six million inhabitants of the British Islands, but, of the total population of the world, three hundred and seventy-six million, that is, more than one-fifth of its inhabitants, were subjects of His Britannic Majesty. In spite of this, the British Imperialists continued to pursue their aims. The great Cape to Cairo railway was to be constructed in Africa, and overland communication established from thence between West and East, via Palestine, Arabia, and Mesopotamia, to India. At the same time, the ever vigilant British Admiralty were endeavouring to secure still firmer control of the high seas, by acquiring fresh naval bases, and preventing such bases being acquired by opponents of the Triple Entente. Just as England ruled over the seas, and the largest number of peoples of various races and religions, so Russia held sway over the most extensive domains. Her vast territorial possessions formed a concrete whole, but many of the peoples united under the Tsar's rule were of foreign origin.

Even small countries like Holland and Belgium owned more extensive and more thickly populated colonies than Germany.

The second charge against Germany, namely that she aspired to " supremacy in Europe ", can equally be refuted. Germany did not want a foot of territory in Europe over and above what she had acquired in 1871. The island of Heligoland, which had been offered by England even earlier, was made over to her by friendly agreement in 1890, in return for extensive renunciation of territory in Africa.

It was otherwise in France and Russia. The belief that, after 1871, France was only bent on recovering Alsace and Lorraine, has proved to have been mistaken. We know now, from the reports of the French Ambassador, Baron Courcel, that, even at the end of 1884, consequently at a time when Germany went particularly far towards meeting the French wishes, leading French politicians still refused to accept the treaties of 1815 as final, and wanted to recover the German Saar district,[1] which, for some inconceivable reason, had been left to France by the Peace of 1814. Delcassé's reports on what he described as the "remarkable" extension of the Franco-Russian alliance he had achieved in the summer of 1899, revealed a third aim, in addition to Alsace-Lorraine and the Saar : in case of the Habsburg Empire breaking up, the union of German-Austria with the great mother country was to be prevented, if necessary by force of arms.[2] Following upon that, it will be seen how Delcassé, Poincaré's right hand, discussed France's territorial aims in Europe with Sazonov in 1913, a year and a half before the outbreak of war. The Sedan defeat had no more succeeded in preventing France from trying to push her frontiers permanently further east than the defeat of Waterloo.

Russia too no longer fixed her attention exclusively on Asiatic territory. The causes which had led her to revert to her former policy of expansion in Europe will be discussed in the chapter on the world situation in 1907. It need only be said here that, at the beginning of 1914, St. Petersburg had adopted the view that the domination of the Bosphorus and Dardanelles, to which Russia aspired, could only be achieved "within the framework of a European war".

Whilst the Triple Entente Powers were making these far-reaching plans, and Germany aspired to a place in the sun, Austria's sole aim was the maintenance of the *status quo*. Although this may be said to have been an unjustifiable anachronism, in view of the fact that there were a certain number of South Slavs who wished for the erection of a Greater-Serbian State, no serious politician can ever have thought of crediting Austria-Hungary with any aspirations to world power, or any wish to dominate Europe.

Thus it will be seen that neither Berlin nor Vienna had aims which could only be realized through a sea of blood and tears. Even the English Imperialists' ambitious

[1] App. I. No. 1, p. 226.   [2] App. I. No. 2, p. 226.

schemes might indeed have been accomplished without a European war, for they were only directed against defence-less nations in other parts of the world. On the other hand, the territorial ambitions of France, Russia, and the nations under Russia's protection, were only attainable on the battlefields of Europe.

3. FAVOURABLE OPPORTUNITIES FOR WAR.

The third charge made by the ultimatum is that Germany had been preparing for a war of aggression for many decades past. Whoever drew up the indictment—it is said to have been an Englishman—forgot that, just ten years before the catastrophe, Great Britain had been most anxious to form an alliance with Germany, an alliance directed against both France and Russia, later on her allies.

To refute this charge, it is hardly necessary to go back to Bismarck's day. The publication of State Papers by the German Foreign Office, including a number of strictly confidential memoranda and written instructions, has revealed the first German Chancellor's most secret aims and intentions to the whole world, which has been amazed to find how very much his policy had been a policy of peace ever since the foundation of the Empire. It was not only a policy of peace for Germany, but for the whole of Europe, based, not on any Pacifist theories, but on practical recognition that this alone could serve the true interests of both Empire and people. Bismarck not only wanted to avoid imperilling the hardly won unity of the German people by military adventures, but he was equally anxious to avert the repeatedly threatened conflict between England and Russia, between England and France, and between Russia and Austria. This anxiety is very clearly shown by his instructions to the German Ambassador in Paris, on the 5th of October, 1884, when war was imminent between England and France over the Egyptian Question. They were as follows :

We have the same interest as France in trying to avert a rupture with England, especially war, and in seeing that the Egyptian question is peaceably solved. An Anglo-French war would be just as great a calamity for us as a war between Russia and Austria, even if we remained neutral.[1]

Field Marshal Count Waldersee complains bitterly, in his memoirs, of Bismarck's determined opposition to the preventive war so persistently urged by certain military circles, particularly in 1887.[2] The January 1923 number of the *Journal of the British Institute of International Affairs* says very truly that, if the documents published really give all that is worth knowing, " they confirm our belief that, from 1871 until his downfall, Bismarck was the pillar of European peace ".[3] It is indeed to be hoped that the legends of Germany's having wanted to invade France in 1875, on account of the rapid reorganization of the French army, and again in 1887, on the occasion of the harmless Schnaebelé incident, will now be discarded by writers of French and English history.

There is no doubt that, after Bismarck's time, Germany's policy was directed by a far less sure hand. Fault may well be found with a great deal in the methods of this period of the Wilhelminic epoch. Many a diplomatic move was made, which would never have been sanctioned by such an excellent pilot as the first Chancellor. The unnecessary prominence given to the person of the Monarch, provocative speeches, bellicose talk, and theatrical gestures, all combined to give malicious people in other countries ample ground for carrying on inflammatory propaganda, while, at the same time, it did not the least alarm Germany's opponents, for they well knew that these demonstrations were not backed by any strength of purpose. According to evidence given on oath by men who had gone through the many thousand volumes of Foreign Office Papers, not one of them contains a single document showing any sign of belligerent intentions.[4] It must further be evident to anyone who reflects at all, that if Germany had wished to embark on a

---

[1] *Die Grosse Politik der Europäischen Kabinette*, 1871–1914 (a collection of German Foreign Office documents), Vol. III. No. 693, p. 431.

[2] App. I. No. 3, p. 227.

[3] Paper by Mr. Gooch published in the *Journal*.—[TR.]

[4] Evidence given by Dr. Friedrich Thimme and Dr. Johannes Lepsius at the Fechenbach-Cossmann trial (with regard to falsifications in the Bavarian Legation reports). *Süddeutsche Monatshefte*, May 1922.

war of aggression, or even only on a preventive war, it
would have been brought about at a time when the political
and military position was favourable. There were certainly
plenty of such favourable opportunities.

First let me recall the position in the autumn of 1898. At
that time France had to haul down the Tricolour at Fashoda
at England's bidding. The ships-of-war in English ports
were in readiness to proceed to the French coasts and colonies.
In addition to that, England had opened negotiations with
Germany in the spring, with a view to an alliance, as a
protection against Russia and France, and would therefore
hardly have stood in the way of the Berlin Government,
had they taken advantage of the opportunity of finally
settling accounts with their western neighbour.

After that came the Boer War, which would have made
it impossible for England to send even a single man or a
single gun to help France on the Continent at any time
between 1899 and 1902. And as the British Government
continued their efforts to bring about an alliance with
Germany, uninterruptedly, till the end of 1901, it may be
assumed, if only for that reason, that it would have been
out of the question for England to adopt an attitude favourable to France as against Germany.

It may be urged that there was no ground for war between
France and Germany, either in 1898 or during the Boer
War. But the answer to that is that it is easy for those
who wish to go to war to find a pretext ; anyhow, this
objection does not apply to far the most favourable opportunity Germany had for a war of prevention. This was
during the Moroccan conflict of 1905–6, when Russia was
absolutely crippled by her defeats in Manchuria and her
revolution, and was incapable of giving France any military
help. It is true that the *Entente Cordiale* between the
Western Powers already existed ; the conversations between
the English and French naval and military experts had
begun in January 1906.[1] The English navy could have
driven the German flag off the high seas and seized the
German colonies, just as during the world war, but the

[1] Grey's speech in the House of Commons, August 3, 1914 (Hansard,
1914), and Viscount Haldane, *Before the War*, pp. 30–1.

few divisions of the British Expeditionary Force could not have compensated at all adequately for the loss of the Tsar's armies, numbering millions, in the decisive European theatre of war. Besides that, in 1906, acccording to the statement made by the War Minister, Haldane, it would have been two months before they could arrive on the Continent, ready for war, and even then their strength would only have been 80,000 at first, half the strength of 1914.[1] There were also serious deficiencies even in the organization of the French army itself, as the French Press pointed out again in 1922.[2] At that time Germany could have thrown the whole of her regular and reserve troops to the west, and have safely left the *Landwehr* and *Landsturm* to protect the east. For that matter, had things gone as in 1914, France would have been absolutely beaten before the first English soldier could set foot on French soil. The Moroccan question provided the pretext for war. In Paris Delcassé wanted it, and in Berlin Holstein was at least no unconditional opponent of such a solution. Nevertheless, Germany pursued an altogether different policy. Much fault may be found with it, particularly with the Kaiser's having been induced to land at Tangier, against his own wish, but an attack on her neighbours did not form any part of the Berlin Government's plans. So far were they from contemplating anything of the kind, that they were, on the contrary, pursuing the phantom of a continental federation. That may be described as foolish or indeed Utopian, but it certainly showed no wish for war. There is also another factor which must not be overlooked. Both the men who pursued a belligerent policy at that time had to resign; Delcassé, who pursued it firmly, and Holstein, who wavered. Delcassé came back to office later on, but Holstein's career came to an end with his resignation.

Thus, during the first fifteen years after Bismarck's fall, Germany, faithful to the first Chancellor's tenets, rejected the idea of a preventive war no less than three times, in spite of the military and political conditions having been favourable. In the following consecutive account of what

---

[1] Haldane, loc. cit., p. 165.
[2] *Eclair* of 17th, and *Gaulois* of March 19, 1922.

took place from 1907 onwards, it will be seen that there were three further opportunities for a war of this nature, which were not turned to account : the Bosnian crisis of 1908–9, the second Moroccan crisis of 1911, and finally the Balkan wars of 1912 and 1913.

A fourth point of the Versailles indictment—the alleged excessive German armaments—will also be dealt with in Part II, the period up to 1907 under the heading of the Hague Conferences, and the period from 1907 to 1914 in a special chapter.

PART II

PRE-WAR HISTORY

1. The Situation in 1907.

At the close of the last century the Imperialism, which at that time had selected the east of Asia and of Africa as its special aim, was at its height. Japan and the United States were taking part in world politics, and had joined the ranks of the great Colonial Powers. Great Britain was engaged in political warfare on two fronts, against Russia in Eastern Asia, and, up to 1899, against France in Africa. The English offers of alliance with Germany did not emanate from English pacifists, who, on the contrary, objected to being bound by any such tie, but from the most pronounced representatives of Imperialism. Chamberlain's speech at Birmingham on the 12th of May, 1898, was almost an appeal for an ally against Russia, the ally being subsequently found in Japan in 1902. It is true that there was violent opposition in England to the Boer War, but it was precisely then that English Liberalism, as a whole, capitulated to the Imperialists. Asquith, Grey, and Haldane, leading members of the Cobden Club, became Vice-Presidents of the Imperial Liberal League. In the summer of 1900 all the Powers acted jointly in China, where the perpetual amputations from the Chinese body politic had given rise to a very natural agitation against foreigners.

Then in 1904 there was, on the one hand, the war between Russia and Japan, over territories to which neither Power had any claim, and on the other, the Anglo-French treaty, equally over countries which did not belong to either of the two Powers, and were in totally different parts of the world. Not only were the published parts of the

treaty a flagrant breach of an international treaty—the
Madrid Convention of 1880—but it was in itself an example
of rare duplicity, for the secret articles, which were made
public in 1911, provided for the allotment and annexation
of territories whose integrity and independence had been
expressly recognized in the published treaty.

After the Russo-Japanese War, by means of which
England had driven her Russian rival out of Eastern Asia
with the help of Japanese arms, the Russian Empire, thus
humbled in the dust, was successfully won over in 1907
by British diplomacy, and, at the same time, kept at a
distance from ice-free seas in the Middle as well as the Far
East. This was done by dividing Persia *de facto* between
the two Powers, and making the coasts English " spheres
of interest ". In addition, England had safeguarded the
" glacis ", north of India, by establishing a Protectorate
over Thibet, and a right of control over Afghanistan. As
a reward for her services, Japan was to be allowed to put
an absolute end to the independence of Korea.[1]

Thus a situation had come about in 1907 entirely different
to what it was when Bismarck retired. In 1890 there
was no alliance in Europe in which Germany would not
have been included, either openly or, as in the case of the
Mediterranean agreement between England, Austria, and
Italy, as a sleeping partner. France stood alone. Seventeen years later a Triple Entente had been established
between France, Russia, and England, with Japan as a
fourth partner in the Far East, and Italy had been virtually
alienated from the Triple Alliance, since 1902, by the
treaty of neutrality with France.[2] Germany and Austria-
Hungary were politically isolated. The distribution of
forces, which the outbreak of war revealed, was already
effectuated. On the one side, three States, vastly superior
in strength on land and at sea, having a total of over
700,000,000 inhabitants of all parts of the world at their
disposal—including Japan and Italy, over 800,000,000; on

[1] The zenith of Imperialism is described in more detail in *Deutschland
und die Schuldfrage*, pp. 78–81. (*Verlag für Politik und Wirthschaft*,
Berlin, 1922.)

[2] French Yellow Book, 1920, *Les Accords Franco-Italiens*, 1901–2, No. 7

the other, two States in the centre of Europe, which would immediately be cut off from all overseas communication in a war in which England took part as an enemy, and which could barely reckon on a total of 120,000,000 subjects.

In this grouping of forces, the elements which imperilled peace were as follows: Russia, seeing the way finally blocked in the Middle and Far East to her long-sought outlet to the high seas, naturally again turned her attention to her former aims in the Near East, which, to the relief of Europe, she had abandoned since 1897: the Balkans, the Straits, and Constantinople. This " return of Russia to Europe " was particularly perilous to peace because, in reverting to her old ambitions, Russia no longer had to fear the opposition from England which had always had a deterrent effect in St. Petersburg, and could count on her neutrality, possibly even on her active support.

A further evil was that, ever since the breakdown of the Anglo-German alliance negotiations, there had been added to the centuries-old Franco-German antagonism, and the antagonism between Russia and Austria, which had existed for decades past, an ever-increasing Anglo-German antagonism, aggravated by Germany's naval policy, and actively fomented in Paris and St. Petersburg. England's antagonism to Germany was subsequently extended to Austria-Hungary, who had so often made common cause with Great Britain in opposing Russian expansion in the Balkans, and might indeed almost have been regarded as her traditional ally against the Russian Empire.

The Anglo-Russian understanding with regard to the Near East was of the more importance because Germany's sole aim of any magnitude, the construction of the Bagdad railway, brought the German Empire into conflict simultaneously with England and Russia, and drew these former rivals more and more closely together. The original idea was purely commercial; it was to offer a fresh field of activity to German intelligence and enterprise, and compensate for the lack of colonial expansion. For this reason this " last open road to the wide world " was a project dear to all who held the legitimate opinion that a people numbering sixty million, whose population was continually increasing, ought not to be permanently tied to the soil of their native country. But the undertaking had political consequences, and overstepped the limits of what was purely commercial, in so far as it was bound not only to increase Turkey's economic strength, but also to strengthen her military position. This did not suit Russia, who foresaw that it might be an obstacle in the way of her historic aims. England, for her part, seems to have feared that Germany might menace India, if she laid a railway to the Persian Gulf, though this is difficult to understand.

Germany was to some extent to blame for a state of affairs having arisen which so seriously menaced the peace of Europe and the safety of the Central Powers. The greatest mistakes she had made were probably her failure to renew the re-insurance treaty with Russia in 1890, and the delay in responding to the overtures made by England during the period from 1898 to 1901. But its essential cause was the Imperialistic rivalry between the great Colonial Powers, their ambition to bring more and more of the world under their domination, which involved the worst possible crimes against the freedom and independence of the Asiatic and African peoples. Germany participated in this rivalry and in these crimes by taking Kiau-chau, by the expedition to China, and the harsh suppression of the Herero rising, but her share was modest as compared with the spoil of the others and their crimes.

2. The Hague Conferences of 1899 and 1907.

The Hague Conferences dealt with two great problems : how to arrest the construction of armaments, and how to find a means of adjusting international conflicts peaceably. Most people in foreign countries, and many even in Germany, still believe that Germany alone stood in the way of a happy solution of both problems. The facts prove that it was not so.

Nor can it any longer be maintained that, in making the proposal of 1898, the Tsar and his Ministers were actuated by pure love of peace. As Dr. Thimme proved to the Reichstag Committee of Enquiry, May 2, 1923, on the authority of German State Papers, Witte, at that time the most influential Russian Minister, aimed at a continental alliance between France, Russia, and Germany, and impressed on the German Ambassador time after time that the money so foolishly spent by the continental Powers in arming against one another might be far better spent on naval armament against England. As a matter of fact, it was precisely in 1898 that the Russian programme of naval construction was considerably extended. It further appears from Witte's Memoirs (French edition, p. 83) that the reason for proposing disarmament was that Austria-Hungary intended considerably increasing her artillery, and Russia had not the means of doing this at the time. A general pause in the construction of armaments seemed to him more advantageous than the understanding with Austria proposed by the War Minister, Kuropatkin, which Witte thought " unpractical " and *bizarre*. Referring to the war with Japan, Witte then says : " In any case we ourselves make it evident that our talk about disarmament and peace meant nothing at all ".

(a) *Armaments.*[1]

From 1871 to 1890 Germany adhered to an army strength of about 1 per cent. of the population, although, as a result of this low rate, many who were fit for service escaped military duty annually. With a population of something over forty million, the peace strength in 1871 was 402,000 non-commissioned officers and men, and in 1890, when the population had increased to forty-nine million, it was 487,000.

France had entirely reorganized her army as far back as in 1875, and brought it up to the same strength as the German army. In 1889 she still adhered to the obsolete five years' period of service, and when she at last changed this to the three years' period that year, universal liability for service, which was only on paper in Germany, came into actual force at the same time. Consequently, the average

---

[1] For further details of the efforts to bring about disarmament in 1899 and 1907, vide *Deutschland und die Schuldfrage*, pp. 73-8 and 81-91.

numbers recruited annually during the period 1890–1892
were :

In Germany, with a population of, in round numbers,
fifty million, 198,000, inclusive of one-year volunteers.

In France, with a population of not quite forty million,
216,000 men, of whom, however, a certain number only
served a year with the Colours.

At the end of another three years, France would have
been able to put 100,000 more trained soldiers of the latest
yearly classes into the field than Germany, in spite of her
population being ten million less. It was on this account,
and having regard to the Franco-Russian alliance which had
been concluded in the meantime, that Germany decided on
somewhat further increasing her army, but at the same time
she reduced the period of regular service, for all but mounted
troops, from three to two years. By the Army Bill of
1893 the rate per cent. on a population of fifty million was
raised to 1·09, bringing the strength up to 557,000 non-
commissioned officers and men. But even the next Bill
of 1899 did not keep pace with the increase in the population. This amounted to four million, the increased strength
of the army being not 40,000, or even half that, but only
16,000 men.

When the first Hague Conference met, the effective peace
strength of the armies of the continental Great Powers was
as follows :

State.	Population in Millions.	Effective Peace Strength, inclusive of Officers, Doctors, and Officials.	Rate Per Cent. of the Population.
Germany ..	55	604,000 *	1·1
Austria	45·3	346,000	0·76
Italy	32	258,000	0·8
France	38·5	574,000	1·49
Russia	130	896,000	0·69

* Without officers, etc., and without one-year volunteers, 570,000 = 1·04
per cent. of the population.

In actual numbers Russia was first by a long way, but

the liability per cent. of the population was far the heaviest in France.

In 1899 the German navy was very weak. In a naval report published by the British Admiralty in 1893, Germany ranked fifth, with 87 ships, while Great Britain had 325, France 220, Russia 130, and Italy 93. It was not till 1897 that Germany brought in her first, very modest Navy Bill. Austria-Hungary was not yet taken into account at all as a naval Power.

The Russian idea of arresting the construction of armaments had been received with the greatest scepticism by all the Great Powers, as is shown by the instructions to the German, American, and English delegates, and the French report of the Conference.[1] The Russian proposals formulated at the Conference were not very happy. They provided for the peace strength of the armies, and the army expenditure, remaining the same for five years, but excepted the colonial troops, under which heading, according to the Russian interpretation, the troops in Central Asia and in the Amur district were included. This, of course, was unacceptable from the start to the Powers which had no colonial troops. The proposals were consequently rejected both by the sub-committee and the plenary committee, all the members voting against the Russian representative, who was completely isolated.

The Russian proposals with regard to navies were of a similar nature, and met with no better fate. There is grim irony in the little known fact that, at the end of July, even before the Conference terminated, the British Admiralty asked for £23,600,000 for the construction of new ships, on the ground that Russia had not modified her programme of naval construction.

There was no further mention of disarmament in the Russian programme for the second Hague Conference ; after the Japanese War the Russians had given up the idea. A public campaign started by Sir Henry Campbell-Bannerman in the spring of 1907, in favour of including the question of disarmament in the programme of the Conference, met with opposition, not only in Germany, but also particularly

[1] Vide loc. cit., pp. 81–2.

in France, where it was bitterly denounced by the *Temps*.[1] It seems that, out of consideration for England, Russia was prepared at all events to deal formally with the matter, but in consequence of the attitude adopted not only by Germany but, as must again be emphasized, especially by France, the problem was not discussed at all at the second Conference, so that once more a meaningless resolution was passed, and there the matter rested.

In 1907 the strength of the armies was :

State.	Population in Millions.	Effective Peace Strength, inclusive of Officers, etc.	Rate Per Cent. of the Population.
Germany	62·0	629,000 *	1·01
Austria	48·2	382,000	0·79
Italy	33·8	284,000	0·84
France	39·2	559,000	1·43
Russia	150·0	1,254,000	0·83

* Without officers, etc., and without one-year volunteers, 585,000 = 0·94 per cent.

Russia is again seen to be first by a long way as regards actual numbers, and France as regards the percentage of those liable for service. Russia was three times as strong as Austria, twice as strong as Germany, and alone more than a match for the two Central Powers. In Germany the percentage of men and non-commissioned officers had fallen seriously below the 1 per cent. of the population maintained from 1871 to 1890. Austria was neglecting her army to an extent hardly consistent with responsibility. She had nine million more inhabitants than France, yet her peace strength was only two-thirds of the French strength ; the fact that a number of *Ersatz* reservists underwent annual military training was of some account, but at that time the course was limited to eight weeks.

Germany had indeed doubled her small naval programme of 1897 in the year 1900, so that in 1917—according to the plans existing in 1907—she would have had thirty-four

[1] Campbell-Bannerman's article in the *Nation* of March 1, 1907, and the reply made by the *Temps*. Vide loc. cit., pp. 86-7.

battleships. In 1906, following England's example, she had also begun to build Dreadnoughts, and had increased the number of her first-class cruisers in the same year. Finally, a Navy Bill was in course of preparation, which was to reduce the length of life of the ships in accordance with the standard of other naval Powers, and consequently speed up the construction of new ships. All these measures certainly did not signify any "menace" to England, who still had vastly superior strength, but as they were regarded as a menace on the other side of the Channel, it would have been wise, from a political point of view, to pacify English public opinion by a naval agreement.

On the other hand, it was certainly not for Germany and her sole remaining faithful ally to take the lead in effectively reducing armaments on land. At the same time it would have been wise to take a broad view of this question, both in 1899 and in 1907. The unfavourable political situation in 1907 ought to have made this evident. Some such proposal, for instance, as that of the Social Democrats' Erfurt programme, namely, that the whole nation should be trained to bear arms, the period of service being greatly reduced, or a proposal that the peace strength of the army, inclusive of officers, etc., should not exceed 1 per cent. of the population, would have won Germany the sympathy of the whole world, and its acceptance would have secured German territory for ever against French occupation. It is true that France, who was making such immense efforts to increase her military strength, would hardly have agreed to such proposals. But this would have shown unmistakably whose fault it was that the continent of Europe could not be relieved of the burden of great standing armies.

(b) Arbitration.

At the first Conference Germany began by objecting to the institution of a permanent Court of Arbitration, but, thanks to the strong representations made by Professor Zorn, she withdrew her opposition, so that a perfectly satisfactory conclusion was reached. The last meeting was "almost of a dramatic nature, in the sense of there being a general wish for peace," and the Conference ended in " perfect accord between all the States ". [1]

It is true that at the second Conference Germany voted with Austria-Hungary, Turkey, Switzerland, and the four Balkan States, against the proposed obligatory arbitration, whilst Italy, Japan, and Luxemburg abstained from voting,[2] so that, in default of unanimity, the motion in favour of compulsion was defeated.

The compulsion only applied, however, to the " Court of Arbitration ", which was primarily intended to adjust legal disputes. There was no question at the second Conference, any more than at the first, of introducing compulsion in the case of institutions which were to adjust purely political disputes, such as " mediation ", " good offices ", and " Commissions of international enquiry ". It was generally agreed that the clauses relating to " circumstances " and " honour " must apply to these methods of adjustment, so that their employment in really serious cases was out of the question from the first.

In addition to that, Germany's experience of two treaties of arbitration she had concluded in 1904, with England and the United States, had been unfortunate. England refused to accept arbitration in the matter of compensation to German subjects for losses incurred in the South African War, on the ground that this was a political, not a legal, question, and that questions of this kind affected the vital interests of the nation. The treaty with America, on the other hand, broke down because the American Senate wanted to reserve the right to accept or reject the award proposed in each particular case.

Thirdly, it must not be forgotten that Germany has inserted a clause providing for arbitration in very many commercial and other treaties of a similar nature ; she has, in fact, concluded seventeen such treaties—more than any other State.

Finally, the great advance made in the matter of arbitration in 1907 was due to Anglo-German co-operation. It

[1] Professor Phil. Zorn, *Die beiden Haager Friedenskonferenzen*, p. 39.
[2] A. H. Fried, *Handbuch der Friedensbewegung*, 1911, p. 252. Zorn gives the proportion of votes rather differently.

was thanks to this that an International Prize Court was set up, according to A. H. Fried, the " first really International Court of Arbitration, with power to make awards without being restricted by clauses of honour ". The regulation of maritime law, formulated in the Declaration of London of February 1909, was equally meritorious. Unfortunately nothing much came of either of these projects, as the British Government had not the courage to ratify them, on account of the militarist and Imperialist opposition in the House of Lords.

It is not true that, at the second Hague Conference, Germany wrecked an agreement which proposed making the adjustment of all disputed questions compulsory, no matter whether they were of a legal or political nature, or whether they affected vital interests and honour. This reproach is based on ignorance or lies. It is the outcome of war propaganda and hatred of Germany, just the same as the legend of excessive German armaments, and of the one-sided, absolutely isolated opposition made by the German Empire to proposals of disarmament, which are alleged to have been practicable. We do not dispute the fact that the tactics pursued by the German Government individually at the Hague were not altogether happy. But the abnormal growth of Imperialism, referred to in describing the world situation in 1907, proves how little Russia, France, England, the United States, and Japan, are entitled to pose as representatives of the peace idea, and protectors of the independence of small nations, on the ground of the policy they pursued from 1899 to 1907.

3. The Annexation of Bosnia and Herzegovina.

It was a factor of far-reaching importance that Austria-Hungary should only have decided on annexing Bosnia and Herzegovina, which she had been occupying since 1878, after Russia had turned back to the Near East, in consequence of her being cut off from an outlet to the ocean in the Far and Middle East, and after the Anglo-Russian differences, which had long been considered irreconcilable, had been composed. Another change was also of importance. Isvolsky, who had been appointed Russian Minister for Foreign Affairs in May 1906, was a very strong advocate of the " European orientation ", and a resolute opponent of all adventures in Middle and East Asia. As far back as at a Cabinet meeting on the 3rd of February, 1908, he stated that the British Ambassador had spoken to him of the community of Russian and British interests in the Near East, and he suggested that it would be quite feasible for the two Powers to carry on combined military operations there. But his question whether the time had come when it would be possible for Russia to go beyond the limits of a strictly defensive policy was answered decidedly in the negative, both by the Minister of War and Stolypin, the Prime Minister, who pointed to the after effects of the war they had lost and of the revolution.[1]

But Isvolsky was destined to reap the firstfruits of his European policy very soon, in the common opposition made by the Triple Entente to Austria-Hungary's absolutely harmless intention—based on the treaties—of constructing a railway to Salonica through the Sandjak of Novi-Bazar, the strip of land between Serbia and Montenegro. Still greater was the success of the meeting that took place between the Russian and English monarchs and their principal Ministers, at Reval, on the 9th and 10th of June, 1908. Persia and Afghanistan, reforms in Macedonia, and the necessity for strong Russian armaments on land and at sea, were all discussed on this occasion.[2]

Isvolsky now turned his attention to the real object of his ambition. This was to solve the question of a passage through the Bosphorus and the Dardanelles in a manner consistent with Russia's interests and prestige. The shameful servitude the Western Powers had imposed on the great Empire in 1856 by the Treaty of Paris, which only allowed her to keep nutshells as ships-of-war on the Black Sea, and no arsenals at all on her coasts, had indeed been abolished by the European Conference of 1871, thanks to

---

[1] Professor M. Pokrovsky (keeper of the Soviet Government archives), *Drei Konferenzen*, pp. 17–30.
[2] *Diplomatische Aktenstücke zur Geschichte der Entente Politik der Vorkriegsjahre*, B. de Siebert (Secretary of the Russian Embassy in London till the outbreak of war), pp. 777–9.

the German victory and Bismarck's diplomatic support ;
but still no ships-of-war could pass through the Straits
without the Sultan's permission. The Black Sea Fleet had
to look on passively, while the Japanese destroyed their
sister ships. In the meantime, knowing well that this
would be less likely to appeal to London than Macedonian
and Persian schemes, the Russian Minister began by trying
to feel his way with the Vienna Government.

An important change in personnel had also taken place in
the Danube Monarchy in 1906. Freiherr von Aehrenthal,
a man of action, had replaced Count Goluchovsky, whose
policy was passive. The new Foreign Minister had long
been of opinion that the persistent Pan-Serbian agitation,
which constituted a serious danger to the continued existence of the Habsburg Monarchy, could only be effectively
checked if the provinces of Bosnia and Herzegovina, which
had been occupied and administered by Austria-Hungary
since 1878, in accordance with the decision of the Berlin
Congress, and at England's suggestion, became integral
parts of the State.

The basis of the understanding reached between the two
statesmen was that Austria-Hungary should annex these
provinces, and Russia should have a free passage for her
warships through the Straits. On the 2nd of July, 1908,
only a few weeks after the meeting at Reval, Isvolsky sent
the Vienna Cabinet an *aide-mémoire*, in which he said that
of course annexation and the passage of the Straits were
European questions, which could only be finally decided
by the Great Powers as a whole, but that Russia was willing
to interchange views with Austria " in a spirit of friendly
reciprocity." [1] It should be remembered that, in this, the
Russian Minister was not making by any means an absolutely
fresh concession. In the Reichstadt agreements of July
1876, the Conventions of January 1877 and July 1878,
and the treaties of neutrality of 1881 and 1884 between
Russia, Germany, and Austria, Russia had over and over
again recognized the Danubian State's right to annex the
provinces. When an agreement was entered into merely
between Russia and Germany, independently of Austria,

---

[1] H. Friedjung, *Das Zeitalter des Imperialismus*, Vol. II. p. 220.

in 1887, M. de Giers explained that this would not deprive the Monarchy of her " liberty to proceed from occupation to annexation " ; it must, however, be admitted that no agreement was reached as to the question of annexation when Russia and Austria came to an understanding over the Balkans in 1897.[1]

The Young Turk revolution in July 1908 had a twofold influence on the questions which had been discussed between London and St. Petersburg and Vienna and St. Petersburg. In England's eyes Turkey suddenly ceased to be a sick man, in need of protection, and became a State blossoming into fresh life, who she thought would gladly exchange the friendship of " autocratic " Germany for that of the Western " democracies ". There was no further question of exerting strong pressure on Constantinople ; the Anglo-Russian agreements respecting Macedonia were at an end. On the other hand, the annexation question had now become really urgent for Vienna. The Young Turks, who showed strong nationalist feeling, were already demanding the restoration of both the provinces to the Sultan. Young Turkey was further to be given a constitution. Consequently the same step must at last be taken in Bosnia and Herzegovina. But the Emperor of Austria could only take that step if, in addition to occupying and administrating the provinces, he became their Sovereign.

Aehrenthal replied to Isvolsky's *aide-mémoire* on the 27th of August. The fact that the Russian Minister was taking the waters at Carlsbad facilitated further negotiations. Whilst there, Isvolsky gave the Serbian Prime Minister, Milowanovich, a hint to submit to " the inevitable ", as early as on the 4th of September.[2] At that time the Serb was of opinion that the annexation would be acceptable to his country if Austria gave up the Sandjak, which Aehrenthal had contemplated doing from the beginning.[3]

---

[1] de Giers' statement, see *Die Grosse Politik der Europäischen Kabinette,* 1871–1914, Vol. V. No. 1074, p. 226 ; Austro-Russian agreement 1897, see Dr. A. Fr. Pribram, *Die Politischen Geheimverträge Oesterreich-Ungarn's* 1879–1914, pp. 18 and 57.

[2] H. Friedjung, *Das Zeitalter des Imperialismus,* 1884–1914, Vol. II. p. 226.

[3] Dr M. Bogitshevich (former Serbian Chargé d'Affaires in Berlin), *Kriegsursachen,* p. 152.

On the 15th of September, Aehrenthal and Isvolsky met at Buchlau, the country residence of Count Berchtold, the Austrian Ambassador in St. Petersburg. The conversations held there were not put into writing, but the reports from both sides agree that the following conclusions were reached :

Austria to act independently as regards the annexation question, but to evacuate the Sandjak ;

Russia to be equally at liberty to set about the diplomatic adjustment of the Straits question as she thought best, Austria to support the Russian wishes ;

When both these questions were settled, the new *status* to be sanctioned at a European Conference ;

The Russian Foreign Minister to be advised beforehand of the impending annexation.

Aehrenthal had already felt his way in advance with Germany and Italy, and had met with no opposition from either.[1] But Isvolsky had not told his Entente colleagues anything about his negotiations, nor had he mentioned his *aide-mémoire* of July 2.[2] It was not till the beginning of October that he began to raise the Straits question in London and Paris, and he met with a very cool reception, for some surprise was naturally felt that such subjects should have first been discussed with the Triple Alliance. How Isvolsky was gradually brought round can be clearly traced. The Serbian Minister reports that while still in Paris, where he received the letter from his Austrian colleague, advising him that the announcement of the annexation (made on the 6th of October) was imminent,[3] Isvolsky said to him :

Serbia and the Serbian people lose nothing, on the contrary; they gain. . . . I foresaw the step Austria-Hungary has taken, and it did not surprise me. This was why I made our consent dependent on the above-mentioned condition (evacuation of the Sandjak).[4]

But a week later, on the 13th of October, when the Russian wishes with regard to the Straits had been ungraciously

[1] Friedjung, Vol. II. p. 227. [2] Loc. cit., p. 220.
[3] Loc. cit., pp. 232 and 247. [4] Bogitshevich, p. 152.

received in London, the Serbian representative there reports in the reverse sense :

Isvolsky did not conceal his annoyance with Austria, and strongly protested against the assertion that he had agreed to the annexation.[1]

They were more Russian in London than the Russians. The Russian Minister, finding himself defrauded of the fruits of his secret agreements, joined in the chorus of indignation, and poured forth loud and violent protests, which were quite incompatible with the Buchlau understanding. Russia would not agree to the annexation ; Austria must be compelled to appear at a Conference. In the diplomatic conflict which then ensued, the Powers were grouped as follows :

England categorically demanded the Conference which would be humiliating for Austria.

Germany resolutely took Austria's part. Italy failed her, and disavowed her previous agreement.[2]

Russia would have been glad to fight, but could not think of it, because her army was not prepared for war.

Finally, France was not so willing to sacrifice her people for Russian aims in the Balkans at that time as later on.

That Russia was not in a position to fight at that time, but, on the other hand, did not intend to give up the idea once for all, and merely wished to postpone it to a more favourable date, is proved by the reports of Professor Koshutich, who had been sent to St. Petersburg as the confidential agent of the Serbian Government. On the 3rd of March he reported that the very influential member of the Duma, Gutchkov, had said to him :

When our military preparations are absolutely complete, then we shall have an explanation with Austria-Hungary. Do not start war now, for it would be suicidal. Say nothing about your intentions and be prepared. The days of your rejoicing will come.[3]

On the 10th of March Koshutich reported the following remark made by Isvolsky :

[1] Loc. cit., p. 157.   [2] App. I. No. 4, p. 227.
[3] German White Book, June 1919, *Deutschland schuldig ?* p. 112.

Serbia will be condemned to a hard life until the moment of
Austria-Hungary's downfall comes. The annexation has brought
that moment nearer, and when it arrives, Russia will raise the
Serbian question and solve it. Isvolsky sees that a conflict with
Germanism cannot be avoided, but for all that, Russia's policy is
absolutely Slavophil.[1]

On the 20th of March he reported the Tsar's having told
the President of the Duma that he felt a conflict with
Germanism was inevitable in the future, and that they must
be prepared for it.

As far back as in November 1908 the Russian monarch
had said to the Serbian Prime Minister, Pashitch :

The Bosnia-Herzegovina question will only be solved by war.[2]

Amidst this conflict of opinion, the compromise suggested
by Germany carried the day. In spite of its tone having
been very peremptory, the proposal did not give dissatisfaction in St. Petersburg, where it was brought forward on
the 23rd of March, for it offered the Foreign Minister an
honourable retreat from a very perilous position. The
Berlin suggestion was that the Powers should each give
their consent to the annexation individually, rather than at
a Conference.[3]

For the moment, it was a great diplomatic success for the
Central Powers. The German and Austro-Hungarian diplomats already believed they had broken up the Entente.
But that was a delusion. It may be said, on the contrary,
that just as the Moroccan crisis of 1904–6 cemented the
Anglo-French Entente, so the annexation crisis of 1908–9
firmly cemented the Triple Entente. Russia's hatred of
Austria was intense. The powerful Russian Empire had
already had to give in three times to the weak and despised
Danubian Monarchy : in the Crimean War in 1854, in
1878 after the Peace of San Stefano, when the Russian
armies were already before the gates of Constantinople,
in 1887 in the Bulgarian question, and now a fourth time.
But the difference was that England had been on Austria's
side the first three times, whereas she sided with Russia the

---

[1] Loc. cit., p. 114.   [2] Bogitshevich, pp. 150 and 151.
[3] App. I. No. 5, p 227.

fourth time. Russia's hatred extended to Germany, who had protected her ally, and it was very clearly expressed in the Russo-Bulgarian Convention of December 1909. Article 5 began with the words :

In view of the fact that realization of the high ideals of the Slav peoples on the Balkan peninsula, who are so dear to Russia, is only possible after a favourable outcome of Russia's struggle with Germany and Austria-Hungary . . .[1]

It should be noted that, according to Article 1 of the treaty, Bulgaria was bound to assist Russia by force of arms in the event of a conflict of arms between Russia and Germany, Austria-Hungary, and Rumania, or between Russia and Turkey, with the express addition " regardless of who may have taken the initiative in the conflict ",[2] therefore even in case of Russia being the undoubted aggressor, Bulgaria was bound to come to her rescue.

If similar documents could be found among the German archives, showing the same will and desire for war, how the enemy would rejoice in exploiting the fact. There is much to which exception may be taken in Aehrenthal's procedure, and the unconditional support Germany gave him during the annexation crisis ; for it was, after all, one-sided notice of the termination of an international treaty, however insignificant the change in the actual position might be. But there was certainly no intention of kindling a general war. On the contrary, no advantage was taken of the fourth opportunity for a preventive war. The military position was no longer as favourable as in 1905–6, but the Russian army had not by any means recovered, the Balkan States had not yet been strengthened by the victory over Turkey, and, above all, France was not yet minded to fight for Serbian aims. A New Year article in the *Temps* said this quite plainly. How little Berlin desired the great conflict at that time is sufficiently shown by the fact that a fresh treaty was concluded with France over Morocco, on the 9th of February, 1909, just when the crisis was most serious.

[1] Bogitshevich, p. 117. (According to Russian sources, the Convention in question was only drafted, not concluded.)
[2] Bogitshevich, p. 115.

According to the three reports of March 3, 10, and 19, the lesser conflict, however, war between Austria and Serbia, would in all probability have been possible then without the interference of a third Power.   The Chief of the Austrian General Staff was sadly disappointed at not receiving the mobilization order against Serbia, which he expected on the 28th of March.   He says in his memoirs :

Thus, never resolved to seize the right moment, the ancient Empire tottered to its fall.[1]

From the purely military standpoint, one can but agree with the General.   But politically speaking, Germany and Austria's leading statesmen were right in not acceding to these wishes.

4. THE RUSSO-ITALIAN TREATY OF RACCONIGI, 1909.

Isvolsky had taken the Italian Foreign Minister and the King of Italy himself into his confidence, with regard to the agreements with Aehrenthal over the Straits and annexation, as far back as between the date of the conversations at Buchlau and his visits to London and Paris.   The change that had come about in the attitude of the Italian Government towards Vienna, under pressure of English public opinion, now drew Italy and Russia even more closely together.   Here, again, common hatred of Austria was the bond of union.   Hitherto, fear that the Italian Socialists might carry out their threats had prevented Nicholas II. from returning Victor Emmanuel's visit.   But, in the autumn of 1909, he went to Italy by sea from Odessa, ostentatiously making a wide détour to avoid Austrian territory, and he met the King at Racconigi, south of Turin, on the 24th of October.   There an agreement was entered into, in which, amongst other things, the two Powers pledged themselves to adopt a benevolent attitude, Italy, if Russia raised the Straits question, Russia, if Italy went to Tripoli.   The days were long gone by when Crispi had declared that Italy " could not under any circumstances allow Russia to gain a footing on the Medi-

[1] Field-Marshal Conrad von Hötzendorf, *Aus meiner Dienstzeit*, p. 174.

terranean," and when he placed 100,000 to 200,000 men at Austria's disposal in case of a Russian attack on the Monarchy, or on Turkey.[1]

The fundamental importance of the treaty lay in the fact that Italy, who had always been on friendly terms with England, and had been closely allied with France since 1902, had now formed similar relations with the third Entente Power. As early as at the end of 1908, the Italian Foreign Minister had declared that Italy was determined to adhere to the Triple Alliance, but had also a " traditional friendship for England, a revived friendship for France, and a new friendship for Russia in the form of an intimate *rapprochement* ".[2]

5. THE LULL IN 1910.

The year 1910 seemed likely to begin with considerable relaxation of the tension. Nicholas II. informed William II. by letter that four Russian Army Corps were to be transferred from the western frontier to the interior of the Empire.[3] In reality, it was a question of quite a different thing. The reorganization of the Russian army, which had been taken in hand in 1910, increased the number of Russian Army Corps from thirty-one to thirty-seven. It is true that simultaneously two, not four, corps were transferred from the western frontier districts to the interior, but this was solely for the purpose of quartering the troops in the districts from which their drafts were supplied, in order to facilitate mobilization, and these two were replaced by two of the newly formed corps. It is difficult to believe that the Tsar was entirely in the dark as to this, and so absolutely misled by his military advisers. Did William II. see through the dishonesty of the communication later on ? Anyhow, if all his letters to the Tsar have been

[1] For full text of the Racconigi Treaty, vide *Un Livre Noir, Diplomatie d'Avant-Guerre d'après les Documents des Archives Russes*, Vol. I., pp. 357–58. For Crispi's statement in October 1887, vide *Die grosse Politik*, Vol. IV., No. 917, p. 352.

[2] Quoted by Haussmann in the *Reichstag*, December 10, 1908, Stenographical Report, p. 6103.

[3] The Kaiser thanked the Tsar on the 11th of January. Vide Professor Dr. W. Goetz, *Briefe Wilhelms II. an den Zaren*, 1894–1914, p. 258.

published, the one in which he thanked him for the information was the last he wrote on political matters to Nicholas II.

The tension between Russia and Austria was in so far relaxed that normal diplomatic relations, which had been suspended during the annexation crisis, were resumed. At the same time an agreement was reached as to the maintenance of the *status quo* in the Balkans. Serbia was reassured by Isvolsky as to this on the 4th of March. There was " no reason for anxiety ", there was no question " either of division into spheres of interest or of reverting to the former conditions . . . the main object was the *status quo* and the peaceful development and independence of the Balkan States ".[1] On the previous day the Russian Ambassador, Nelidov, had written rather more clearly to Isvolsky, that the agreement would enable Russia " to perfect her military strength unmolested, and prepare for events which were inevitable ".[2] Russia required a few more years to complete her " great programme ".

Even the death of Edward VII., on the 6th of May, and Isvolsky's resignation of the Foreign Secretaryship, which was given to his former " assistant ", Sazonov, did not have the effect hoped for in the interest of peace. The German Emperor's presence at his uncle's funeral was very much appreciated by the English public, certainly, but England's foreign policy was still directed by the King's docile pupil, Sir Edward Grey. Isvolsky went as Ambassador to Paris, and exerted his influence no less zealously at the Quai d'Orsay than hitherto at the Nevsky Prospekt, as the mortal enemy of Austria-Hungary, and consequently of Germany too.

But, in spite of this, the tension was genuinely relieved by the so-called Potsdam agreements, on the occasion of a visit paid by the Emperor Nicholas to Potsdam in November. In them, Germany acknowledged Russia's special influence in northern Persia, whilst Russia undertook not to make any difficulties in the way of German trade there, abandoned her opposition to the Bagdad railway, and agreed to the construction of a German branch line from Bagdad to the Turco-Persian frontier. In addition, and this was of the

[1] De Siebert, p. 120. [2] Loc. cit., p. 118.

utmost importance, the conversations extended to discussion of a pledge that " neither party would embark on anything that might have an aggressive aim against the other ". But Sazonov refused, later on, to have this particular point committed to writing, in consequence of the threefold opposition made to a serious *rapprochement* between Russia and Germany by the Russian intelligentsia, French public opinion, and the British Foreign Office.[1]

6. THE SECOND MOROCCAN CRISIS, 1911.

The Franco-German Moroccan treaty of 1909 (p. 37) did not lead to the desired result. No sooner had the French and German Governments paved the way for an economic understanding, than capitalist groups in both countries complained that the interests of their respective countries had been sacrificed. The French colonial politicians became impatient, and urged advantage being taken of the secret treaties of 1904. England had long since reaped the benefit of them in Egypt, why should France wait so long for Morocco ?

The year 1911 brought the desired pretext for action. In January a French column was attacked, and in February an insurrection against the Sultan broke out. The Government having announced, on the 9th and 10th of March, that they would be satisfied with the punishment of those who had taken part in the attack, the French Press demanded a Protectorate a week later. In April reports were spread that the capital of the Shereef's territory was besieged by rebels, and that the European colony was in danger. The day after the English Government had stated in the House of Commons that " the Europeans were not in danger " they were rescued by the French.[2] When the fact that Fez had been occupied, which had at first been kept secret, became known, there was great rejoicing throughout France.

In vain had the official *Norddeutsche Allgemeine Zeitung* explained that the independence of the Moroccan Sovereign

---

[1] App. I. No. 6, p. 227.
[2] Hansard's Parliamentary Debates, 1911, Vol. 24, p. 1601, and French Yellow Book on Morocco, Vol. VI. No. 255.

formed " an essential part of the Algeciras Act ", and announced that, in case of any alteration in the conditions, as a result of the French procedure, " the Powers would be free to act ". Paris did not even consider it necessary to discuss the matter with the Berlin Foreign Office, which was becoming politically more and more isolated. Finally, in consequence of the increasing dissatisfaction of public opinion in Germany, a section of which went so far as to demand the acquisition of western Morocco, the French Ambassador, Jules Cambon, was instructed to negotiate with the Secretary of State, Kiderlen Wächter, as to compensation. Orders were given at the same time to evacuate Fez. These orders were not carried out till July, and then only by the peculiar method of leaving French garrisons at every important point between the capital and the coast. In the meantime Spain, in order not to forego the advantages of the secret treaty, had sent troops into the Moroccan zone she had been promised, to the great and not very logical indignation of the French Press. The French Government's long silence had decided the Berlin Cabinet to send the gunboat *Panther*, a small vessel of a thousand tons, with a crew of 125 men, to Agadir, on the west coast of Morocco, where she cast anchor on the 1st of July. Until the German State Papers are published it is impossible to say whether the original intention was to take possession of the port as security. In reality nothing of the kind was done. Not a man was landed. A German Note presented to the French Government, stated that " the interpretation of the Act of Algeciras, respecting the sovereignty of the Sultan and the integrity of Morocco, was incompatible with the actual position. The German Government were prepared to enter into a friendly exchange of opinion with regard to a solution of the Moroccan question, and willing to discuss any proposal made by the French Government." [1]

The excitement caused by the appearance of the *Panther* off Agadir was greater in London than in Paris. Sir Edward Grey regarded the German action as a menace to British interests, and announced that Great Britain must take

[1] French Yellow Book on Morocco, Vol. VI. Nos. 418 and 421.

part in the Franco-German negotiations. From this it appears that he feared France might concede rights to Germany which would imperil England's economic interests, or—by the surrender of a naval base on the north coast of Africa—her strategic interests.[1] In reply to a French enquiry in London, he seems even to have said that " it might be advisable to silence the German interloper by a counter-demonstration, and compel him to retreat."[2] Fortunately a new Ministry had come into power in Paris on the 26th of June, with Joseph Caillaux as Premier, a man who aimed at economic co-operation with Germany, and consequently did not lend a willing ear to advice which must lead to war, but continued the conversations already begun.

In the course of these conversations Kiderlen Wächter took up an idea which had already been considered by the German Foreign Office in 1905. He offered Jules Cambon an entirely free hand in Morocco, and, in addition, Togo and a portion of the Cameroons, and demanded as compensation the part of the French Congo which separated the Cameroons from the great river. If there had previously been any intention in Berlin of asking for compensation in Morocco itself, it was at all events abandoned now. But France would only transfer parts of her Congo colony which were not on the coast.

When the negotiations came to a standstill towards the middle of July, England suddenly intervened, taking an extraordinarily high hand. *The Times* sounded the alarm on the 20th of July, and went so far as to assert that Germany was claiming absolute European predominance. At the time, France's possessions in Africa were three times greater than those ruled over by Germany, reckoned both territorially and according to population.[3] The following day

[1] This is evident from Grey's statement, in his speech of November 27, 1911, that he had told the German Ambassador that England had given France a free hand in Morocco, but had made certain economic and strategic stipulations.

[2] Freiherr v. Schoen, *Erlebtes*, p. 136. The French Yellow Book only contains, in Nos. 437 and 440, a question of July 8, whether England could not induce Germany to recall the *Panther*.

[3] Germany's possessions in Africa comprised 2·7 million qkm., with a population of 11·16 million ; and those of France 9·58 million qkm. with a population of 35·63 million.

Grey told the German Ambassador that Germany appeared to be making impossible demands, there were rumours of a German landing at Agadir, and of the intention being to make it a naval base, and he said that it would be advisable to invite England to take part in the conversations. In the evening, after consultation with Asquith and Grey, Lloyd George made a speech at a public banquet, in which, after extolling England's love of peace, he uttered the following threat :

But if a situation were to be forced upon us, in which peace could only be preserved by the surrender of the great and beneficent position England has won by centuries of heroism and achievement, by allowing Great Britain to be treated, where her interests were vitally affected, as if she were of no account in the Cabinet of Nations, then I say emphatically that peace at that price would be a humiliation intolerable for a great country like ours to endure.

Such language towards a Great Power is only customary on the eve of war. The German Government made no public reply at all, and only protested through the Foreign Office. Berlin had already sent a conciliatory reply to Grey's peremptory message of the 21st, and said that Germany did not ask anything exorbitant of France, and had neither landed at Agadir, nor had she any intention of doing so. But after the text of Lloyd George's speech had become known, Sir Edward Grey's question whether he could quote these assurances in Parliament was answered in the negative. A strong protest was made against the " insinuations " which emanated from the anti-German party, and the " hallucination " that the Germans proposed establishing a naval base in Morocco, and it concluded by saying : " If the English Government intended complicating and upsetting the political situation, and leading to an explosion, they certainly could not have chosen a better means than the Chancellor of the Exchequer's speech." As many of Grey's colleagues in the Cabinet and Party friends thoroughly disapproved of the threatening speech, the British Secretary of State replied with great moderation to this well-deserved lecture.

The general public, however, did not hear all this. The

excitement continued. The French were absolutely trans-
ported with joy over Germany's humiliation, but the Quai
d'Orsay would not agree to England's taking part in the
negotiations. The conversations between Kiderlen and
Cambon were continued, but came to a standstill again,
soon after the middle of August. The excitement rose to
fever heat throughout Europe ; a good deal transpired
subsequently as to the preparations for war made by England
in particular. But a hint from Russia, who gave it as her
opinion that Germany wished for an understanding,[1] had
a sobering effect on her Entente colleagues. The Russo-
German agreements respecting Persia and the railways in
Asia Minor were signed on the 19th of August, 1911, consequently the Potsdam agreements of the previous year
(p. 40) had a satisfactory result after all, just at a
critical moment, and, on the other hand, semi-official statements in Austria laid stress on the fact that the Moroccan
dispute did not concern the Danubian Monarchy. For
all that, considerable anxiety was still felt until finally,
on the 4th of November, two treaties were concluded, in
which France was given a free hand in Morocco, in return
for a guarantee that Germany's economic interests would be
safeguarded, and Germany received territorial compensation
in the Congo.

For our present purpose, the question is what value to
attach to the Agadir incident in relation to the Versailles
indictment. The *Panther* coup was certainly anything but
a skilful diplomatic move. It was calculated to wound
French pride, and, at the same time, as a naval demonstration, to bring England upon the scene. But it is self-
evident that a military operation cannot be undertaken by
a vessel of only a thousand tons, with a crew of 125 men.
As soon as the position became serious, the German Government preferred a diplomatic defeat to a breach of the peace.
For the rest, the reports of the Russian Ambassadors in
London and Paris may be allowed to speak for themselves.[2]
On the 16th of August, Count Benckendorff reported Grey's
having said to him :

[1] French Yellow Book on Morocco, Vol. VI. Nos. 518 and 527. Siebert,
p. 408.
[2] Siebert, pp. 435 and 445.

I do not believe that the Emperor William wanted war when this incident occurred, nor do I believe that he wants war now.

On the 13th of October Count Osten-Sacken wrote :

To begin with, the Emperor William decided, directly the crisis arose, not to let it come to war.

But, with regard to the other side, the Serbian Chargé d'Affaires in London reported on the 8th of September :

M. Cambon is of opinion that the present negotiations with Germany will be conducted to a conclusion, and that an agreement will be reached. But this agreement will not, and cannot permanently avert the peril threatened by Germany's policy of sudden attack. The only result would be to postpone war for three or four years. . . .

France is convinced that war will be forced upon her. . . . But both France and her allies are of opinion that the war must be postponed till later, that is to say, until 1914–15, even at the cost of still greater sacrifices. This postponement is necessitated less by the state of France's material preparation for war, which is complete, than by the organization of the Supreme Command, which has not yet been brought to perfection. This respite is also a necessity for Russia. England alone will gain nothing by it, as her naval superiority over Germany diminishes with every year. In consideration of her allies' preparations, France advises an understanding being reached now.[1]

With France in 1911, as with Russia in 1908–9, it was only a question of postponing war to a more favourable time, not of abandoning the idea. But Lloyd George's speech had been a plain threat of war. A Germany looking to armed conflict as a means of attaining European supremacy had a fifth opportunity for a war of prevention. The military conditions, it is true, were no longer so favourable, by a long way, as in 1905–6, and were also less favourable than in 1908–9. But Russia had only just begun to carry out her great armament programme, Serbia was only half as strong as in 1914, France had not yet started the three years' service period, and the French army was not at that time stronger than the German by 40,000 men. Lastly, in case of things becoming serious, Austria-

[1] Bogitshevich, pp. 141–2.

Hungary's loyalty could be relied upon, in spite of the lukewarm diplomatic support she had given her ally.

7. THE TRIPOLITAN WAR OF 1911.

The French action in Morocco led to the Tripoli enterprise. What the Italians wanted in this part of the world had been conceded in the second Triple Alliance treaty of 1887, and even more definitely by Germany, consequently by Austria-Hungary too, in the third treaty of 1891. In 1901 the following agreement was entered into with France : Morocco for France, Tripoli for Italy.[1] The agreement with England was probably concluded at the same time, anyhow at the latest, when the two Kings met at Gaëta in April 1907. Russia had given her consent at Racconigi in 1909 (p. 38). Then, in the autumn of 1911, when it was certain that a French Protectorate would be established over Morocco, there was some fear at the Consulta, lest France, being sure of her booty, might grudge Italy hers, and it was decided to lose no time in seizing it. Prince Bülow relates how one day the Marquis di San Giuliano took out his watch and said to his secretaries :

Note the hour and the date. It has been decided to-day that we go to Tripoli. We have been left no alternative. . . .[2]

On the 28th of September an ultimatum was presented to the Porte, which only left the Turks a choice between Italian occupation and war. The time given for an answer was limited to twenty-four hours. The ultimatum stated that it was in Italy's vital interest that Tripoli and Cyrenaica should be raised to a high level of civilization, and that, as Turkey was not equal to the task, nothing remained but for Italy to occupy both provinces. The Porte conceded the economic demands, but refused to agree to the occupation, and war began. England appeased the conscientious objections to the violation of international treaties she had so loudly and vehemently proclaimed in 1908, by occupying the Gulf of Sollum, situated on the Egyptian

[1] French Yellow Book, *Les Accords Franco-Italiens*, 1901-2, No. 1.
[2] Prince von Bülow's *Deutsche Politik*, 1917 edition, p. 107.

frontier, and belonging to Tripoli, presumably basing her action on previous agreements. France did not take her romantic sister-nation's expansion on the shores of the Mediterranean so calmly. French policy, it is true, was no longer guided by the views Napoleon III. held when he told Bismarck in 1857 that he did " not exactly want to make the Mediterranean a French lake, only something very similar ", [1] but the idea was to effectually maintain France's position as the second Mediterranean Power after England, and probably at the same time to aim a blow at Italy, as Germany's ally, although the alliance was only nominal. It was hardly possible to adopt this attitude openly, consistently with the treaty of 1901, but smuggling arms for the Turks was secretly encouraged, and, after the seizure of two French ships by the Italian navy, this led to diplomatic negotiations, in which Italy decided to yield, although she was unquestionably in the right.

Whilst Austria-Hungary was not sorry to see Italy turning her attention to the southern shores of the Mediterranean, the Tripoli enterprise was a serious blow to Germany's position in Constantinople. The pro-German politicians had to make way for those who favoured England. The military campaign their ally had embarked upon could not be booked as a diplomatic gain to the Central Powers. Germany had neither been able to protect her friend, Turkey, against a breach of the peace by her ally, nor to protect her ally, Italy, against French rapacity.

8. German Efforts to approach England and France at the Beginning of 1912.

The events that had taken place in the summer of 1911 produced very opposite results in France and England. People on the other side of the channel began to see where the path that had been pursued since 1908 must lead. The Radical wing of the Liberal Party protested against a diplomatic system which had brought Europe to the verge of a general war. There was even a distinct demand for Grey's resignation. The pacifist, E. D. Morel, known for his

---

[1] *Die Grosse Politik*, Vol. VI. No. 1207, p. 103.

courageous campaign against the cruelties practised on the natives in the Belgian Congo, was one of the most ardent champions of this school of thought. It is true that public opinion for the most part approved the main lines of the policy pursued hitherto, but, apart from the Jingo militarist party, no one wanted war. Grey decided to change his methods.

In France it was the reverse. Caillaux's Ministry, which had been prepared to enter into an economic understanding with Germany, was overthrown. January 1912 saw the advent of the " second great Ministry of the third Republic," so called because it reckoned ten former Ministers among its members, of whom two were former Premiers. The leading men were : Poincaré, the Lorrainer, as Premier and Minister for Foreign Affairs, the *ci-devant* Socialist, now Militarist, Millerand, as War Minister, and Delcassé, the soul of the alliance with Russia, and author of the *Entente Cordiale*, the man who had wished for war in 1905, as Minister of Marine. Well might the Russian Ambassador, Isvolsky, write towards the end of the year :

If the crisis comes, which may God forbid, the decision will be in the hands of the three strong personalities at the head of the Cabinet : Poincaré, Millerand, and Delcassé. We are fortunate in the prospect of having to deal with these men, and not with one or other of the chance politicians who have succeeded one another in the French Government in the course of the last few years.[1]

This impression continued to exist among the diplomatists in Paris, for as recently as on the 16th of January, 1914, the Belgian Minister, Baron Guillaume, made the following report :

Ce sont, en effet, MM. Poincaré, Delcassé, Millerand, et leurs amis, qui ont inventé et poursuivi la politique nationaliste, cocardière, et chauvine dont nous avons constaté la renaissance. Or, cette politique constitue un danger pour l'Europe et la Belgique.[2]

The first step taken in the new direction by the British Government was a visit paid by the well-known financier, Sir Ernest Cassel, to Berlin, where he submitted an unofficial

[1] *Livre Noir*, Vol. I. p. 364, Isvolsky to Sazonov, December 5, 1912.
[2] *Zur Europäischen Politik*, 1897–1914, edited under the direction of Bernhard Schwertfeger, Vol. IV. p. 174.

memorandum, on behalf of Grey, Lloyd George, and Churchill, suggesting that Germany should limit her naval construction ; that England would then support the German wish for colonial expansion, and an English Minister could come to Berlin to discuss the matter.[1] The German Government said that they were willing to acquaint the London Cabinet with their new Navy Bill before publishing it, but whether they could modify it to meet any wish or objection England might express, must depend on her being willing to enter into a political agreement which would give Germany a certain amount of security, in case of a continental war. After this preliminary conversation, the British War Minister, Haldane, arrived in Berlin on the 8th of February, 1912.

The Chancellor, von Bethmann Hollweg, was prepared to make the greatest possible concessions in the matter of the Navy Bill, if this were counterbalanced by a political agreement. But it was precisely with regard to the political agreement that no formula could be found which was satisfactory to both parties, although, after Haldane's departure on the 12th of February, the negotiations were continued till the end of March. Germany's first demand : " England's neutrality in a war in which Germany might be involved " undoubtedly went too far, for it would have pledged England to neutrality even in case of a German war of aggression. On the other hand England's first counter-proposal " not to take part in an unprovoked attack on Germany " did not go far enough. When this formula was amplified by adding " refrain from an aggressive policy towards Germany ", the Chancellor expressed what must be regarded as a legitimate wish that the words " benevolent neutrality, in case of war being forced upon Germany," should be added. According to a report sent by the German Ambassador, Count Metternich, on the 17th of March, Grey, however, stated that " a direct treaty of neutrality would be certain to offend French susceptibilities, and that the British Government must avoid this." On the 20th of March, Metternich reported that the British Secretary of State had said : " Any advance

[1] Bethmann Hollweg, *Betrachtungen zum Weltkrieg*, Vol. I. pp. 49–50, and Viscount Haldane, *Before the War*, p. 55.

beyond the existing Navy law would debar the British Government from entering into a political agreement with Germany, but presumably complete abandonment of the Navy Bill is outside the realm of discussion." To this Berlin replied that " as no satisfactory treaty of neutrality could be obtained, there was no further possibility of altering the Navy Bill to meet England's wishes. The German Government were willing to continue the inter-change of views with regard to territorial and colonial questions."[1]

Grey's statement, reported on the 17th of March, points to the probability of his having come to an understanding with France, and reports from the Russian Ambassador in Paris confirm this. According to a telegram sent by Isvolsky on the 1st of March, 1912, Poincaré was not averse to an Anglo-German agreement at first, but French military men were of a different opinion, as they were afraid that if Germany reduced her naval expenditure she would spend more on her army.[2] Poincaré seems to have fallen in with this view at once, for, later on, Isvolsky sent the following report, on the strength of communications from Poincaré and Paléologue, at that time Director of the political department :

The London Cabinet informed Poincaré of the proposal, and were obviously uncertain whether to accept or reject it. Poincaré expressed a very decided opinion against such an agreement ; he pointed out to the English Government that the signature of such an agreement with Germany, at a time when there was no agree-ment of a general political nature between England and France, would at once put an end to the existing Anglo-French relations. This protest had the expected result : the London Cabinet rejected the German proposal, thereby causing great dissatisfaction in Berlin.[3]

---

[1] The Ambassador's report and the German Government's reply are quoted from unpublished German Foreign Office records in *Deutschland und der Weltkrieg*, pp. 598 ff., by Hintze, Meinecke, Oncken, Schulmacher (B. G. Tarbner, second edition, 1916).

[2] Siebert, p. 761–2.

[3] *Livre Noir*, Vol. I. pp. 365–6, Isvolsky to Sazonov, December 5, 1912. A written Anglo-French agreement of a general political nature existed in December, in the form of a correspondence of the 22nd and 23rd of November, 1912, between Cambon and Grey, but not at the time of Haldane's mission.

According to Haldane, the feeling in England changed, because the British Admiralty considered that the new German Navy Bill went too far. In reality both causes probably contributed to bring about the change, the French Premier's protest, and the objections made by the Admiralty. The negotiations which had begun earlier between London and Berlin, with regard to the Bagdad railway and the allotment of the Portuguese colonies in Africa, were continued.

According to an official French source, Germany tried to approach France on the basis of far reaching autonomy for Alsace-Lorraine, soon after the failure of Haldane's mission. At that time Poincaré said to the French Ambassador in Berlin :

> The only thing of interest in all this is the attitude of the German Government. They seem to be pertinaciously endeavouring to bring about a *rapprochement* which would really be impossible unless the former *status* were completely restored. If we entertained such proposals we should fall out with England and Russia. We should lose all the advantages we have gained, thanks to the sound policy France has pursued for many years past.[1]

Consequently Poincaré is at least partly responsible for the failure of the Anglo-German *rapprochement*, and he is solely responsible for the failure of the Franco-German *rapprochement*.

The English author, Begbie, who was certainly not pro-German, said of the attitude of the German Government at that time :

> It is not history, it is not even romance, it is wild nonsense to suggest that the German Government was not striving for peace at this moment. The Emperor wanted peace, the Chancellor wanted peace, and a *rapprochement* with England was the ideal to which the Foreign Minister, Kiderlen Wächter, was devoting his energies (as the *Daily Mail's* correspondent in Berlin assures us). The war party, of course, was working for war, but the responsible Government of the country was earnestly working for peace.[2]

---

[1] Report to the French Senate, No. 704, of the year 1919 (*Rapport de la Commission d'Enquête sur les Faits de la Guerre*, Vol. I. p. 363.
[2] *Vindication of Great Britain*, by Harold Begbie, 1916, p. 142.

9. THE FIRST BALKAN WAR, AUTUMN OF 1912.

The storm which had hung over the Balkans in 1909 without bursting, now travelled back there via Morocco and Tripoli. Just as the destruction of Morocco's independence had been the cause of the expedition to Tripoli, so Turkey's being involved in war with a Great Power inspired the Balkan States' decision to liberate their kinsmen who were still under Turkish rule, a perfectly legitimate decision from their point of view. The advocates of an active policy in St. Petersburg were also urging action. The majority, led by Hartwig, the Russian Minister in Belgrade, were in favour of a Balkan League against Turkey; the Russian Ambassador in Constantinople, Tcharikov, on the other hand, advised including Turkey in the League, in return for concessions to Russia as regards the Straits. But rumours of the negotiations with the Porte reached the public; the Foreign Minister, Sazonov, denied all knowledge of them, and the matter was dropped.[1]

The advocates of a Balkan alliance against Turkey had carried the day. The Serbian Minister, Milowanovich, now showed special zeal in helping to found the League, and directed it against Austria as well, from the first. His view was that the downfall of the Danubian Monarchy would very much "simplify" a solution of the pending territorial disputes between the Balkan States. This is what he said to the Bulgarian Premier, Guechov:

> If the break up of Turkey and the downfall of Austria-Hungary could take place simultaneously, the solution would be very much simplified; Serbia would be given Bosnia and Herzegovina, whilst Rumania would have Transylvania, and we should have no interference to fear from Rumania in our war with Turkey.[2]

The Serbo-Bulgarian treaty, concluded with Hartwig's alleged co-operation, was signed on the 13th of March, the second article being as follows:

> Both the contracting Parties pledge themselves to support one another with all their available forces, in the event of any one of

---

[1] Vide Part II. sect. 12, on The Development of the Straits Question.
[2] Vide Friedjung, Vol. III. pp. 174 and 175, and the authorities he quotes.

the Great Powers attempting, even only temporarily, to seize, or occupy, or send troops to occupy any territory situated in the Balkans, and at present under Turkish suzerainty, even if only one of the two States considers such act injurious to its interests, or a *casus belli*.[1]

This referred to a possible re-occupation of the Sandjak by Austria-Hungary. A secret rider appended to the treaty appointed Russia arbiter, both for any disputes that might arise out of the treaty, and to fix the date for the commencement of hostilities against Turkey. It was a remarkable coincidence that the day before the treaty was signed, the 12th of March, the following order had been issued in Russia :

In accordance with His most gracious Majesty's decision, a telegraphic command to order mobilization in the European military districts, on account of political complications on the western frontiers, is to be regarded simultaneously as an order to commence hostilities against Austria and Germany. As far as Rumania is concerned, hostilities are not to be commenced without a direct order.[2]

In May and June the Serbo-Bulgarian agreements were supplemented by military conventions, which stipulated that Bulgaria should place 200,000 men at Serbia's disposal, not only in case of Austria-Hungary invading the country, but also in case

Austria-Hungary, by agreement with Turkey, or without such agreement, should march her troops into the Sandjak of Novi-Bazar under any pretext, and thereby compel Serbia either to declare war on Austria-Hungary, or to send troops to the Sandjak to defend her interests there, whereby Serbia would bring about a conflict with Austria-Hungary.[3]

A treaty Bulgaria concluded with Greece, at the end of May, merely provided that the two States should help their fellow countrymen in Macedonia to obtain their rights, and

---

[1] Bogitshevich, p. 130.

[2] Instruction sent by the Russian General Staff to the Commandant of the Warsaw military district, April 11, 1912, No. 545. Original in the archives at Potsdam.

[3] Bogitshevich, pp. 130, 132, 134, 136–8. The Serbo-Bulgarian agreements are not given in full in the German White Book of June 1919 (*Deutschland schuldig ?*), pp. 137 and 139.

support them by armed force if this should lead to war with Turkey.[1]

In June, between the conclusion of the first and second Serbo-Bulgarian military conventions, the Kings of Bulgaria and Montenegro visited Vienna, where Count Berchtold had succeeded Aehrenthal in February. They were received with blind confidence, and the greatest friendliness. A meeting took place the same month between the German and Russian Emperors at Port Baltic, after which a semi-official Russian account announced that the meeting vouched, on the one hand, for the firm and enduring friendship between the two Empires, and, on the other hand, it indicated the peaceable principles which determined their uniform policy. Did the Tsar and his Ministers really believe that the power conceded to Russia to fix a date for the commencement of war would enable them to maintain peace ?

The purport of the Serbo-Bulgarian treaty went too far even for Russia's French ally. When Poincaré looked into it in St. Petersburg, in August, he wrote to Paris :

Le traité contient donc en germe, non seulement une guerre contre la Turquie, mais une guerre contre l'Autriche. Il établit, en autre, l'hégémonie de la Russie sur les deux royaumes slaves, puisque la Russie est prise comme arbitre dans toutes les questions. Je fais remarquer à M. Sazonov que cette Convention ne répond aucunement à la définition qui m'en avait été donnée, qu'elle est, à vrai dire, une convention de guerre, et que, non seulement elle révèle des arrières-pensées chez les Serbes et chez les Bulgares, mais qu'il est à craindre que leurs espérances ne paraissent encouragées par la Russie, et que le partage éventuel ne soit un appât pour leurs convoitises.

According to Poincaré, Sazonov admitted that, in transmitting the treaty to St. Petersburg, the Russian Minister in Sofia had himself described it as a war treaty, but he said that as the Serbs and Bulgarians had pledged themselves not to declare war or even to mobilize without Russia's consent, Russia could exercise a right of veto, and would not fail to do so.[2]

---

[1] Friedjung, Vol. III. p. 178.
[2] *Ministère des Affaires Etrangères, Documents Diplomatiques, Les Affaires Balkaniques* 1912–14, Vol. I. No. 57, p. 38. Sir Arthur Nicolson also considered that the Convention was " directed against the possibility of Austrian aggression " (Siebert, p. 552).

At that time, Poincaré also gave St. Petersburg to understand that public opinion in France would not permit the Government of the Republic to take up arms for Balkan questions, if Germany did not intervene,[1] but he did not urge an alteration being made in the objectionable treaty, although he believed that Austria would not, under any circumstances, allow it to be carried into effect, if she heard of it. There was no ground for anxiety on this score, for when the Vienna Government learnt of the existence of the treaty, in the middle of September, they merely transmitted the information to Berlin.

Reliance on Russia's right of veto proved delusive. Ominous clouds having given warning of the approaching storm since the beginning of August, Bulgaria, Serbia, and Montenegro mobilized on the 30th of September, and Greece a day later. On the same 30th of September, the VIth Army Corps at Warsaw, and no doubt other Army Corps as well, were informed of the order that " an announcement of mobilization would also be an announcement of war against Germany".[2] The Russian army was simultaneously strengthened by test mobilizations on an extensive scale on the frontier, which were not officially notified (to Germany [Tr.]) beforehand, as formerly.[3] The order shows what general mobilization in Russia would have meant ; its coincidence with the Balkan States being ready for war, and the simultaneous reinforcement of the army, further prove that the authorities in St. Petersburg cannot have been altogether taken by surprise. But the political leaders did not wish for the great war then ; they joined in the efforts made by the other Powers to exorcise the evil they had themselves let loose, in Poincaré's opinion, for they feared that " a prolonged war would not be at all advantageous to the Balkan States, whose resources were limited."[4]

Even after the 30th of September the Great Powers imagined that they could still save the situation by a formula

---

[1] Siebert, p. 549 ; comp. *Affaires Balkaniques*, Vol. I. No. 184, pp. 111–14.
[2] App. I. No. 7, p. 228.　　　　[3] *Deutschland schuldig ?* p. 141.
[4] *Affaires Balkaniques*, Vol. I. Nos. 181 and 184. The latter shows that Poincaré's conscience reproached him for having concealed the ‚' war treaties " which he now communicated to London.

threatening the peace-breakers, and decreeing the maintenance of the *status quo*. When this interdiction was communicated to Cettinje, on the 8th of October, King Nicholas
replied that he had just declared war on Turkey. On the
17th and 18th the three allies followed his example.

The Turks did not gain the victory expected in Berlin
and Vienna, and feared in Russia and France. Instead of
acting on the advice formerly given by Field-Marshal von
der Goltz, and waiting till their fighting forces, which could
only be gradually brought up from distant parts of the
country, were all assembled, they took the offensive on all
the enemy frontiers. While still far inferior numerically,
they were decisively defeated in Rumelia by the Bulgarians,
and in Macedonia by the Serbs and Greeks. The badly
planned Bulgarian attack on the strongly fortified Tchataldja
line, which protected Constantinople, failed, it is true, and
King Ferdinand's dream of planting the cross on the Mosque
of St. Sophia was not fulfilled. But the Porte, whose forces
were absolutely exhausted, had to ask for an armistice.
This was concluded with Bulgaria and Serbia on the 3rd of
December, but Adrianople and Scutari were still besieged,
and Greece did not suspend hostilities.

By the end of October it was evident that the Balkan
States were the victors, and this produced a fundamental
change in French policy. Whilst the responsible leaders in
Paris at first endeavoured to avert, or at least to localize
the conflict, they now recognized what a valuable ally the
victorious Balkan League might be against the Central
Powers. In contrast to the attitude adopted during the
annexation crisis of 1908-9, French policy now followed
absolutely in Russia's wake. Now and again, indeed,
France supported the wishes of the Russian war party and
the aims of the Balkan States more zealously than the
political leaders in St. Petersburg. The formula proposed
by Poincaré on the 30th of October, that the Great Powers
should declare their "absolute *désintéressement*",[1] was
obviously aimed against Austria. This is quite evident
from a letter written by the French Premier to Isvolsky
a few days later, in which he says that in agreement with

[1] Loc. cit., Vol. I. No. 210.

the Cabinet, he considers it advisable " to decide on a common line of action, in case of Austria's endeavouring to add to her territorial possessions ".[1] The reply from St. Petersburg thanked him for taking the initiative and anticipating Russia's wishes, but described the general formula " absolute opposition to any annexation of Turkish territory by a great Power " as " too positive ",[2] on account of their own wishes as regards the Straits.

From his conversations at the Quai d'Orsay the Russian Ambassador became more and more convinced of the change in France's policy, so much so that he sent the following report on the 7th of November :

> Whereas France has told us hitherto that local occurrences, so to speak exclusively Balkan concerns, could only cause her to take diplomatic steps, and on no account to intervene actively, she now seems to recognize that acquisition of territory by Austria would jeopardize the general balance of power in Europe, and therewith France's own interests.[3]

A few days later, Sazonov was informed by the French Ambassador that, in the event of Austria marching on Serbia, the position to be adopted by France would depend upon Russia's attitude.[4] But the statement Poincaré made to Isvolsky on the 17th of November went still farther :

> In a question in which Russia is the party chiefly interested, it is for Russia to take the initiative. France's rôle consists in giving her the most effective support.

And he added :

> What it all amounts to is simply that if Russia goes to war France will do the same.[5]

This promise was explained the following day, it is true, as only meaning that France would march " in the case provided for by the alliance, that is to say, if Germany were to support Austria-Hungary against Russia by force of arms ". The provisions of the treaty of alliance restricted

---

[1] Loc. cit., Vol. I. No. 226.   [2] *Livre Noir*, Vol. I. p. 345.
[3] Loc. cit., p. 342. Siebert, p. 575.
[4] *Affaires Balkaniques*, Vol. I. No. 257.
[5] *Livre Noir*, Vol. I. p. 346.

the obligation to the case of an Austro-Hungarian *offensive* against Russia, supported by Germany, but this restriction was not mentioned.[1] The following statement was made to the Italian Ambassador on the 20th of November, equally without any such reservation :

If the Austro-Serbian conflict should lead to a general war, Russia can absolutely rely on France's armed support.[2]

It is assuredly not a mere chance that just about this time, on the 22nd and 23rd of November, the Cambon-Grey correspondence took place, on the French initiative. This correspondence supplemented the conversations which had been customary since 1906 between the English and French naval and military experts, by a diplomatic agreement of a general nature, if only in the form of an exchange of notes.[3] Lloyd George spoke of it in Parliament on the 7th of August, 1918, as a " pact," and in reply to interruptions, as an " obligation of honour ". It was in fact the agreement whose absence Poincaré had regretted in the spring (p. 51).

Some interest also attaches to a report from the German Embassy in Paris, on the 11th of November, that, according to information from an absolutely reliable agent, the French Premier had represented in confidence to his Ministerial colleagues the necessity for

getting the start of the Germans and securing the first moral success, so important for the French temperament, by advancing across our frontiers the moment an armed conflict becomes inevitable. With this object constitutional considerations must be boldly disregarded, for the sake of gaining time, and Parliament must be confronted with a *fait accompli*, without being asked whether to declare war.[4]

These spontaneous assurances of loyalty to the alliance, the communication made to Italy as to France's readiness for war, and the establishment of her relations with England on a firmer basis, are the more remarkable, seeing that a much calmer view was taken of the situation in St. Peters-

---

[1] App. I. No. 8, p. 228.   [2] *Livre Noir*, Vol. I. p. 348.
[3] English Blue Book, 1914, No. 105. *Collected Diplomatic Documents.*
[4] German Foreign Office unpublished Documents.

burg. Sazonov said on the 14th of November : " Serbia must not hope to carry Russia with her, for she (Russia) is determined not to go to war for the sake of a Serbian port on the Adriatic," and on the 18th of November he said he did not believe there was any immediate danger, or that Austria wished for a rupture ; there was a tendency in Belgrade to exaggerate the Austro-Hungarian military preparations. If he was uneasy, it was, on the contrary, only " because of the difficulties there would be in the way of a settlement, and the excessive susceptibility of a section of public opinion ". In Paris, however, the necessity for advising Belgrade to give in, on account of Russia's attitude, was almost unwelcome, and the French representative was instructed to " word the advice in the most friendly spirit, to let Russia take the initiative, and not to say anything that might give rise to a belief that it was owing to the French attitude that Russia counselled moderation ".[1]

The calm view Sazonov took was thoroughly justified, for Austria had drawn the conclusion " the Balkans for the Balkan peoples " from the victories won by the Balkan States, and had accepted it with resignation. The aspirations to Salonica, if they still existed at all, were finally buried when the Greeks occupied the town on the 8th of November. Berchtold's modest programme, which was communicated on the 30th of October to Berlin and Rome, where it met with approval, and was then conveyed to the other capitals, only stipulated that Serbia should not have access to the sea, that Serbia and Montenegro should enter into commercial agreements with Austria-Hungary which would guarantee their ceasing to pursue a policy hostile to the Dual Monarchy, that Albania should be given a form of government which would make her independent, and Salonica declared a free port.[2] Rumania was to be suitably compensated, and the Bosnian frontier rectifications demanded were of purely local importance.

The only one of these demands to which exception can be taken is the opposition to Serbia's having access to the Adriatic. But this, and the creation of an independent

[1] *Affaires Balkaniques*, Vol. I. Nos. 258 and 260.
[2] Loc. cit., Vol. I. No. 247.

Albania, were precisely the points most approved of in Rome, where the establishment of the South Slavs on the eastern shores of the Adriatic would have given as much dissatisfaction as in Vienna. This unanimity facilitated the renewal of the Triple Alliance on the 5th of December, 1912, all the more as Italy was annoyed with France because the whole French fleet had been assembled in the Mediterranean, and also because of the difficulties she had thrown in the way of the Tripoli enterprise by smuggling arms. But the anxiety shown by Poincaré regarding Austria's alleged intention of adding to her territories can only be put down to ill-will, as Berchtold's programme had been communicated to Paris as far back as at the beginning of November.

It is true that, in view of the steps taken to reinforce the Russian army not having been cancelled, precautionary measures were also taken in Vienna. The strength of the three Army Corps in Galicia, and of the troops on the Bosnian frontier, was increased by calling up reservists and *Ersatz* reservists. Those were the orders which were erroneously described, even in official documents, as "mobilization." The re-appointment of General Conrad von Hötzendorf to be Chief of the Staff was also of political importance.

As far as the attitude of the Berlin Cabinet is concerned, they were not by any means willing to be as absolutely guided by Austro-Hungarian policy as the French Republic by the policy of the Russian Empire. On the contrary, they endeavoured to mediate both with regard to a Serbian port on the Adriatic and the question of Albanian expansion. In writing to the Foreign Office on the 7th, 9th, and 11th of November, the Emperor William said :

From the attitude of the Austrian Press it appears to me that Austria intends to make serious opposition to Serbia's wish to establish herself on the Adriatic coast. Serbia wants an outlet to the sea, the same as her neighbours. It is, after all, what all inland States want. I see absolutely no menace to Austria's existence or prestige in a Serbian port on the Adriatic.

Have discussed the matter exhaustively with the Chancellor, and told him definitely that nothing will induce me to march on Paris and Moscow for the sake of Albania and Durazzo.

The Triple Alliance only safeguards the mutual territorial rights of the three States, it does not bind them to take part unconditionally in disputes over the territory of others. If Austria were attacked by Russia the *casus fœderis* would arise certainly, but even then, only if Austria had not provoked Russia to attack her.[1]

On the occasion of a shooting party at Springe, near Hanover, November 22, " the Archduke Franz Ferdinand tried to show the German Emperor how necessary it was to take strong measures against Serbia. The Emperor did not dispute this, but he wished that at the same time nothing should be done which might lead to a rupture with Russia ".[2]

On the same occasion General von Moltke, Chief of the German General Staff, replied to the Archduke's question whether he thought it likely that Russia would attack Austria :

If Austria wishes to avoid war, she must first inform the Cabinets plainly what she demands of Serbia, and if her minimum wishes were stated, she would assuredly gain the sympathy of the Powers. Steps must then be taken to expedite a renewal of the Triple Alliance, without regard to Austria's private wishes. That will have the effect of restraining Russia.[3]

The French Minister in Belgrade reported on the 27th of November that, according to official information, the German Government were endeavouring to " find a compromise between the irreconcilable Austrian and Serbian views ".[4] Three days later, the Belgian Minister in Berlin, no longer the very pro-German Baron Greindl, but his more unapproachable successor, Baron Beyens, wrote :

There is no doubt that the Emperor, the Chancellor, and the Foreign Secretary are strongly pacifist.[5]

On the 2nd of December, the Chancellor pointed out in the Reichstag that if, contrary to his hopes, there should be

[1] German Foreign Office unpublished Documents, quoted in the *Süddeutsche Monatshefte*, May 1922, pp. 99–100, in connection with the Fechenbach-Cossmann trial.
[2] Friedjung, Vol. III. p. 228.
[3] German Foreign Office unpublished Documents.
[4] *Affaires Balkaniques*, Vol. I. No. 296.
[5] *Belgian Diplomatic Documents*, 1905–14, No. 96, p. 112.

disputes which could not be solved, it would be for the Powers directly concerned to vindicate their claims, and he added : " But if, contrary to all expectation, our allies should be attacked by a third party, and their existence threatened, when defending their rights, we should then stand by them resolutely, true to our obligations ". France tried to agitate against Germany in London and Paris, on account of these last words, and not altogether without success, in the case of Sir Edward Grey. But Sazonov said he saw nothing in the speech that had not already been said to Russia, namely, " Germany will only side with Austria, if the latter is attacked.[1]

Lastly, Germany found an unexpected witness for her defence in Poincaré, who said, during the debate on the question of responsibility for the war in the French Chamber, on the 6th of July, 1922 :

There can be no doubt that during the whole of the year 1912, Germany made honest efforts to act with us in the interest of Europe in general, and with a view to the maintenance of peace.[2]

The addition " she was not ready ", after a studied pause, was an unworthy insinuation. The lack of logic in representing that Germany wanted a war in the summer of 1911, according to Poincaré, for which she only prepared after 1912, escaped his undiscerning hearers.

10. THE SECOND BALKAN WAR, FEBRUARY TO MAY 1913.

A change of historical importance had taken place in the south-east of Europe in the months of October and November 1912. Turkey, who had in reality a leaning towards Germany, in spite of many a lapse, was almost entirely thrown back towards Asia Minor ; the victorious League of fifteen million Serbs, Montenegrins, Bulgarians, and Greeks, cut off the Central Powers from the East by land, thus bringing a considerable accession of power to the Triple Entente. The sole, perhaps only temporary, compensation for this was that, on account of her opposition to

[1] *Affaires Balkaniques*, Vol. I. No. 309, and Vol. II. No. 8.
[2] *Annales de la Chambre des Députés*, 1922, Vol. II. p. 717.

South Slav expansion, Italy approached Germany and Austria again. Even in September 1912, the experts in France had viewed the prospects of Russia and France, in the event of a general conflagration, " with considerable optimism "[1]; how favourably they must now have regarded the possibilities of a conflict, after the unexpectedly great successes of the Russian troops. In the eyes of the world, the defeat of Turkey was also a defeat for the German instructor, and of course it was said that the superiority of the French guns over the Turks' German artillery equipment had been proved beyond the possibility of doubt. The wildest hopes of the Pan-Slavists seemed to be nearing fulfilment, and the French nationalists saw the day approaching within measurable distance when Alsace-Lorraine would be won back again, as the Royalist Comte de Mun announced in a public speech. Russia, and with her the combined Powers of the Triple Entente, were amply avenged for the diplomatic defeat of 1909. The Russian Ambassador in London, Count Benckendorff, expressed this feeling on the 24th of November in the following words :

If I am not mistaken, public opinion in Russia appears to be guided above all by the thought of revenge for 1909; I myself have this feeling too strongly to be in a position to condemn such a feeling in Russia. But it also seems to me that we have already achieved our revenge to a very great extent.[2]

Two conferences, presided over by Sir Edward Grey, were held in London, with the object of restoring peace, one a conference of representatives of the belligerent States the other an Ambassadors' conference. The modest task allotted to the latter was to fix the future boundaries of Albania, and apportion the islands of the Archipelago. A disquieting factor was that not only the armies of the belligerents naturally remained on a war footing, but neither Austria nor Russia cancelled the steps which had been taken to raise theirs above peace strength. In Paris people were very full of the question of war. Towards the middle of December Russia had advised Serbia to accept the decision

---

[1] *Livre Noir*, Vol. I. pp. 326, 342, and 346. Siebert, pp. 575-6 and 586.
[2] Siebert, p. 594?

of the Powers respecting the Adriatic port, Nicholas II. had expressed a most decided wish for peace, the Russian War Minister was so confident that peace would be maintained that he intended going abroad, and the Russian General Staff declared that Austria was only taking defensive measures on the Russian frontier, it was highly improbable that she would attack Serbia, and that even in this case, Russia would not draw the sword. But the French statesmen were reckoning " seriously with the possibility of war ", on the strength of alarming reports from their representatives in Vienna and Belgrade, which found no credence in London, and were " very much upset and alarmed " by the view taken in St. Petersburg, as they were convinced " of the belligerent character of the Austrian preparations, and feared a sudden attack on Russia, which would facilitate German military operations against France ".[1] Not having received an immediate answer to his report of this, despatched on the 14th of December, Isvolsky reported as follows four days later :

Whereas only a short time ago the French Government and Press were inclined to blame us for egging on Serbia, and the dominant note was : " La France ne veut pas faire la guerre pour un port Serbe," our indifference to the Austrian mobilization is now regarded with astonishment and undisguised anxiety.

He repeated his former statement that the news from St. Petersburg had very much surprised Poincaré and all the Ministers, adding that the French mobilization had been tested on the eastern frontier, and that even material was in readiness.[2]

The nervousness felt in France now extended to Russia. Sazonov threatened to strengthen the Russian army if Austria did not cancel her "mobilization measures", and declared that the General Staff had gone too far in saying that Russia would not go to war, even if Austria attacked Serbia. He had never spoken so decidedly before. On the 23rd of December it was further stated that Russia's neutrality could " no longer be guaranteed ", unless the

---

[1] *Affaires Balkaniques*, Vol. II. Nos. 9–14. Also Isvolsky to Sazonov, December 14, 1912, *Süddeutsche Monatshefte*, July 1922, pp. 207–8.
[2] *Livre Noir*, Vol. I. p 369.

Porte gave up Adrianople, Scutari, and Janina. This statement was contradicted later on, but subsequently repeated.[1] The restraint Russia showed at first was based, it is true, not on innate love of peace, but on her confidence that there would be still more favourable opportunities in the future. On the 13th of November, 1912, the French and Russian Ministers in Bucharest had advised their Serbian colleague to be patient as regards the outlet to the Adriatic, on the ground that it was better

for Serbia, who would be at least twice as large as before, to wait, and in the meantime strengthen and pull herself together, so as to be as prepared as possible for the important events which must take place amongst the Great Powers.[2]

On the 27th of December Sazonov assured the Serbian representative in St. Petersburg that

after Serbia's great successes he had confidence in her strength, and believed that she would deal Austria a shattering blow ; for this reason Serbia ought to be satisfied with what she would receive, and regard this as only a stage, for the future was hers.[3]

In spite of the advice to give in as regards the Adriatic port, the St. Petersburg statesmen had no wish to see Austria and Serbia sincerely reconciled. A report sent by Benckendorff on the 30th of October makes this perfectly evident. With reference to the Austrian proposals (p. 60), the Ambassador considered a commercial agreement in particular, " imposed as a condition ", " incompatible with Russia's interests ", but went on to say that Russia must not let it appear that she did not wish for this understanding, for

if we allowed it to be foreseen that we should try to prevent Austria from concluding an economic agreement with the aggrandized Balkan States in the future, the rôles would be exchanged. I doubt whether we should have any substantial support from the Western Powers in this case. For if an economic agreement between sovereign States, which serves their mutual interests, can avert the danger of a European war, it seems to me that both public opinion and the Governments of the Western Powers will approve of such an agreement.[4]

[1] *Affaires Balkaniques*, Vol. II. Nos. 33, 34, 37, 39, 40 and 45.
[2] Bogitshevich, p. 127. [3] Loc. cit., p. 128.
[4] Benckendorff to Sazonov, October 30, 1912. Siebert, pp. 559–60.

At the turn of the year 1912–13, the political world was looking forward with great suspense to the Presidential election which Poincaré was contesting. Isvolsky was torn with anxiety, for according to him, the late Premier's defeat would be a " catastrophe " for Russia, and " the beginning of a Combes era ". [1] His faithful ally was elected, however, thanks to Royalist support, although he had been defeated at the trial ballot a few days earlier. This decision was regarded by many people in France as almost equivalent to war,[2] and it certainly was responsible for a very dangerous programme of foreign policy. The new President of the Republic assured the Ambassador that he could continue to influence the method of dealing with foreign questions, and pointed out that

it was of the greatest importance for the French Government to be able to prepare public opinion in advance for participation in the war which might be caused by the Balkan question.[3]

Isvolsky was now sure that " men like Caillaux, Cruppi, and Monis " would not come into power during the next seven years. Conversations with Poincaré and the Foreign Minister, Jonnart, not only assured him that the new Cabinet would carry out the obligations of the alliance in full, but they also

admitted, with full confidence of what it implied, and all the necessary *sang froid*, that the final result of the present complications might perhaps be France's necessarily having to take part in a general war.[4]

Poincaré took up his abode at the Elysée on the 18th of February, and on the 19th he decided to recall the French Ambassador in St. Petersburg, George Louis, who was replaced in March by Delcassé. This step was a bombshell,[5] as the Belgian Minister in Paris put it, for Louis had exerted a pacifying influence in St. Petersburg. In a personal letter to Nicholas II., the President recommended the new

[1] *Livre Noir*, Vol. II. p. 9.
[2] *Considérations sur les Responsabilités de la Guerre*, Gustave Dupin, Paris, 1921.
[3] *Livre Noir*, Vol. II. p. 15.   [4] Loc. cit., Vol. II. p. 26.
[5] *Belgian Diplomatic Documents*, No. 99.

Ambassador, who was to cement the alliance between the Republic and the Russian Empire still " more firmly," and urge the " construction of certain railway lines on the west frontier of Russia being expedited ". These were railways of which Poincaré had spoken when he was in St. Petersburg the summer before, and which had become still more necessary ", in consequence of the great effort France intended making to maintain the balance of power in Europe ".[1] This referred to the introduction of the three years' period of service.

In the meantime the labours of the two London Conferences had not been attended with success. The Conference between the representatives of the belligerents came to an abrupt end as far back as on the 7th of January, as Turkey refused to surrender Adrianople, which was to be given to Bulgaria, as an inducement to her to make further concessions to Serbia in Macedonia than had been provided for in the treaty of 1912. This demand was now taken up by the Ambassadorial Conference, and even Germany associated herself with it, for the sake of unanimity. The Turkish Government made the sacrifice with a heavy heart, but was overthrown by Enver Pasha on this account.

The Young Turks came into power again, and rejected the Balkan League's peace proposals. On the 2nd of February the second Balkan war began.

Russia did not welcome the renewal of hostilities, as she was afraid that the Bulgarians might yet enter Constantinople, which they had long called " Zarigrad ". Even King Ferdinand's undertaking only to remain there for two days, as at least some small concession to the wish of the army and people, did not satisfy Sazonov. On the contrary, he sent word to the Bulgarian Minister that he need not call upon him, as his Government would be certain to do as they liked.[2] On the other hand, the following extract from a report sent by Benckendorff, on the 25th of February, throws a remarkable light on the French attitude at the London Conference :

Whereas it was agreed that England's support would be purely diplomatic, although without prejudice to what might ultimately

[1] *Livre Noir*, Vol. II. pp. 52–4.   [2] Friedjung, Vol. III. p. 241.

happen, no reserve of this kind was made by France. So much so—there must be no mistake as to this—that, however great the wise, though never enigmatic, moderation shown by M. Cambon at the meetings, he was in reality taking his cue from me, rather than acting on his own initiative. On the contrary, when I think over all his interviews with me, and what passed between us, and take M. Poincaré's attitude into consideration as well, I have a feeling, amounting to a conviction, that, of all the Powers, France is the only one who, I will not say wishes for war, but would envisage it without great regret. Anyhow, I saw nothing to indicate that she was actively contributing to the endeavour to find a compromise. *Or, le compromis, c'est la paix, en dehors du compromis, c'est la guerre.*

The position, as far as I can see, appears to be that all the Powers are really working for peace, but, of them all, France is the one who would accept war with the most philosophy.[1]

This was the impression made on her ally by the attitude of France's representative in London. But Delcassé did not confine himself when in St. Petersburg to discussing the construction of strategic railways, in return for the reintroduction of the three years' service period ; he also carried on negotiations with Sazonov concerning the objects of war with Germany. The following telegram sent by Isvolsky on the 13th of October, 1914, when the French Government had fled to Bordeaux, and Delcassé was again in charge of foreign affairs, as in 1898–1905, incidentally reveals what the French intentions were, as far back as in the third month of the war :

Delcassé has talked to you very often and quite frankly, and has been able to satisfy himself that the aims of France and Russia are identical. France seeks no territorial gains for herself in Europe, with the exception, of course, of the restoration of Alsace-Lorraine, nor does she aspire to any fresh territorial gains in Africa ; she will be satisfied with the destruction of what remains of the Act of Algeciras, and the rectification of some colonial frontiers. After that, France's main object—and as to this the three allied Powers are absolutely of one mind—is that the German Empire should be overthrown, and Prussia's military and political strength weakened as much as possible. The matter must be so managed as to give the individual German States an interest in this.[2]

[1] *Livre Noir*, Vol. II. pp. 303–6.
[2] Isvolsky to Sazonov, October 13, 1914, No. 347, *Berliner Tageblatt*, December 28, 1922, No. 589.

After going into details as to the future disposition of the German States, and making general suggestions with regard to Russia's territorial demands and the Straits, the Ambassador continued :

Delcassé referred to the negotiations which took place in St. Petersburg in 1913, and earnestly besought me to call your attention to the fact that, except for her necessarily wishing for the destruction of Germany's political and economic strength, France's wishes and demands remain what they were.

The possibility of war was faced with far less equanimity in Berlin than in Paris. On the 20th of January, the day after Bulgaria and Serbia had re-opened hostilities with Turkey, the Chancellor, von Bethmann Hollweg, said to Jules Cambon, in discussing Turkey's fate :

If war were to break out in Europe, it would be a terrible disaster for the whole world, with the exception of Japan and the United States, and generations to come would look upon us as fools if we did not succeed in averting it.[1]

The Chancellor had been assisted, since the beginning of 1913, by von Jagow, who was appointed Secretary of State for Foreign Affairs after Kiderlen Wächter's sudden death, and was more inclined to favour a " western orientation " than his predecessor. In consequence of this, greater efforts seem to have been made to expedite the negotiations with England concerning the respective naval strength of the two countries, for Admiral Tirpitz stated in the Reichstag, on the 7th of February, that Germany would not exceed the proportion of ten to sixteen Dreadnoughts. There was friendly Anglo-German co-operation in the interest of peace at the London Conference ; Grey endeavoured to exert a moderating influence on Russia, and not only the politicians, but the military circles in Berlin were also doing their best to prevent Austria-Hungary from taking any rash step. At the beginning of February, Bethmann Hollweg sent the Chief of the General Staff a letter from Duke Albert of Würtemberg, according to which the heir to the Austrian throne had spoken very strongly against war with Serbia, and said that at the

[1] *Affaires Balkaniques*, Vol. II. No. 90.

best the only gain would be unreliable subjects and " a lot of plum-trees ". General von Moltke replied that this view was in keeping with former statements made by the Archduke, he even remembered the remark about the plum-trees, and he concluded his letter as follows :

Your Excellency's chief task should be to prevent Austria from doing anything foolish, neither a pleasant nor an easy task.[1]

Moltke wrote about the same time to his Austrian colleague, General Conrad von Hötzendorf, that if Austria had pronounced the occupation of the Sandjak to be a *casus belli*, everyone would have understood it, just as everyone understood that Austria could not agree to Serbia's having a port on the Adriatic without sacrificing her most vital interests. But these two points had now been settled. The Chief of the Staff was pessimistic, it is true, as to the general position, and believed that, sooner or later, there would be a European war, for which they were bound to prepare, but he added :

The aggression must, however, come from the Slavs.[2]

Similarly, Bethmann told Count Berchtold, on the 10th of February, that he would regard a forcible solution at the present time as

a mistake of incalculable importance.[3]

In the meantime Austria had taken a step which went a long way towards meeting Russia. When the differences of opinion between St. Petersburg and Vienna, over the territory to be allotted to Albania, became acute at the Conference, towards the end of January, the Emperor Francis Joseph decided to send Prince Gottfried of Hohenlohe with a personal letter to the Emperor Nicholas II. " in order to remove the misunderstandings which, it seems, have arisen in Russia with regard to our policy, and put an end to foolish tales, which might prejudice the excellent relations fortunately existing between our countries ".[4]

[1] German Foreign Office unpublished Documents.
[2] As No. 100, mentioned in the Fechenbach-Cossmann trial.
[3] As No 100.
[4] Letter from the Emperor Francis Joseph, dated February 1, 1913. Bogitshevich, p. 139.

Hohenlohe's mission, which began unpleasantly, ended by bringing about an improvement. Russia conceded one or two places to Albania, and the question of reducing the Austrian and Russian armies to the normal establishment was taken in hand. With a view to promoting this, the Emperor William wrote personally to the Archduke Francis Ferdinand on the 20th of February :

> I should be glad to think that you would have no objection to the measures taken being cancelled by degrees, of course assuming that Russia does the same. According to my information that would certainly be the case. Perhaps Hohenlohe's mission may have already smoothed the way as regards this. I should be very glad of it. By doing this, Austria-Hungary would show the world that she is not nervous, and at the same time win over the sympathy of all to her side.[1]

The Archduke Francis Ferdinand told the German military attaché, Count Kageneck, that he was very glad the tension was relaxed, and reiterated his political creed :

> Dreikaiserbund, as far as possible in conjunction with England.[2]

The German Ambassador, von Tschirschky, reported on the 23rd of February :

> I see people in authority almost every day, and I lose no opportunity of pointing out to them the advantages of a policy of peace. In so doing I invariably harp on the theme that the famous idea of " a reckoning " with Serbia is merely the expression of a vague feeling, and that one cannot base a sound policy on such feelings.[3]

In concluding that Germany would not allow Austria to give in, even if she wished to do so,[4] merely from Tschirschky's remark, a fortnight later, that Austria certainly would not give way as regards Scutari, his French colleague, M. Dumaine, represents the situation almost upside down. Germany was the restraining, not the driving force. The Austrian Chief of the Staff was again complaining, as before,

---

[1] Friedjung, Vol. III. p. 244, presumably taken from Austrian State Records. February 24th should read February 22nd.
[2] Unpublished Military Report from Vienna.
[3] German Foreign Office unpublished Documents.
[4] *Affaires Balkaniques*, Vol. II. No. 160.

of the " obstructive element, emanating from Berlin ". In
March 1913 he made the following entry in his journal :

Not only the Kaiser, but Moltke's letter also gives one a feeling
that they want to play a waiting, defensive part.

His Imperial Highness (the heir to the throne) ought not to
allow himself to be so much influenced by the Kaiser ; they held
us back in 1909, and are putting a spoke in our wheel again now.[1]

In the theatre of war, the fall of the two fortresses, Janina
and Adrianople, in March, was a great gain to the allies,
but the Bulgarians did not succeed in making their entry
into Constantinople, which they were now trying to do by
marching on the Gallipoli peninsula, instead of storming
the Tchataldja line. Nor would Russia have willingly
allowed her ambitious protégé to score such a triumph.
On the contrary, she was determined to send her Black
Sea fleet to the Bosphorus in this event.[2] On the 16th of
April a fresh armistice was concluded, both sides being
weary of war.

Montenegro alone continued to besiege Scutari at heavy
cost, with all her forces and the help of a Serbian auxiliary
corps, although the town had been promised to Albania
by the Conference of Ambassadors. On the 1st of April
the diplomats in London had gone so far as to decide on
a joint naval demonstration, in order to put an end to the
slaughter described by Grey in Parliament as " criminal
folly." But although Sazonov was personally very angry
with the King of the Black Mountains, who " wanted to
set the world on fire, to boil his eggs ", he was afraid to take
any steps against Serbia, having regard to public opinion
in St. Petersburg, where demonstrations were taking place
in favour of the Bulgarian and Serbian Ministers, and of
the Grand Duke Nicholas, the King of Montenegro's son-
in-law.

On account of Russia's holding aloof, France also refused
to take part in the naval demonstration, and was only
induced to do so by Sir Edward Grey's threat that otherwise
England would not send her ships either, and that he

[1] Field-Marshal Conrad von Hötzendorf, *Aus meiner Dienstzeit*, Vol. III.
pp. 167 and 169.
[2] *Affaires Balkaniques*, Vol. II. Nos. 193 and 220.

himself would not attend any further meetings of the Ambassadorial Conference. Finally France wrecked the undertaking by demanding that there should only be a " peaceful " blockade. Consequently the concentration of the ships-of-war of five Great Powers at the mouth of the Drina resolved itself into a comedy, which did not intimidate Montenegro. It merely tied Austria's hands by an apparent concession. The investment of the fortress was continued, and on the 22nd of April Scutari was compelled to hoist the white flag.[1]

This announcement caused great rejoicing throughout the Slav countries (with the exception of Poland), not only in Russia, but also in the Habsburg State itself ; there was great exultation over Austria-Hungary's humiliation, and the difficulty in which she had been placed, through having considerably strengthened her armed forces in the southeast of the Empire, and then been afraid to employ them, owing to the attitude of the Triple Entente. The Ambassadorial Conference now began to see the absurdity of the position, and demanded that Scutari should be handed over to the commanders of the Fleets. But Montenegro defied the whole of Europe, well knowing that Russia and France were at heart on her side. Count Berchtold then sent word to the Powers that if they did not decide on taking military measures, Austria would compel the evacuation of Scutari independently. Germany also represented in London, on the 28th of April, that Austria had already subordinated most vital interests to the maintenance of the European Concert, since the commencement of the crisis, and that the Powers consequently owed it as much to the Danubian State as to their own dignity to put an end to the intolerable situation. If general action was not possible, Austria and Italy should be authorized to act jointly against Montenegro, and if Italy refused, then Austria alone.[2] General Conrad von Hötzendorf's notes at this time are to the effect that the Archduke Francis Ferdinand was " coming round, but the Emperor William was still opposed to war ". On the 2nd of May he thought indeed that " Germany

---

[1] Loc. cit., Vol. II. Nos. 199, 205, 208, 209, 211, 218, 228 and 265.
[2] Loc. cit., Vol. II. No. 268.

was entirely with Austria, and in favour of a decisive conflict ", but he had to admit two days later that this feeling had evaporated.[1] At the end of April the French Ambassador in Berlin also reported that Germany had exercised a moderating influence on the Vienna Cabinet, who were now prepared to compensate Montenegro, as soon as she evacuated Scutari.[2] But, as regards the other side, the Serbian Minister in Paris reported that, according to information from a competent authority, there had been imminent danger of war as far back as at the beginning of April—that is, at the time of the negotiations over the naval demonstration—and that the danger had only been averted at the cost of certain moral sacrifices, because, " amongst other things, they wished to give the Balkan States an opportunity of recuperating, and preparing for events which might occur at no very distant future time ".[3]

If the " competent authority " was correctly informed, this would again have been merely postponing the conflict of arms to a more favourable opportunity, not opposition to war. In the meantime, however, King Nicholas recognized that Austria was in earnest, and that the other Powers would leave her free to act. Consequently he at last gave in, and evacuated Scutari on the 4th of May, handing it over, not to Austria, but to the Powers in general, to save appearances. The Serbians withdrew from Durazzo the same day, and towards the middle of the month an international detachment occupied Scutari, and steps were taken to safeguard the Albanian frontiers. The Monarchy was also now able to place the Austro-Hungarian troops in the south-east on a peace footing.

At the end of May, six months after the Conference of belligerent States had assembled in London, the Turkish and Balkan States delegates at last affixed their signatures to the preliminaries of peace. Bulgaria, who had been denied the right to establish herself on the Bosphorus, had hoped she would at least be allowed to obtain a footing

---

[1] Conrad, Vol. III. pp. 275, 294 and 298.
[2] Jules Cambon to Pichon, April 30, 1913, *Affaires Balkaniques*, Vol. II. No. 271.
[3] Report of April 9, 1913, Bogitshevich, p. 168.

on the sea of Marmora. But Great Britain and Russia had decided otherwise. The frontiers of Turkey in Europe were to be drawn from Enos, on the Ægean Sea, to Midia, on the Black Sea, so that the shores both of the Dardanelles and of the Bosphorus remained in possession of the Turks. The other Powers agreed to this. Bulgaria gave in, as a conflict with her other allies was already impending, the preliminary peace having only fixed the territory that was to be taken from Turkey, without arranging how it was to be distributed amongst the victors. The Bulgarian delegate confined himself to suggesting that the frontier should be slightly advanced in the south, to Cape Ivridge (40 km. east of Enos) ; but Russia did not want the Bulgarians to be so near the Turkish capital.[1]

In order fully to understand the excitement which held Europe breathless during the first few months of 1913, it must be remembered that the great armament Bills, which will be discussed in Part II, Section 15, were brought forward simultaneously in the French and German Parliaments, and gave rise to an exceptionally violent press feud between the two countries.

11. The Third Balkan War, Summer of 1913.

After the break up of Turkey in Europe, the territories gained would have satisfied the Bulgarian and Greek national aspirations. But Serbia and Rumania aspired not only to a share of those territories, but also to Austro-Hungarian territory. Serbia wanted to expand northwards, and Rumania westwards. In addition to that, Serbia's share in the territory taken from Turkey was very much reduced by the erection of the Albanian State desired both by Austria and Italy. However, as the hour for the dissolution of the Habsburg Empire, so ardently longed for by the Slav world, excepting the Poles, had not yet struck, the Serbs and Rumanians tried to obtain compensation in the meantime in the south, at Bulgaria's expense. Rumania, hitherto a passive onlooker in the struggle, demanded a strip of the right bank of the Danube, as compensation

[1] *Affaires Balkaniques*, Vol. II. No. 308.

for the aggrandizement of the other Balkan States. Serbia demanded a modification of the treaty of 1912 (p. 53), which had promised Bulgaria five-sixths of Macedonia. Greece also laid claim to this province, which had been conquered and occupied by Greek and Serbian troops, and into which Greeks, Serbs, and Bulgarians had been thrown pell-mell, to the point of inextricable confusion, for centuries past. Bulgaria, on the other hand, obstinately adhered to the letter of the treaty, which had been concluded under other conditions, that is to say, without taking Albania into consideration, and which, in the altered circumstances, would have given Bulgaria the rank of First Power in the Balkans.

This produced the following disposal of forces : Serbia, Greece, and Rumania against Bulgaria.

Towards the middle of April, six weeks before the London preliminaries were signed, the tension between the two groups had become very acute. At this juncture, King Ferdinand appealed to the Tsar to decide the matter without delay. Russia saw the menace to the Balkan League, and, fearing the destruction of the fruit of her diplomatic work of the last few years, tried to smooth over the difficulties. Efforts were made to influence Serbia, in particular, by pointing out that portions of the moribund Danubian Monarchy must soon fall to her share. Sazonov wrote to the Minister Hartwig, to this effect on the 6th of May :

Serbia has only passed through the first phase of her historical rise. In order to attain her object, she must go through another frightful struggle, which will imperil her whole existence.

Serbia's promised land is situated in the territory of present-day Austria-Hungary, not where she is now aiming, and where the Bulgarians are standing in her way. In these circumstances, it is vital to Serbia to maintain the alliance with Bulgaria on the one hand, and on the other to work patiently and perseveringly with a view to being prepared in the necessary degree for the conflict which is inevitable in the future. Time is working for Serbia, and for the ruin of her enemies, who are already showing evident signs of disintegration.[1]

A week later the Serbian Minister in St. Petersburg telegraphed :

[1] *Deutschland schuldig ?* p. 99.

Sazonov has again told me that we must work for a future time, as we shall get a great deal of land from Austria-Hungary. My reply was that we shall willingly give the Bulgarians Monastir (Bitolia) if we get Bosnia and other Austrian provinces.[1]

But Serbia did not intend to be put off entirely with future hopes. The Prime Minister, Pashitch, the successor of Milowanovich, whose death had taken place in July 1912, not only made this clear in St. Petersburg at the end of May, but also in public speeches, which cut off the possibility of retreat, and he concluded an alliance with Greece. A meeting between the Serbian and Bulgarian Prime Ministers at the beginning of June did not result in a settlement. The Tsar then requested the four Balkan States to send their Prime Ministers to St. Petersburg to receive his decision, although only Bulgaria and Serbia had recognized him as arbiter beforehand. Even they, in accepting the invitation, reserved the right to preserve their interests by a military decision, whilst Greece wished that Russia should only act as arbiter in conjunction with a second Power.[2] The anxiety in St. Petersburg grew. Russian experts thought a Bulgarian victory possible, even over the combined Serbian and Greek forces. But it was not desirable that the self-confident State, whose claims to Turkish territory had already been opposed, as being fraught with peril to Russian interests, should gain too much strength. Serbia's defeat in this conflict would even have been regarded as " a catastrophe for Pan Slavism " by men like Hartwig.[3] In vain had King Ferdinand hoped to incline Russia more favourably towards the Bulgarian cause by recalling the pronounced pro-Russian, Danev, to the head of the Ministry, after the failure of the Conference at the beginning of June. The Tsar insisted on the Ministers' coming to St. Petersburg. Pashitch finally agreed to go, and, after hesitating for a long time, Danev also decided on obeying the summons. This, however, fell through in consequence of a decision which had apparently been taken without his knowledge.

[1] Bogitshevich, p. 129.
[2] Friedjung, Vol. III. p. 291 ; *Affaires Balkaniques*, Vol. II. Nos. 332–4.
[3] Loc. cit., Vol. II. Nos. 326 and 345.

As they had to reckon with the fact that, in addition to Serbia and Greece, Rumania and Turkey would also take arms against Bulgaria, King Ferdinand's Generals conceived the bold plan of freeing their hands for the struggle against their fresh enemies, by a rapid offensive against their former allies. This scheme having been sanctioned by the King, the Bulgarians attacked half-heartedly, on the evening of June 29, on the strength of confused orders. The fortune of war decided against them. The Serbs, who were both ready and determined to do battle, threw them back by a frontal counter-attack, whilst at the same time the Greeks were preparing to deliver a decisive blow by means of an enveloping offensive from the south. Russia, who had notified the Bulgarians, as recently as in September 1912, that in case of a Bulgaro-Rumanian conflict she could not remain a passive onlooker, now informed them, in spite of the 1909 treaty with Bulgaria, that " in the existing circumstances she would not stand by them ".[1] On the 11th of July the Rumanians crossed the frontier and the Danube on the march to Sofia. The Turks, for their part, set out for Adrianople, and entered the town, which had been hastily evacuated by the Bulgarians, on the 22nd.

Threatened on four sides, Bulgaria, who, six months earlier, had dreamt of a great Empire, with control of the Bosphorus, was obliged to haul down her Colours. At King Ferdinand's request, Austria and Russia arranged an armistice, which was concluded on the 30th of July. The Peace of Bucharest, signed on the 10th of August by the five Balkan States, robbed the country, which had been ruined by over-ambition, of the greater part of its gains. Whereas Serbia and Greece increased their population by about one and a quarter million inhabitants, Bulgaria only increased hers by a third of that number. Nothing remained to her on the Ægean coast but a narrow strip. In vain she tried to secure at least the port of Kavala. Austria supported this demand, and so did Russia at first, for in spite of her preference for Serbia, she did not want Bulgaria to be too much weakened But Germany spoke in favour

[1] App. I. No. 9, p. 228.

of Greece, and so did France, whose consideration for
Russia was outweighed by her anxiety lest Germany shouid
cut her out in Athens.[1] It is a strange satisfaction now,
that, on the 5th of August, 1913, the German Under-Secretary of State for Foreign Affairs should have expressed a
hope that the Franco-German solution would be accepted
by the countries concerned, and, with faint irony, added
a further hope that " the new friends, Russia and Austria,
would acquiesce in the *fait accompli* ". Shortly before peace
was signed, Russia changed her mind, Italy's attitude was
undecided, and Austria alone stood by Bulgaria.[2]

The Berlin and Vienna Cabinets had not always acted
entirely in agreement on Balkan questions in the course
of the year. At a meeting in March, von Jagow propounded
a plan of bringing Rumania, Turkey, and Greece into
rapprochement with the Central Powers, and also con-
ciliating Serbia as far as possible, but dropping Bulgaria,
who was indissolubly bound to Russia. Berchtold, on the
other hand, was of opinion that Bulgaria was tired of
Russia's guardianship, and would be willing to join the
Central Powers, whereas the Monarchy had reached the
limit of what could be done to meet Serbia. Friendly
relations with Greece would certainly be desirable, but she
was at enmity with Italy, on account of Albania, so that
there were difficulties in the way of remaining on good
terms with both countries simultaneously. Subsequently,
at the beginning of May, when Montenegro was prepared
to let loose a world war for the sake of Scutari, with Serbia's
support, von Jagow admitted that Berchtold's estimate
of the Serbo-Montenegrin policy had been more correct
than his own.[3]

Nor were Germany and Austria of one mind at the time
of the Bulgaro-Rumanian conflict. Rumania had wished
to take part in the first Balkan war, in order to prevent
Bulgaria from gaining the upper hand in the Balkans.
But the Central Powers succeeded in dissuading her from

---

[1] *Affaires Balkaniques*, Vol. II. Nos. 441 and 467.
[2] Loc. cit., Nos. 452, 456 and 462.
[3] A conversation between Jagow and Berchtold in March 1913, quoted
by Friedjung, Vol. III. p. 275, probably from the Austrian State Papers.

this, by promising that Bulgaria would give her ample compensation. Thanks to this promise, the Rumanian treaties with the Triple Alliance were renewed at the beginning of February. But as the Austro-German efforts in Sofia proved fruitless, the Rumanians began to feel that they gained very little from the alliance, and, actively encouraged by the French, they turned to Russia. An Ambassadorial Conference, held in the Russian capital, also decided that Silistria and its environs should be ceded to Rumania.[1] When it appeared that the Bulgarians were still resolved not to give way, the Germans were very angry, and entirely sided with Rumania. But, in spite of that, the Vienna Government continued to mediate between Bucharest and Sofia, in the hope that it might yet be possible to establish overland communication with Turkey, via Rumania and Bulgaria, and by this means keep Serbia in check. But this plan was defeated by King Ferdinand's obstinacy.

The greatest difference of opinion between the Wilhelm-strasse and the Ballplatz arose, however, when the following telegram of July 3 was received from the German Ambassador in Vienna, von Tschirschky, after the failure of the Bulgarian attack on the Serbian lines :

Count Berchtold asked me to call on him to-day. The Minister said he considered it his duty not to leave the German Government in the dark as to the gravity of the position for the Monarchy. The South Slav question, that is to say, undisturbed possession of the provinces inhabited by South Slavs, is a vital question for the Monarchy as well as for the Triple Alliance. The Monarchy's South Slav provinces could not be held if Serbia became too powerful. As to that, all competent opinions here agree. The Monarchy might accordingly possibly be compelled to intervene, in the event of Serbia inflicting a crushing defeat on Bulgaria, in conjunction with Rumania and Greece, and annexing tracts of country in excess of the territory of former Serbia, or something approximating to that. Serbia cannot be left in possession of Monastir, in any case.

To my question, when and how he thought of intervening, the Minister replied that it would no doubt be possible to find the psychological moment. Naturally he could not say anything now as to the method of procedure, that would depend on circumstances.

[1] *Affaires Balkaniques*, Vol. II. Nos. 239 and 297.

He thought they would have to begin with a diplomatic conversation in Belgrade, which must be supported by military pressure, if it led to no conclusion. Then, if Russia came into the arena, St. Petersburg would become the scene of action.

The Minister again expressed a hope that the Monarchy's difficult position would be understood in Berlin. Far from wishing to pursue an adventurous policy, or being bent on conquest, her only object was to safeguard her South Slav possessions, which of course included Trieste. Naturally the most acceptable solution of the question would be a small Serbia, defeated by the enemy, and he would very much prefer this to a possible occupation of Serbia by the Monarchy. But, failing the first alternative, the Monarchy would be compelled to take action, in order to safeguard her possessions. There must be no mistake as to the danger of a great " Piedmont ", which would be of military importance, on the frontiers of the Monarchy.

Count Berchtold will have a talk with the Chief of the Staff this evening, and leave for Ischl to-morrow.

The plan did not at all meet with approval in Berlin, and the following instructions were sent to the Ambassador by return of post :

For your guidance and information. The Minister in attendance on His Majesty was commissioned to submit Your Excellency's telegram No. 162 to His Majesty, and at the same time to represent the following standpoint : There can hardly be any occasion for special anxiety in Vienna for the moment, as it is too soon to speak of danger of a Greater Serbia. Our business should be to allay Austria's anxiety, prevent her from doing anything hasty, and see that she keeps us regularly informed of her intentions, and does not come to any decision without having consulted us. Herr von Treutler reports : His Majesty approves of the policy outlined by Your Excellency, but thinks Count Berchtold makes a great mistake in now committing himself definitely with regard to Monastir, as he did before in the case of Durazzo.[1]

As the Marquis di San Giuliano happened to be in Germany, where he had had a talk with von Jagow at Kiel, on the 2nd of July, Italy only replied a week later than Germany, and equally refused to countenance the Austrian suggestions.[2] On this, Berchtold gave up the idea of precipitate action.

[1] Both telegrams, taken from the German Foreign Office Documents, were published by the author in the *Deutsche Allgemeine Zeitung* of March 7, 1920, No. 123.
[2] Pribram, Vol. I. p. 301.

In spite of conclusive proof to the contrary having repeatedly been given publicity, both by Austria and Germany, this incident has always been incorrectly represented in Entente countries, as though Germany had assented at that time to the Vienna plans, and it was only Italy's opposition which prevented their being carried out. This calumny is based on the " Giolitti revelations," so called because the former Italian Premier made the following statement in the Chamber, on the 5th of December, 1914 :

In the course of the Balkan war, to be more exact, on the 9th of August, 1913, I received the following telegram from my colleague, the Marquis di San Giuliano, during my absence from Rome :
" Austria has communicated to us, and to Germany, her intention of taking action against Serbia, and she defines such action as defensive, hoping to bring into operation the *casus fœderis* of the Triple Alliance, which, on the contrary, I believe to be inapplicable. I am endeavouring to arrange for a combined effort with Germany to prevent such action on the part of Austria. It may, however, become necessary to state clearly that we do not consider such action, if it should be taken, as defensive, and that therefore we do not consider that the *casus fœderis* arises. Please telegraph to me at Rome whether you agree."
I replied as follows :
" If Austria intervenes against Serbia, it is clear that a *casus fœderis* cannot be established. It is a step which she is taking on her own account, since there is no question of defence, inasmuch as no one is thinking of attacking her. It is necessary that a declaration to this effect should be made to Austria in the most formal manner, and we must hope for action on the part of Germany to dissuade Austria from this most perilous adventure ".[1]

This statement does not in any way suggest that Germany had agreed to Austria's attacking Serbia at that time, it only says that Italy had wished to come to an understanding with Germany, in order to prevent Austria from taking any precipitate step, and had reckoned on Germany's effective support. In reality, there was still more to be said for Germany, as is evident from the above mentioned instructions to Tschirschky, for she had immediately sent a very blunt refusal on her own initiative, without first communicating with Italy. It is difficult to understand

[1] App. to Serbian Blue Book, *Collected Diplomatic Documents*, p. 401.

Giolitti's having made the mistake of giving the date as August instead of July.[1]   At the beginning of August an Austro-German plan to relieve Bulgaria by an Austrian attack on Serbia would have been quite out of the question, in the first place, because hostilities had been suspended on the 30th of July, and further because Germany took part against, not with Bulgaria, in the Kavala question. The incident to which Giolitti referred, and which he did not personally turn in any way to account against Germany, proves the exact contrary of what the enemy war propaganda made out of it.   The truth is that in July 1913 Germany prevented Austria from drawing the sword, as she had so often done before.   There are also French witnesses to the very different attitude of the Central Powers at that time.   For example, the Minister of the Republic in Belgrade was describing the opposite views taken of the Serbian victory by his German and Austrian colleagues, on the 24th of July, and he remarked that " the principle of non-intervention Germany had so carefully upheld, had sown the seeds of a liking for her, which increased with the growing distrust of Russia ".   A week later Delcassé wrote from St. Petersburg that Count Pourtalès spoke of Austria " with irritation, which he made less and less effort to conceal ".[2]

The Peace of Bucharest fixed frontiers on principles for which there was nothing to be said, either from the national or the geographical point of view.   Austria and Russia proposed their revision for different reasons, certainly : Austria wished the Serbo-Bulgarian frontiers altered, and Russia the Bulgaro-Greek frontiers.[3]   Rumania made the strongest opposition to this, on which Russia withdrew her proposal.   Again Austria was left to grumble alone.   The view taken in Berlin did not coincide with hers,[4] on account of the German anxiety to cultivate friendly relations with Rumania, and particularly with Greece.   The Emperor William demonstrated that clearly by appointing King Constantine to be a Field-Marshal in the German army, and in a way that was particularly painful for Austria,

---

[1] Giolitti makes the same mistake in his book *Memorie della mia Vita*.
[2] *Affaires Balkaniques*, Vol. II. Nos. 422 and 438.
[3] Loc. cit., Vol. III. No. 7.   [4] Loc. cit., Vol. II. No. 466.

namely, in a telegram of congratulation to King Carol. The ill-feeling between Berlin and Vienna reached such a pitch at that time, that the Austrians would not send any representative to the German manœuvres.[1] All these events took place in the first half of the month of August, and are a further proof of the impossibility of the conclusion, falsely drawn from Giolitti's statements, namely, that Germany had agreed to an Austrian attack on Serbia at that time. Another indication of the general character of German policy is Sazonov's having rejected the English suggestion that Germany and Russia should come to an understanding as to the measures to be taken to compel Turkey to evacuate Adrianople, in the following words :

How can Sir Edward Grey think of wanting us to embark on a conversation with Germany ? That is just what Germany wants. No day passes without her inviting us to come back to the *Dreikaiserbund*, but we belong to the Triple Entente and not to the Triple Alliance.[2]

It is characteristic of the French point of view, however, that, in November, France should have wished to confine the negotiations with Germany, respecting the Turkish finances and the Bagdad railway, entirely to the economic sphere, and was absolutely determined

to avoid an agreement of a general nature, which might be regarded by public opinion as sanctioning the present conditions, consequently, as France's final renunciation of the provinces lost in 1870.[3]

The Balkans did not quiet down till long after the Peace of Bucharest. Bulgaria only concluded peace with Turkey at the end of September, when she too had to give up Adrianople, and Serbia not till the middle of the following March, whilst Greece never came to any final agreement with the Porte at all, in spite of a temporary treaty in November, so that a resumption of hostilities was still considered possible in July 1914. The Serbs were very slow in evacuating Albania, set fire to the villages, according to French reports, and massacred the Mussulman popula-

---

[1] Conrad, Vol. III. p. 429.
[2] *Affaires Balkaniques*, Vol. II. Nos. 426 and 433.
[3] Isvolsky's report of November 18, 1913, *Livre Noir*, Vol. II. p. 175.

tion. The Serbian Minister in Vienna tried to justify the illegal occupation by talking of a " dangerous initiative " on the part of the expeditionary corps, and the " massacres and disturbances " by representing them as revenge for the alleged devastation of " Serbian " (?) territory by Albanians.[1] In order to put a stop to this behaviour in the territory of an independent State, erected by international decision, Austria presented a demand to the Belgrade Government, on the 18th of October, for its evacuation within eight days. The Serbian Government, knowing that they were in the wrong, decided to give in the very next day, without waiting to see whether they would be supported against the Austrian ultimatum. The French State Papers are very silent about the attitude of the Powers towards this step. General Conrad von Hötzendorf writes : " Russia was taken aback, but it was unlikely that she would take any counter measures ; France began by thinking it unjustifiable, but was subsequently convinced of the contrary ; Germany had promised her whole-hearted support, and even Italy sided with Austria ".[2] The assurance the Emperor William gave Conrad at that time, which was in direct opposition to the statements of the responsible Chancellor : " I agree with you. The others are not ready, they will make no objection to it. You must be in Belgrade within a day or two. I was always an advocate of peace, but there is a limit to that ",[3] was interpreted by the French Press as meaning that Germany had consented to Austria's taking military action against Serbia. But the course of events shows that the Kaiser bowed to the Chancellor's opinion.

What importance is to be attached to the result of the third Balkan war, as regards its effect on the balance of power in Europe, the agreed aim of the Franco-Russian alliance, and the ostensible *leitmotiv* of British policy ? The dream of Catherine the Great and Joseph II., of dividing the Balkan peninsular into a Russian east and an Austrian west, was finally shattered, and the later, more moderate solution proposed by Bismarck, namely, that it should be

---

[1] *Affaires Balkaniques*, Vol. III. Nos. 100 and 108.
[2] Conrad, Vol. III. p. 474.   [3] Loc. cit., Vol. III. p. 470.

divided into two spheres of interest, was equally knocked on the head. The Balkans belonged to the Balkan people. To whose advantage was that ? The Balkan *bloc* Russian diplomacy had steadily aimed at establishing had broken up, and the balance of power was no longer as much to the disadvantage of the Central Powers as it had been at the end of November. In spite of that, the position of the Triple Entente was very much stronger than before the first Balkan war. Notwithstanding her having recovered Adrianople, Turkey was practically driven out of Europe. Serbia, Russia's favourite protégé, had been considerably aggrandized, and her self-confidence had increased to an inordinate extent. She had held the temporary compensations, at Bulgaria's expense, by the sword, but this did not prevent her hankering for further aggrandizement at the expense of Austria. Rumania had turned her back on the Central Powers ; the President of the French Chamber, Deschanel, publicly commended the Minister, Blondel, for having induced his country to declare war on Bulgaria, saying that this had been the means of bringing the conflict to such a speedy and happy conclusion, and of arousing Rumanian sympathy for France.[1] A German loan was gladly accepted in Bucharest, but the preference for France remained the same. King Constantine emphasized the fact that, whilst he owed his military successes to German military training, there were French instructors in his army, and English instructors in his navy. In addition to that, the want of unanimity that existed in the Triple Alliance in important questions had become evident. Austria was driven from the Ægean Sea, which Lord Salisbury had said in 1887 would be incompatible with her interests,[2] her helplessness against the Balkan *bloc* favoured by Russia had seriously damaged her prestige, and the main item of the Vienna programme, an Albania capable of being independent, had only been very imperfectly carried out. The Coalition, to which France and Russia belonged, had consequently

---

[1] Friedjung, Vol. III. p. 296 ; quotation from an article by Professor F. Gheorgov of Sofia, in the *Oesterreichische Rundschau*, 1916, second number. Compare also Schebeko to Sazonov, April 3, 1914, Siebert, pp. 622–4.

[2] *Grosse Politik*, Vol. IV. No. 913, p. 346.

gained a good deal, in spite of the blow Slavism had sustained in the break up of the Balkan League.

The Russian Ambassador in Vienna, Schebeko, expressed that opinion on the 24th of April, 1914. He said that the last Balkan war had been regrettable, certainly, from the Slav point of view, but it had been advantageous as far as Russia's special interests were concerned. If the voice of reason had carried the day in Bulgaria, the result would have been unfavourable to Russia, for

> Bulgaria would have become the greatest of the Balkan States, as far as the extent of her territory and number of her population are concerned ; Rumania, and probably Turkey also, would have hastened to form ties with her, and if, in addition to that, there had finally been a *rapprochement* to Austria—which I always thought possible, even before the war with Serbia—a *bloc*, hostile to us, would have been formed in the Balkans, consisting of Austria, Bulgaria, Rumania, and Turkey. Under the existing conditions, however, Austria is now entirely isolated in the Balkans, and any attempt on her part to alter the *status quo* would be resolutely opposed by the *bloc* composed of Rumania, Serbia, and Greece.[1]

Consequently, the balance of power remained strongly against the Central Powers, even after the third Balkan war.[2] A policy honestly and impartially based on the principle of maintaining the balance of power would necessarily have opposed, instead of supporting, the Russo-French coalition. But what the Powers forming the Triple Entente understood by " maintenance of the balance of power " was only preventing its shifting in favour of Germany and Austria. They invariably welcomed its shifting in any other direction. The danger of war had increased again. What Poincaré had correctly estimated, in August 1912, as a danger, in the case of the first Balkan League, namely that their hopes " seemed to be encouraged " by Russia, and that, consequently, their ambition to secure what they coveted had grown, now applied to the new *bloc*, Rumania, Serbia, Montenegro, and Greece. The result was that the possibility of the world war, the most fatal of all, succeeding the Moroccan, Tripolitan, and Balkan wars, had increased.

[1] Siebert, pp. 622–4.   [2] App. I. No. 10, p. 229.

12. The Development of the Straits Question.

In 1908 Isvolsky only asked for the following solution of the Straits question : ships-of-war belonging to the States on the shores of the Black Sea to be allowed to pass through the Straits in both directions, so long as Turkey is not at war, but not more than three ships belonging to one State to be *en route* between the Black Sea and the Ægean at the same time ; the Straits to remain closed to the ships-of-war of all other States. Aehrenthal agreed to this at Buchlau (p. 34), but the Cabinet in London did not. In a note of the 14th of October, 1908, Grey said that, after protesting against the annexation of Bosnia and Herzegovina, Russia surely could not take advantage of the opportunity of securing such a prerogative. A one-sided treaty of that kind would make the whole Black Sea " an impregnable fortress for the States on its shores, from which cruisers and torpedo boats could emerge as they pleased, without fear of being pursued by one of the belligerents ". The British Government was not opposed " in principle " to the Straits being thrown open, but an agreement as to this must be based on reciprocity, and treat the belligerents, " in case of war, on a footing of equality, as regards passage through the Straits ". Turkey's consent must also be a prior condition of any arrangement.[1] The English counter-proposal, that the Straits should be thrown open to the ships-of-war of all the nations, was precisely the arrangement most favourable to England, which Russia had formerly least desired ; for then the powerful British fleet could again block and bombard the Black Sea ports as in the Crimean War. This answer of Grey's shows clearly why he so strongly opposed the annexation of Bosnia and Herzegovina at the time ; it was not out of regard for Serbian and Russian interests, or inherent respect for treaties ; he was considering England's interest in the Bosphorus and Dardanelles. This accounts for Isvolsky's defeat in the autumn of 1908. It is remarkable that the

---

[1] *Livre Noir*, Vol. II. pp. 457–8. According to Siebert, Grey's answer was dated October 18th. Benckendorff's reports on the Bosnian crisis in Siebert's collection only begin in November.

fundamental difference between the Russian and English view is not strongly emphasized in later reports from the Russian Embassy in London ; Count Benckendorff always refers merely to the " time not having come " for fulfilment of Russia's wishes, and the desirability of a prior understanding with Turkey, as being England's main objections.[1]

The question was not revived till three years later, in the autumn of 1911. The Russian Ambassador in Constantinople, Tcharikov, was instructed to take advantage of Turkey's difficulties, owing to the war with Italy and the Franco-German negotiations over Morocco, to make a fresh experiment. A draft treaty of October 12 proposed to the Porte that Russia should " give Turkey effective support in upholding the conditions regarding the Straits, and extend this support to the adjacent territories, in case of their being menaced by enemy forces ". In return, Turkey was to pledge herself " not to oppose the passage of Russian ships-of-war through the Straits, either in peace or war time, on condition that these ships should not anchor in the waters of the Straits, except by special agreement ".[2] This draft consequently provided that Russia should guarantee Constantinople and the surrounding country to the Porte.

Difficulties were again made in London. It is true that, after some hesitation, the objection that the time was " ill chosen " was dropped, but Grey still contemplated the solution suggested by his answer of the 14th of October, three years before. Benckendorff was very mistakenly less afraid of objections on the part of England to " the Black Sea being turned into a great harbour of refuge for the Russian fleet in case of war ",[3] " than on the part of Europe as a whole ". Out of consideration for England, France, whose policy was not yet directed by Poincaré, also adopted a rather ungracious attitude towards her Russian allies, and on the 4th of January, 1912, after three months' correspondence, she only stated that she was willing to exchange

---

[1] Siebert, p. 678 and elsewhere. Benckendorff was apparently trying to smooth over the differences of opinion between St. Petersburg and London.

[2] *Livre Noir*, Vol. II. pp. 463-4.

[3] Siebert, pp. 675-6, 678, 681, 682, 684.

views, " if fresh circumstances should make it necessary
to examine the question of the Straits ".[1]

Germany's attitude was far more obliging. As early as
on the 11th of November Count Osten-Sacken was able
to report from Berlin that the German Government " was
not in any way opposed to the agreements with Turkey ".
Soon after that, Austria also recognized Russia's special
interests in the Straits, with the proviso that she must
be guaranteed against attack by the Russian fleet.[2] Thus
the Central Powers adopted a more benevolent attitude
towards Russia, in one of the questions most vital to her,
than her two Entente allies. Germany acted in accordance
with the Bismarck tradition that the problem of the Straits
must be settled by treaty between Russia and the Porte.[3]
Had there been any suspicion in Berlin and Vienna that
Russia was simultaneously contemplating the formation of a
Balkan League, including Turkey, against Austria (p. 53),
the answers would no doubt have been different. The
negotiations again came to a standstill, however, as the
general public heard of them prematurely, on which
Sazonov telegraphed to the Embassy in Constantinople at
the beginning of December that it was impossible to continue the conversations on the lines agreed upon.[4] After
this, nothing further was done in St. Petersburg in the
direction of a treaty with Turkey, and a Balkan League
in which she would be included. Instead of that, Russia
turned her attention to the formation of a Balkan League
directed *against* the Porte.

Eleven months later, at the beginning of November 1912,
when it became necessary to reckon with the possibility
of the Bulgarians entering Constantinople, after their
astonishing military successes, Sazonov contemplated
sending the Black Sea fleet to the Bosphorus, in such an
eventuality, to compel King Ferdinand's troops to with-

[1] *Livre Noir*, Vol. II. p. 466.
[2] Loc. cit., pp. 469 and 470. Siebert, p. 686.
[3] *Grosse Politik*, Vol. V. No. 1074, p. 227, marginal note 3 ; Vol. VI.
No. 1175, p. 45, marginal note 1. Further, *Gedanken und Errinnerungen*,
Vol. II. p. 300. Kiderlen Wächter pursued Bismarck's policy in opposition
to the opinion of the Ambassador in Constantinople, Freiherr von Mar-
schall ; vide Karl Helfferich, *Der Weltkrieg*, p. 93.
[4] *Livre Noir*, Vol. II. p. 462.

draw. Grey, on the other hand, proposed to neutralize Salonica and Constantinople, and make them international ports.[1] That would have finally wrecked Russia's hopes for the future. A lengthy memorandum of the 28th of November, from the Russian Foreign Minister, then pointed out that such international guarantees would not suffice to protect Russia's interests, as they could always be evaded, on the one hand, and, on the other, they might be an obstacle, in the future, in the way of finally solving the question of the Straits consistently with Russian interests. It would therefore be better that they should confine themselves to further consideration of the 1908 idea.[2] Grey thereupon agreed to the Russian 1908 proposal ; at all events Benckendorff reported to that effect, but he still thought a prior understanding with Turkey necessary.[3]

The Anglo-Russian differences respecting the entrances to the Black Sea were consequently by no means adjusted at the end of 1912. The fact of the Dardanelles having been permanently closed during the war with Italy and the three Balkan wars, had been just as injurious to Russian commerce as to the prestige of the Empire, as it had prevented the export of wheat from the southern provinces. The result was that the number of Russian politicians who would no longer be satisfied with a passage through the Straits, and aspired to full control, steadily increased. When the proposal to put the Turkish finances under international control was under consideration, in May 1913, Tcharikov's successor, M. de Giers, for instance, wrote that

the introduction of an international element into the relations which have existed hitherto between us and Turkey can only hinder and delay our historic efforts to secure possession of the Straits.[4]

In spite of the differences which still continued to exist, the English and Russian Governments constantly found it necessary to co-ordinate their Turkish policy, in view of their common opposition to Germany's efforts to revive

[1] *Affaires Balkaniques*, Vol. I. No. 234, and Siebert, p. 688.
[2] Siebert, pp. 687–90.   [3] Loc. cit., p. 691.
[4] Loc. cit., p. 695.

the strength of the Ottoman Empire, after its serious loss of power and prestige. England no longer had any cause to fear the establishment of a German naval base on the Persian Gulf, it is true, as the terminal section of the Bagdad railway was to be under English administration, and Russia had concluded an agreement in 1911 respecting the apportionment of the railways in Asia Minor (p. 45), but the completion of a line from Stamboul to the mouth of the Shat-el-Arab was bound to strengthen the Turkish Empire very considerably, in due course, both from the military and economic point of view. This was not desired, either in St. Petersburg, where they aspired to possession of the Straits, or in London, where they hoped to secure the overland route from Egypt to southern Persia.

Therefore, when the head of the new German military mission, General Liman von Sanders, was appointed to command the Constantinople Army Corps, on the 2nd of December, 1913, the Triple Entente objected strongly. Their Ambassadors represented this to the Porte, but in vain. The instruction to the British Ambassador pointed out that " the Diplomatic Corps in Constantinople would be subordinate to Germany, the key of the Straits would be in German hands, and a German General would be able to traverse the Sultan's sovereignty ",[1] an amazing exaggeration. In order to reduce the Turks to submission, Russia demanded the appointment of Russian officers to command the Armenian gendarmerie, the use of the Russian gauge on the Armenian railways, and suspension of the construction of fortresses on the Straits. By the middle of December Isvolsky was able to report from Paris that Doumergue's new Cabinet had also expressed their " solidarity " with Russia, and their intention of giving her " the most active support ". The Ambassador further commended the French Press, because the " only fault it finds is with our efforts to adjust this question by means of friendly conversations with Germany ".[2] *Rapprochement* to Germany was one of the greatest imaginable offences in Paris, and had been considered so ever since the fall of Caillaux's Ministry.

[1] *Affaires Balkaniques*, Vol. III. No. 157.
[2] *Livre Noir*, Vol. II. p. 212.

Thus, as regards Turkish finances and the Bagdad railway, France, as already mentioned, had been careful to restrict the negotiations with Germany to economic questions, and " in no circumstance to enter into an agreement of a general nature, which might be regarded by public opinion as sanctioning the present conditions, and, consequently, as France's final renunciation of the provinces lost in 1870 ".[1]

On the 1st of February, 1914, France even went so far as to propose that Russia should send a battleship to the Bosphorus, and announce that " she would only leave when the agreement with Liman von Sanders and his officers was modified ".[2] Is it possible that the French did not realize that this flagrant breach of the treaties of 1856 and 1871 would have been the signal for war ? True, the proposal, which is carefully suppressed in the French Balkan Yellow Book, continues : " The Sultan would not venture to give orders to fire on her ".[3] But what guarantee had they for that ?

These were the kind of suggestions made in Paris, where the Agadir incident had been taken so much amiss. Four days later, Isvolsky reported that, in the existing circumstances, France was determined not to evade the obligations imposed upon her by the alliance with Russia.[4]

On the 12th of January, a week later, it was publicly announced that, for the sake of peace, Germany had completely given in, and had agreed to Liman von Sanders being relieved of his command of the Constantinople Corps and appointed Inspector-General of the Turkish Army without any direct command. A Russian Ministerial Council therefore decided not to go to war with Germany,

[1] Loc. cit., Vol. II. p. 175.

[2] Loc. cit., Vol. II. p. 223. This provocative advice is suppressed in the French Yellow Book, which does not mention the Liman Sanders affair at all between the 3rd of December and 21st of January.

[3] According to the *Livre Noir* (Vol. II. p. 223), the suggestion that Russia should send a battleship to the Bosphorus was made by M. Bompard, the French Ambassador in Constantinople, in a private conversation with Paléologue, who repeated it to Isvolsky, laying stress on the fact that it was Bompard's personal opinion and not to be regarded in any way as official advice. On Isvolsky's remarking that the Sultan would hardly be likely to give the necessary firman, Paléologue said a Russian cruiser could enter the Bosphorus without a firman, and that the Turkish batteries certainly would not decide to open fire.—[Tr.]

[4] Siebert, p. 669.

although the Russian War Minister and the Chief of the Staff had stated positively that Russia was " perfectly prepared to fight Germany, not to speak of Austria, single-handed ".[1] A few days afterwards, Nicholas II. told the German Ambassador, Count Pourtalès, how glad he was that the matter had been adjusted.[2] France had once more been prepared to support Russia unconditionally, by force of arms. Germany had once more preferred a diplomatic defeat to an armed conflict.

The minutes of a later Ministerial Council, held on the 21st of February, and an accompanying memorandum from the Russian Foreign Office, give even more food for reflection than the resolution of the meeting held on the 13th of January. In these two documents the following views are expressed :

1. Russia's historic mission demands that she should no longer be satisfied with the free passage of the Bosphorus and Dardanelles, but should endeavour to secure control of both waterways.

2. Possession of the Straits cannot be achieved by a localized war against Turkey, but only " within the limits of a European war".

3. At present the business of the Foreign Office is to prepare a favourable political atmosphere " for operations leading up to the occupation of the Straits ".[3]

This did not show that anyone necessarily wished the great war to come about in the near future, certainly, but it meant, at least, that it was considered an historic duty to pursue an aim, which could admittedly only be achieved through a European war. What consideration was primarily responsible for this fatal decision must remain uncertain. Was it belief that Germany would side with Turkey in any circumstances, or was it that they thought England would oppose a localized Russian war against Turkey, but would consent to the Straits being transferred to Russia in the event of a general conflagration, as she actually did six months after the outbreak of war ?

A remark made by Nicholas II., in April 1914, showed that he was imbued with the same ideas as those expressed

---

[1] Pokrovsky, p. 42. [2] *Deutschland schuldig ?* p. 167
[3] Pokrovsky, pp. 49 and 50, and *Deutschland schuldig ?* pp. 171, 172, 173.

at the Ministerial Council of February 21. He was talking
to Sazonov about the possibility of a fresh outbreak of
hostilities between Greece and Turkey, and agreeing that
Russia could not allow the Straits to be closed again.
" I would even resort to force ", said His Majesty, " to
re-open them ". They then discussed the possibility of
Germany siding with Turkey. In order to prevent this,
the Tsar was most anxious for the speedy conclusion of an
Anglo-Russian agreement [1] (similar to the Anglo-French
diplomatic and military agreements). Thus it will be seen
that the Tsar's plan, in the event of the Dardanelles being
closed again, was to re-open them by force, at the risk of
a European war.

13. THE MIRAMAR, KONOPISCHT, AND PARIS MEETINGS.

The year 1914 had begun under gloomy auspices, on
account of the differences of opinion with regard to the
German military mission in Constantinople, and the Russian
demands as regards Armenia. The continued tension
between Greece and Turkey was an added source of anxiety,
and finally there was the dispute over Albania, Serbia
claiming the north of the newly erected principality and
Greece the south. Prince William of Wied had accepted
the position of Prince of Albania in November 1913, but
an insurrection broke out in March, which was encouraged
by Greece, if only indirectly. At the end of the same month
the Serbian Prime Minister announced the conclusion of
a treaty between Serbia, Greece, and Montenegro. Visits
paid by the Crown Prince and Princess of Rumania to
St. Petersburg, and by the Russian Imperial Family to
Costanza, considerably increased the influence of the Entente
in Bucharest. The whole of the Balkans was still in a
state of ferment, Serbia being, as ever, the most restless
element. [2]

Under these conditions it is perfectly comprehensible

---

[1] Paléologue to Doumergue, April 18, 1914, vide *Livre Noir*, Vol. II.
p. 258. For the nature of the Anglo-Russian Agreement, vide loc. cit.,
p. 260.

[2] For details of the position at the turn of the year 1913–14, vide Friedjung, Vol. III., postscript by Professor Hoetzsch, pp. 311 ff.

that the Balkan question should have been the principal
subject of discussion when the German Emperor met the
Emperor Francis Joseph in Vienna in March, and again
when he met the Heir to the Austrian Throne at Miramar
in the course of the same month, and at Konopischt in
June.

Rumania's attitude was causing anxiety in Vienna. The
Austrian Emperor and Berchtold already considered her
practically lost to the alliance, whereas the German Emperor
hoped things might improve. His opinion of the Russian
military preparations was that they were not mainly inspired by belligerent intentions towards Germany and
Austria. He thought Russia merely wished to secure her
Austrian and German frontiers against attack in the possible
event of her marching against Turkey. Count Tisza gave
reassuring accounts of the relations between the Monarchy
and the Hungarian Rumanians. He considered the union
of Serbia and Montenegro inevitable, but said it was none
the less important, in the interests of Austria-Hungary,
that Serbia, as a Russian outpost, should be kept at a
distance from the Adriatic. His advice was that the Triple
Alliance should act systematically together in the whole
realm of policy, the same as the Triple Entente, particularly
in the Balkans. There was no doubt that the Balkan
States were to be employed as a battering-ram against
Austria-Hungary in the event of a great European war.

At Miramar the first thing discussed was the King of
Italy's presence at the great German manœuvres. It was
next agreed that it would be very desirable for Rumania
and Greece, and if possible Turkey, to form a coalition in
the Balkans against the Slavs. Finally, Austria-Hungary's
difficulties with the Slavs within the Monarchy were discussed.

At Konopischt the serious differences between Turkey
and Greece formed the principal topic of conversation.
The Kaiser and the Archduke were of one mind in their
personal dislike to the King of Bulgaria, and were equally
unanimous in disapproving of the Italian procedure in
Albania. The Archduke then spoke very strongly about
the behaviour of the Hungarian Government to the non-

Hungarian elements. The official German report of this visit concludes with the sentence : " The Archduke's opinion is that there is nothing to be feared from Russia ; her internal difficulties are too great to allow of her pursuing an aggressive foreign policy ". Those were the Archduke's last words on political subjects to the German Emperor before his assassination a fortnight later. Not a word about plans for war, let alone desire for war, not even any expression of anxiety lest there should be war. As the most foolish tales have been spread abroad about these meetings by ignorant and malicious people, the full text of the reports of the conversations, as recorded in the German Foreign Office Documents, is given in the appendix.[1]

On his return from Konopischt the Emperor William found the well-known article, " Russia is ready, France must be ready too ", inspired by the Russian War Minister, on his writing table. He now realized whom Russia's military preparations concerned, and concluded that France and Russia were directing their efforts towards war with Germany at an early date. Anyone contemplating a preventive war would now have plainly emphasized the urgent necessity of forestalling the Franco-Russian offensive, in marginal notes, which as far as any human being could judge would never be made public. Instead of that, the marginal notes refer to fresh taxation, and enlisting the fit men in Germany who were liable for service, the full number not having yet been called up. This would involve a new Army Bill, which could not be passed by the Reichstag till the spring of 1915, consequently the first trained recruits would not be available till the spring of 1916.[2] Thus, only a month before the outbreak of war, the principle of a preventive war was rejected, as it had been systematically in the past. The same disinclination to adopt it had been shown in the course of a conversation between the Chancellor and the Bavarian Minister. After expressing rather a pessimistic opinion of the general political situation, they discussed the question of the preventive attack many military men advocated. Both the politicians considered

[1] App. I. No. 11, p. 229.
[2] *Deutsche Dokumente zum Kriegsausbruch*, No. 2.

that the right moment had gone by for an action which would have had the best chances of success in 1905, and the Chancellor added :

The Kaiser has never waged a preventive war, and never will.[1]

There was much more talk about war on the occasion of the visit paid by the King and Queen of England to Paris, from the 21st to the 24th of April, to celebrate the tenth anniversary of the Entente Cordiale, than at Miramar and Konopischt. Doumergue and Poincaré took advantage of the opportunity to point out to King George and Grey the necessity for closer alliance between Russia and England, on the lines of the Anglo-French " political conventions ". In the toasts allusion was not only made to peace, but very great stress was laid on the " balance of power in Europe ", which, it is well known, had been so successfully upset in the Balkans. Doumergue took special pains to advise the conclusion of an Anglo-Russian naval agreement, which would set a portion of the British fleet free, and enable it to show greater activity, not only in the North Sea and the Baltic, but also in the Mediterranean. Grey quite agreed, but pointed out that some of the members, not only of the Government Party, but even of the Cabinet itself, were not at all inclined to form closer ties with Russia. The military agreements must be confined entirely to the Navy, as all England's land forces had already been allotted their places in the theatre of war, and could not co-operate with the Russian army.[2] In May negotiations regarding the Anglo-Russian naval convention were started. Russia was also informed of the correspondence of November 1912 between Grey and Cambon.[3] When rumours of the naval convention began to reach the general public, Grey was very much concerned as to how to deny them. He took counsel with the Russian Minister, who pronounced the evasive answer the Secretary of State thought of giving in Parliament excellent. The somewhat differently worded explanation Grey gave the German Ambassador, who was

[1] *Bayerische Dokumente zum Kriegsausbruch,* p. 113.
[2] *Livre Noir,* Vol. II. pp. 259–61.
[3] Loc. cit., Vol. II. pp 265–7 ; compare also pp. 315 and 321.

away on a holiday, was equally ingenious ; in it he stated that the Straits question had not been discussed between London and St. Petersburg for five years. When the negotiations rather hung fire towards the end of June, Benckendorff thought that perhaps Grey wanted the excitement in Berlin to subside before continuing them, as it was really " not at all easy for the Secretary of State to deny and carry on the negotiations simultaneously ". He had to play this part, however, both towards Germany and towards a considerable section of his party and the English Press.[1]

14. AUSTRIA-HUNGARY AND SERBIA.

The battle of Kosovo had given the Serbian kingdom its death-blow. Seventy years later it was a Turkish province. Prince Eugene made the first attempt to emancipate the Serbs from this yoke. The capture of Belgrade in 1717 raised their hope of liberation, but twenty years later the crescent waved once more from the Ægean to the Danube.[2] But the Austrian feats of arms had inspired them with a desire for independence, which continued to be a living force, fostered at one time by Russia, at another by Austria. Step by step they strove for independence, till at last, in 1867, acting on Austria's advice, the last Turkish troops evacuated the Serbian fortresses. The Russian victory in the Turkish war completed their independence, and brought them an accession of territory. Still, it was generally assumed, at the Berlin Congress, that, just as the Eastern Balkans belonged to the Russian, so the Western Balkans ought to belong to the Austrian sphere of interest. At England's suggestion, the Congress gave Austria the right to occupy Bosnia and Herzegovina, and secret agreements with Russia, which were valid till 1887, and frequently confirmed, also gave her the right to annex these provinces. From 1881 till 1891 there was even an

---

[1] Loc. cit., Vol. II. p. 326 and note 2, pp. 327, 328 and note.

[2] For details of the development of the Greater-Serbian idea, vide H. Delbrück, "Serbia, Austria, and Russia," in *Deutschland und die Schuldfrage*, p. 95.

Austro-Serbian treaty of alliance in force,[1] on the strength of which the Monarchy came to Serbia's rescue in 1885, by calling on the victorious Bulgarians to halt. But Russian and Austrian influences continued to contend against one another in the Royal Palace (*Konak*) of the " White City ". When the last of the Obrenovich dynasty, the young King Alexander, with his wife and Ministers, had been done to death by the sword-thrusts of pro-Russian officers, on the terrible night of the 11th of June, 1903, Russia had won the upper hand. The House of Karageorgevich, which the Russian Foreign Minister, de Giers, had said in 1884 " could never reckon on support from the Russian Government ",[2] turned the helm towards St. Petersburg. A Serbian Government programme of March 1904 laid down the following line of policy :

Action in Bosnia with a view to its union with Serbia. The Austro-Hungarian administration to be discredited by systematic press propaganda, and by encouraging the discontent of the orthodox population in Bosnia and Herzegovina.[3]

The Greater-Serbian idea, which aimed at uniting Croats, Slovenes, Dalmatians, and Bosniacs, as well as Serbs, under one empire, gained more and more ground. The prospect of realizing schemes of this kind increased when England and Russia had effected their reconciliation in 1907. England, whose representative had been recalled from Belgrade after the King's assassination, protested more loudly than anyone against the annexation, five years later, though this may have been from selfish motives (p. 35). But as the Russian sword was not yet whetted, Serbia had to moderate her pretensions at that time, and pledge herself solemnly, in March 1909, to " change the policy she had directed against Austria, and live on friendly and neighbourly terms with her ".

It is evident that promises of that kind are worthless. It was only now that spiritual preparation for the great things to come began in real earnest. The Serbian Press did its best to stir up public feeling, the schools inculcated

[1] Pribram, Vol. I. pp. 18, 57 and note 2.
[2] *Grosse Politik*, Vol. III. No. 646, p. 371.
[3] L. Mandl, *Oesterreich-Ungarn und Serbien*, p. 15.

the idea of war, the agitation spread across the frontier, and worked upon the Croats and Slovenes. The Serbian Officers' Association, popularly called the " Black Hand ", started a newspaper, *Piémont*, which systematically instigated murderous attacks on leading Austro-Hungarian politicians, and honoured the murderers as national heroes.[1] An attempt was made to assassinate the Governor of Bosnia in 1910, and in 1912, 1913, and 1914 similar attacks were made on the Ban of Croatia.

The counter measures taken in Vienna and Budapest were not happy. The Hungarians took the strongest political measures against the Croats, which achieved the opposite of what was desired. The Serbs were not allowed an outlet to the Adriatic ; they were to remain dependent exclusively on the Danube waterway, and consequently on Austria-Hungary as their only market. The Serbian peasants could only sell their products with the greatest difficulty, whilst on the other hand the Austrian industrialists wanted to control the whole Serbian market. From the spring of 1906 to the autumn of 1908, and again from the spring of 1909 to the beginning of 1911, there was open tariff warfare. This chicanery undoubtedly immensely intensified the difficulties, but it is questionable whether a satisfactory solution could have been found by economic means alone. A strong people with pronounced national feeling does not renounce its ideals for a mess of pottage in the form of economic advantages. Not only that, but Russia did not at all wish for an Austro-Serbian understanding of the kind (p. 66). Perhaps it might have been possible to reconcile Serbia's right to national development with the right of the Habsburg State to maintain the *status quo*, by changing the Dual Monarchy into a Federal State, composed of three or more members, which the Kingdom of Serbia would join as a Federal State.[2] The Archduke Francis Ferdinand, who had ideas of this kind, was destined not to ascend the Habsburg throne.

The great advantages that had accrued to her, as a result of the Balkan wars, did not by any means have the

---

[1] Loc. cit., p. 32.
[2] This is H. Delbrück's opinion, loc. cit., p. 97.

effect of inducing Serbia to abandon her more ambitious aims. Pashitch, who had succeeded Milowanovich as Prime Minister in July 1912, kept his great object in view with iron consistency. He, the man who had voted for war against Austria as far back as in 1908, said, after the signature of the Bucharest peace in August 1913 :

The first game has been won, the second game against Austria must now be prepared.

Soon after that he confided to a Serbian diplomat that, in order to gain possession of Bosnia and Herzegovina, he might have taken the risk of the first Balkan war developing into a European war, but

as I was afraid that in that case we should have had to make greater concessions to Bulgaria in Macedonia, I wanted first to secure Macedonia for Serbia in order then to be able to take steps to acquire Bosnia and Herzegovina.[1]

Pashitch also spoke of a Greater-Serbian Empire to the Tsar on the 2nd of February, 1914. He began by saying he thought that some concessions might be made to Bulgaria, " if she were willing to help in solving the Serbo-Croat question ", in plain English, if she would take part in war against Austria. Then he said to the Tsar of all the Russias :

If it should fall to our lot to have a daughter of the Emperor of Russia as our Queen, she will have the affections of the whole Serbian people, and if God and circumstances permit, she may become Tsaritza of the South Slav, Serbo-Croat people. Her influence and her prestige will extend throughout the Balkan peninsular.

Nicholas II. did not cut him short ; on the contrary he listened with obvious pleasure, and at the end of the audience assured him that Russia would do everything in her power for Serbia. His parting words were :

Greet the King from me, and tell him that we will do everything in our power for Serbia.[2]

[1] Bogitshevich, p. 65 and note.
[2] Loc. cit., pp. 177, 179, and 180.

Six months later the Russian monarch kept his word, yielding to the pressure put on him by his *entourage*, although probably with a heavy heart. He did everything in his power for Serbia, and in so doing brought disaster on himself, his country and people, and the whole of Europe.

15. ARMAMENTS, 1907–14.

(a) *Armaments on Land.*

The additions to the German army in 1911 and 1912, after the second Hague Conference, did not keep pace with the increase in the population. The peace strength in 1912 was only 623,000 non-commissioned officers and men, with a population of sixty-five million. It had accordingly fallen from 1·09 per cent. in 1893 to less than 1 per cent. of the population, and the percentage was even lower than in 1871 !

In Austria-Hungary, with ten million more inhabitants than France, the quota of recruits was 126,000 up to 1910, half the number furnished by the French, and up to 1912 it had only risen to 175,000. Some additional strength was provided by raising the period of training for *Ersatz* reservists from eight to twelve weeks.[1]

The change that the first Balkan war had brought about in the balance of power in Europe meant that, in a war between the Central Powers and the Triple Entente, the latter could count on the armed help of more than half a million tried soldiers from the Balkan States, which were still united at that time. This would have involved the retention of considerable Austro-Hungarian forces in the south-east, so that only quite an inadequate number of troops would be available against the Russian hordes. It was consequently incumbent on the responsible authorities in Berlin and Vienna to consider how this immense accession of power to the Triple Entente could to some extent be counterbalanced. In Germany, a memorandum drawn up by the General Staff, at the end of November, proposed increasing the yearly number of recruits by

---

[1] For exact confirmation of the figures, vide Reichstag Committee of Enquiry, Sub-Committee I, Part 1, p. 100, and Part 2, p. 152.

150,000, so that 300,000 non-commissioned officers and men would consequently have been added to the peace establishment within two years, and forming at least three new Army Corps.[1] The Army Bill of 1913 did not add to the number of Army Corps, however, and only provided for 60,000 additional recruits.

Austria also strengthened her army to some extent, and raised the number of recruits to 200,000, about four-fifths of the French quota.

On the other hand, Russia had increased the number of men to be enlisted yearly from 337,000 to 445,000, as far back as 1905, shortly before summoning the second Hague Conference. In 1913 the number was further increased to 580,000 by the " great programme ", which had been drawn up even before that.[2] In addition, the period of service was lengthened by six months, so that, in the case of the infantry, four, and in the case of other branches of the service, five annual recruit contingents were serving with the Colours in winter.

France had only reduced the period of service to two years in 1905, that is, twelve years later than Germany, and in 1913 she reintroduced the three-year service period. In my opinion, there is no certain proof that this had been decided upon before the terms of the German Army Bill were known in Paris, but the Bill providing for it must have been drafted some time before that, for it was submitted to the Chamber directly the news of the addition to the German army became public.[3] At the same time, the age limit was lowered, for the enlistment of recruits, to twenty from twenty-one, and raised, as regards liability for service, from forty-five to forty-eight, a gain, at one stroke, of fully four additional annual classes in case of mobilization. An attack made by the Socialists on the proposal to lengthen the period of service was defeated.

---

[1] Ludendorff, *Französische Fälschung meiner Denkschrift von 1912 über den drohenden Krieg* (Berlin, 1919, Mittler und Sohn). The memorandum is grossly falsified in the French Yellow Book, No. 2. The fact that Jonnart is still spoken of as Foreign Minister, on the 2nd of April, 1913, although he had resigned on the 22nd of March, is sufficient in itself to show how carelessly it is drafted.

[2] Vide App. I. No. 12, p. 235.

[3] Vide App. I. No. 13, p. 235.

On the 13th of June, 1914, the Chamber sanctioned, not only the retention of the three-year service period, but also important measures providing for the military education of the rising generation, and reorganization of the reserves.

The peace strengths in the summer of 1914 were :

State.	Population in Millions.	Actual Peace Strength, including Officers, etc., and One-year Volunteers.	Percentage of the Population.
Germany	66	761,000*	1·15
Austria	51	478,000	0·94
Italy	36	273,000†	0·76
France	39·15	794,000‡	2·0
Russia	170	1,445,000 (winter : 1,845,000)	0·85

* Without officers, etc., and one-year volunteers, 695,000 = 1·05.
† Without natives.
‡ Without 86,000 natives, and without foreign legionaries.

The steady increase of the Franco-Russian superiority over the Central Powers, from the time of the first Hague Conference till 1914, is shown by the following statistics (the numbers in brackets are those of the Triple Alliance, including Italy) :

Year.	France and Russia.	Central Powers.	Franco-Russian Superiority.
1899	1,470,000	950,000 (1,208,000)	520,000 (262,000)
1907	1,813,000	1,011,000 (1,295,000)	802,000 (518,000)
1914	2,239,000	1,239,000 (1,512,000)	1,000,000 (727,000)

As regards war strength, the French General Staff had calculated, as far back as in 1892, that France and Russia could put 700,000 more men into the field than the Central Powers.[1] The regular war strength of the first and second line troops in 1914 was :

[1] French Yellow Book, *L'Alliance Franco-Russe*, pp. 38–9. On p. 45 the superiority over Germany and Austria (without Italy and Rumania) is even given as 800,000 men.

| France and Russia | .. | .. | .. | .. | 5,070,000 |
| Germany and Austria | .. | .. | .. | .. | 3,358,000 |

| Franco-Russian superiority | .. | .. | .. | 1,712,000 |

Or, after deducting 500,000 men, representing
the non-European Russian troops, who would
not arrive till later   1,212,000

As regards comparison between the Russian and French
military preparations in particular, France's first military
expert, General Buat, writes :

> It is not only incorrect to say that Germany made the greatest
> possible total effort of which she was capable in 1914, but it is
> absolutely false to assert that Germany had drawn as much on
> her reserves as France.[1]

Buat then strongly criticizes the inadequate enlistment
of recruits in Germany, and their exemption from military
service on account of very trifling physical defects. He
admits that the French peace establishment was stronger
than the German, and that the total number of men available for service, in case of mobilization, was the same in
both countries, and says, with regard to the relative forces
on the west front at the beginning of the war, that

> as regards the number of divisions, France alone was at least
> equal, if not superior, to her formidable enemy, independently of
> English and Belgian help.

As a matter of fact, only 50 to 55 per cent. of the men
liable for service were enlisted in Germany up to 1912,
inclusive, and about 65 per cent. in 1913, but in France
the percentage was 78 to 82. Consequently five to six
out of every ten men were serving with the Colours in
Germany as against eight in France. In order to compare
the last military preparations made in 1913, it should be
noted that the revival of the three-year service period,
and addition of four classes to the reserve forces in France,
took full effect at once, and left the French with no further
military resources to fall back upon. The same applied
to the extended period of service in Russia, in the event

[1] Vide App. I. No. 14, p. 235.

of a winter campaign. On the other hand, it would be many years before the full effect of the additions to the recruit contingents in Germany, Austria, and Russia could be felt. The position in Germany on the outbreak of war was that the first additional 60,000 men had only been enlisted in October 1913, the second increased quota would not fall due till the autumn of 1914, and the full effect on the reserves would only be felt in 1919, on the *Landwehr* and *Landsturm* in 1931 and 1936. It was a measure which could not take effect for a long time to come, not one which could be turned to account at once.

Germany was also less prepared in the matter of munitions than her western neighbour. France, who had only to fight on one front, had over 340 million rounds of ammunition, and half a million more field artillery shells than Germany, who had to fight on two fronts. There was only a small advantage on the German side as regards munitions for heavy field artillery.[1] On the 18th of June, the Prussian War Minister wrote to the German Chancellor that the experiences of the Balkan wars showed that it was absolutely essential to increase the supply of field artillery munitions, and proposed to insert the sum of 20,000,000 marks required for that purpose, in three instalments, in the 1915, 1916, and 1917 estimates, so that the supply, demanded as an urgent necessity, would only have been available at the beginning of 1918.[2] On the same 18th of June, the Ambassador in St. Petersburg, Paléologue, who had replaced Delcassé on the 12th of January, and was in Paris at the moment, said to the new Premier, and Minister for Foreign Affairs, Viviani :

I think we are on the verge of war, and that we must prepare for it.[3]

He was given the reassuring information that the pacifist majority of the Chamber had capitulated to the Nationalists, and passed the Bill providing for three years' service.[4]

[1] Vide App. I. No. 15, p. 235.
[2] Von Falkenhayn to Bethmann Hollweg on the 18th of June, 1914, No. 1150/14g A4, Confidential Estimates, 1915. Records of the former Prussian War Ministry.
[3] Paléologue in the *Revue des deux Mondes* of January 15, 1921, p. 230.
[4] Vide App. I. No. 16, p. 235.

(b) Naval Armaments.

After the second Hague Conference, Germany carried on her naval construction within the limits of the naval programme, which was to be completed in 1917. The Bill providing for a reduction of the duration of life of ships (p. 28), which had been accepted by the Reichstag in 1908, necessitated accelerating the pace of ship-building, and this caused a tremendous and quite unreasonable panic in England, partly kept up by very exaggerated reports. At that time the German Government discussed the possibility of retarding the rate of construction, and the advisability of defending the coasts by increasing the number of submarines, mines, and fortifications, rather than of Dreadnoughts. But the Minister of Marine, Admiral von Tirpitz, firmly adhered to the theory that every additional ship was a bulwark of peace. After the Agadir incident, the Admiral proposed to make amends for the diplomatic defeat by adding to Germany's naval strength still further.[1] The fundamental idea of the Bill of 1912 was, not indeed to increase the number of ships, which was quite inconsiderable, but to commission a reserve squadron, so that instead of two squadrons there would always be three in readiness. However expedient the proposal may have been from the professional point of view, the political argument was surprising, so it is difficult to understand the Chancellor's having agreed to it. He did not do so very willingly, it is true. As a matter of fact, the Bill had disastrous political consequences. It was mainly responsible for the failure of Haldane's mission (p. 50), and for the army not having been adequately increased in 1912, an omission which could not be fully repaired in 1913. The net result of the German naval policy was to cast a shadow over Germany's relations with England, and prevent the *per centum* increase of the German army. The verdict of history in days to come might well be that Germany strengthened her navy unnecessarily, particularly her High Seas Fleet, but kept her army on too weak a footing, in proportion to the allied French and German armies,

[1] Von Tirpitz, *Errinnerungen*, p. 182.

after the failure to reach any agreement as to a general diminution of armaments, and only tried to repair the omission when too late.

But although Germany's naval policy may be considered mistaken, it is quite certain that no will for war can be deduced from it. A naval Power with thirty-five battle-ships, and a total tonnage of 1·02 million, could not be a menace to Britannia, who ruled the seas, with her sixty battleships, and a tonnage of 2·17 million.[1] According to these figures England had seventeen to every ten German battleships. Churchill had described even sixteen to ten as sufficient, on the 18th of March, 1912 ; Tirpitz stated on the 7th of February, 1913, that this proportion would not be exceeded.

(c) *Military and Naval Conventions.*

The Triple Entente were not only numerically superior to the opposite side as regards man power, guns, and ships, but their very precise military agreements gave them a further advantage.

Germany and Austria had not concluded any military convention, in spite of an alliance which had existed for thirty-five years. The conversations which Bismarck had with difficulty been induced to hold with the General Staff in the eighties were not of a binding character, and were very indefinite. After 1896 no further exchange of views with regard to the conduct of operations, in case of a general war, took place for fully twelve years. The practice was revived during the 1908–9 crisis, but even then no binding agreements were reached as to the date of mobilization, and the forces to be employed on the various fronts. General Conrad von Hötzendorf gives a detailed account of his last interview with Moltke on the 12th of May, 1914, when the latter was taking the waters at Carls-bad, and is so frank that he certainly would not have omitted to give full particulars of such agreements.[2] As lately as on the 22nd of July, 1914, the Austrian Chief of

---

[1] The figures refer to the strength of 1914, and are taken from *Nauticus*.
[2] Vide App. I. No. 17, p. 236.

the General Staff refused to give the German Military
Attaché any information as to the Corps to be mobilized
against Serbia, in case of need.[1] Italy alone had entered
into a military convention with Germany, and a fresh
naval agreement was concluded between Germany, Austria,
and Italy in 1913. This agreement was in consequence of
the French having increased their naval strength in the
Mediterranean, a measure which was regarded in Rome as
a menace.[2]

France acted quite differently to Bismarck in concluding
her alliances. She invariably attached most importance to
the military element. The military agreements Bismarck
feared might tie the hands of the politicians in the hour of
danger were exactly what the French favoured. The
diplomatic agreement with Russia, in 1891, was followed
the very next year by the military convention which was
such a menace to peace, and which will be discussed later
on. The General Staffs met very often, finally they went
so far as to meet annually, for a thorough discussion of all
details at joint conferences. From 1911 onwards their
decisions were ratified by the Governments, and thus became
politically binding.[3]

Between France and England the military agreements,
which had begun as far back as in the winter of 1905–6,
had even preceded the exchange of diplomatic notes by as
much as six years. Their purport is still carefully kept
secret in the archives, but Isvolsky was able to report,
in the spring of 1914, that they were " technically more
complete " than the Franco-Russian convention, although
they were not of a binding character.[4] Poincaré's object
in concluding the Franco-Russian naval convention in
1912 was at first only, on the one hand, to exert pressure
on Italy by concentrating the main French naval forces
in the Mediterranean, and on the other, to meet Russia's
wishes, as far as possible, with regard to the Straits—in

---

[1] German Military Report from Vienna, July 22, 1914.
[2] Pribram, Vol. I. p. 308.
[3] Protocol of the Conferences of 1911, 1912, and 1913 in the so-called
Russian Blue Book, p. 697. German translation in the August 1922 number
of the *Süddeutsche Monatshefte*.
[4] *Livre Noir*, Vol. II. p. 249.

marked contrast to the reserved attitude maintained by his predecessor towards this question in 1911 (p. 90). But this dislocation of the French fleet, which at that time withdrew its very last cruiser from the English Channel, was of extraordinary importance, because it had been decided upon in agreement with England, on whom it consequently imposed at least a moral obligation to defend the north coast of France in any war, no matter how it might originate.[1]

As the understanding of 1907 was not at all in the nature of a covenant, a military agreement was also to have preceded a diplomatic agreement between England and Russia. Russia went so far as to wish the terms of the proposed naval convention to bind England to send transports to the Baltic ports in peace time, for landing troops on the Pomeranian coast, a demand Benckendorff thought so unreasonable that he strongly advised its not being made.[2]

[1] Loc. cit., Vol. I. p. 326.   [2] *Livre Noir*, Vol. II. p. 325.

PART III

THE CRISIS

1. THE SARAJEVO MURDER.

THE assassination of the Heir to the Throne and his consort, on the 28th of June, 1914, by Austro-Hungarian subjects of Serbian nationality, was the incendiary torch which was hurled into an atmosphere charged with combustible material. The Greater-Serbian agitation, which had increased beyond all bounds, as a result of the Serbian successes in the Balkan wars, had instigated Nationalists to commit this crime.

The preamble to the English Blue Book says:

No crime has ever aroused deeper or more general horror throughout Europe, none has ever been less justified. . . .

Austria was under provocation. She had to complain of a dangerous popular movement against her Government.

Viviani made the following admission in the French Chamber on the 5th of July, 1922:

One would be expected to think the next day

> On aurait pu penser que, le lendemain, dans un moment d'exitation, l'Autriche addressât à la Serbie un ultimatum, même brutal.[1]

" would address " equally

In a memorandum published by permission of the Russian censor in 1915, the Serbian Consul in Odessa expressed himself as follows, with regard to the effect of the murder:

From 1908 till 1914, the small, helpless Slav State continually risked upsetting the strongly armed peace of Europe. The South Slavs never ceased saying to the Hungarians and Germans: "We are not afraid of you, for we have Serbia behind us, and behind Serbia Russia and her friends!" The South Slavs forced little Serbia into war with Austria-Hungary by bringing about

[1] *Annales de la Chambre des Députés*, 1922, Vol. II. p. 758.

8

the Sarajevo incident. The shots fired at Sarajevo set the whole world on fire.[1]

An Austrian official sent to Sarajevo to enquire into the question of who was responsible for the tragedy, reported that there was no proof, nor did it even seem likely that the Serbian Government knew who had carried out or organized the murder, or that they had supplied the weapons. There was, on the contrary, every reason to regard this as out of the question. On the other hand, it was almost indisputably established that the plot was hatched in Belgrade, and that a Serbian civil servant, and a Serbian officer, had supplied the necessary bombs, munitions, and poison. It was definitely proved that the bombs came from a Serbian arms depôt, but there was no evidence that they had been taken expressly for this purpose. According to statements made by the persons accused of the crime, there seemed no doubt that the bombs and arms had been secretly smuggled across the frontier to Bosnia by Serbian Customs officials and frontier guard officers.[2]

Since then it has transpired that the head of the Intelligence Department of the Serbian General Staff, Colonel Dimitrijevich, arranged the whole thing. At a meeting of the " Black Hand " on the 15th of June, he announced that, in his opinion, the impending Austrian manœuvres in Bosnia were only the prelude to war against Serbia ; the Archduke Francis Ferdinand was the soul of this enterprise, consequently he (Dimitrijevich) had made all the necessary arrangements to dispose of the Heir to the Throne, and so prevent the war. As all but two of those present expressed themselves against the plan, the Colonel promised not to carry out his project, but in reality he left the preparations already made to take their course. During the war, in the spring of 1917, Dimitrijevich was condemned to death by court-martial, and shot, with a few other officers, apparently for having conspired against the Prince Regent of Serbia. But, according to trustworthy information, he was condemned and shot because his responsibility for the murder had been established, and the Serbian Government

[1] Friedjung, Vol. II. p. 189.   [2] Vide App. I. No. 18, p. 236.

wanted to pave the way to a separate peace with Vienna by punishing him. Even this does not prove the complicity of the political leaders—all the less, as in 1914 the relations between them and the " Black Hand " were strained rather than otherwise.[1] But it would have been very important, as far as public opinion throughout the world is concerned, if it had been known, during the critical days before the war, that a distinguished Serbian General Staff officer, in a very responsible position, had instigated the murder.

Immediately after the armistice in 1918, Serbian officers in Vienna requisitioned all the documents relating to the Sarajevo trial and the Greater-Serbian agitation. The substance can hardly have been creditable to Belgrade, otherwise it would certainly have been published. The Serbian Government afterwards honoured the murderers as national heroes, at a Church service held on the spot where the murder took place.

2. THE HOYOS MISSION.

The whole world expected that Austria-Hungary would deal severely with Serbia. The German Government were also of opinion that it would be advisable to take strong measures. The Emperor William's infatuation for Serbia, which Count Tisza had complained of as recently as on the 1st of July (A I. 2 [2]), was at an end, as many very drastic marginal notes clearly show. Berlin took the view that the Serbian Government were behind the intrigues which had instigated the murder.

On the 5th of July Count Hoyos arrived in the German capital as Count Berchtold's emissary, bringing with him an autograph letter from the Emperor Francis Joseph, and

---

[1] All the evidence against Dimitrijevich, as reported by the former Reichstag Deputy, Wendel, who knew Serbia well, is amongst the Reichstag Committee of Enquiry Documents.

[2] A = Austrian Red Book.
 D = *Die Deutschen Dokumente zum Kriegsausbruch.*
 E = English Blue Book.
 F = French Yellow Book.
 R = Russian Orange Book.

The figures appended give the numbers of the documents, not the numbers of the pages.

a memorandum from the Austro-Hungarian Government (D 13 and 14). The memorandum started by assuming that the Central Powers were pursuing a conservative policy, whilst the aims pursued by the Franco-Russian alliance were offensive, and it then proceeded to strike a balance of gains and losses resulting from the Balkan wars. The erection of an independent Albania, Greece's friendly attitude towards the Triple Alliance, and the liberation of Bulgaria from Russian influence, were reckoned as gains. But the losses were greater : Turkey having been weakened, Serbia having been so immensely aggrandized, her possible impending union with Montenegro, and, above all, Rumania's *rapprochement* to Russia and Serbia, which would make it hardly possible for the Central Powers to place any further reliance on Rumania, or derive any advantage from the former alliance with her. In consequence of this change in the balance of power, the " military superiority " of the Central Powers, the main guarantee of European peace, was becoming a thing of the past. In addition to this, the result of the Balkan wars, favourable as it had been to France and Russia, had not satisfied them; they were now trying to form a fresh Balkan League, in order to put an end to the superiority of the two Central Empires, with the help of troops from the Balkans, a prospect being held out to the Balkan States of enlarging their borders at the expense of Austria-Hungary, by " gradually shifting the frontiers from east to west ". In order to meet this danger, the Vienna Government proposed making Bulgaria the " Balkan exponent " of the Central Powers, instead of Rumania, and concluding a treaty with her, which might be supplemented by a Bulgaro-Turkish alliance. The only military measures proposed were " making fresh dispositions in case of war, and considering the question of constructing fortifications against Rumania ". Both were measures which could not be completed for some time to come, particularly the construction of fortifications. The only thing said about Serbia was in a concluding paragraph, which stated that " indisputable proof had now been given of the impossibility of bridging over the differences between the Monarchy and Serbia, and of the danger and intensity

of the Greater-Serbian efforts, which would stick at nothing ".
It was consequently necessary for the Monarchy to strike
firmly at the root of the plot which was being hatched for
its destruction by the enemy. In earlier drafts of the
memorandum, which covered a long period of history,[1]
the possibility of a fresh *rapprochement* between Serbia and
Austria-Hungary being brought about through Rumanian
mediation, was taken into consideration, but this proposi-
tion had now been struck out. The view that the Central
Powers had the advantage in military strength before the
Balkan wars, and that their superiority was only now
ceasing to exist, is strange.

The Emperor Francis Joseph's letter expressed the same
train of thought, and proposed first and foremost the
formation of a new Balkan League, friendly to the Central
Powers. In saying that the Government in Vienna must
in future direct its efforts towards isolating Serbia, and
reducing her territory, he was not suggesting that Austria-
Hungary should go to war for the sake of territorial gains,
but merely referring to the vain attempts made, in his
time, to revise the Bucharest Peace in favour of Bulgaria.
The Bavarian Chargé d'Affaires's celebrated report of
July 18 (D, App. IV. 2) shows that the aim of the Monarchy
was to redistribute the territorial possessions of the Balkan
States between them, not to make extensive annexations.
The gist of the report was shockingly misrepresented, when
it was first published in November 1918, both through
the suppression of the whole part dealing with the Balkans,
and many other omissions.[2]

The official German answer to the Austrian memorandum,
and detailed explanations of it, form the substance of the
despatch sent to the Ambassador in Vienna, on the 6th
of June, by the Chancellor, as the responsible director of
German policy, after reporting to the Emperor.

It stated that the Emperor William was not blind to the
danger the agitation, carried on by Russian and Serbian
Pan-Slavists, constituted to Austria-Hungary, and conse-

---

[1] Dr. Roderich Gooss, *Das Wiener Kabinett und die Entstehung des Weltkrieges*, p. 3.
[2] *Süddeutsche Monatshefte*, May 1922.

quently to the Triple Alliance. The proposal that an effort should be made to draw Bulgaria into the alliance was agreed to, and an assurance was given that Germany would do her best to induce Rumania to fulfil the obligations of her alliance, and put a stop to the Rumanian agitation against Austria-Hungary. The only remark made about Serbia was that the Emperor naturally could not take any part in the questions pending between that country and Austria-Hungary, as they were not within his competence. But the Emperor Francis Joseph could rest assured that His Majesty would be true to their old friendship, and stand by Austria-Hungary, conformably with the obligations imposed on him by the alliance.

The Chancellor struck out the words "in all circumstances", which had been inserted in the draft, with his own hand. Although the instruction (D 15) was only intended for von Tschirschky's "personal guidance", it must be regarded as the German Government's official reply to the Austrian memoir, as it absolutely tallies with the statements the Chancellor made to the Austro-Hungarian Ambassador on the 6th of July, which were very correctly reported by the latter (A I. 7).[1]

It will be seen that the Berlin Government left the allies a free hand, and stated that they agreed to all measures, consequently also to a war against Serbia. That undoubtedly denoted a change of policy. Just a year earlier Germany had strongly opposed the Vienna Cabinet on this point. What had brought about this change? In the first place, the view that the existence of the Monarchy was so seriously menaced by the Pan-Slav agitation, that further inactivity was inconsistent with the duty of self-preservation. A second reason was the belief that the Tsar could not take Serbia's part. It was not surprising that a man of the Emperor William's character should overestimate the feeling of monarchical solidarity, but the same view was taken in other quarters. At all events the Belgian Minister reported that people were saying in Berlin: " Serbia will not let things come to such a pass, unless she is sure of

[1] Count Szögyény's report of the preceding day (July 5th) on the interview with the Emperor, vide Part IV. sect. 1, p. 204.

being backed up by Russia. And the Tsar's Government will not support her, for they must themselves share the horror and fear the Sarajevo crime has excited ".[1] Added to this there was, thirdly, the mistaken belief that Russia was not by any means prepared for war, a belief for which there was no justification, according to all the information to hand from military quarters. Finally, the optimistic view taken of the situation was based largely on the fact that there had recently been a steadily increasing improvement in the relations between England and Germany. The important Anglo-German agreement with regard to the Portuguese colonies and the Bagdad railway was on the point of conclusion. If England adopted an attitude friendly to Austria and Germany in a possible diplomatic conflict, the chances were that France would not make up her mind to fight, and Russia would not start hostilities without French armed support. Three mistakes—overestimation of the Tsar's feeling of solidarity, underestimation of France and Russia's preparations and will for war, and a false estimate of the attitude England would be likely to adopt—were responsible for Germany's having underestimated the magnitude of the risk Austria's action against Serbia must involve.

After the conference with the Imperial Chancellor in the afternoon of the 5th of July, the Emperor sent for the War Minister. Although he was not instructed to do so, General von Falkenhayn informed the Chief of the General Staff, who was taking the waters at Carlsbad, of what he had been told. From what the Austrian Ambassador had said, the Emperor understood that Austria-Hungary would not put up with Serbia's machinations any longer, and intended marching on the country " if necessary ". Falkenhayn remarked, however, that he did not gather from the Emperor Francis Joseph's autograph letter, and the Austrian Government's memoir, which had been read to him, that the Vienna Cabinet had taken any definite decision ; both documents spoke, not of war as the issue, but of active political steps, for instance, the conclusion of a treaty with Bulgaria, for which Vienna wanted to secure support in Berlin. Neither

[1] *Belgian Diplomatic Documents*, No. 119.

did the Chancellor believe, any more than he did himself, that Austria was in earnest, although she spoke more firmly than on former occasions. In any case, nothing was likely to be decided within the next few weeks, so there was no need for General von Moltke to curtail his stay at Carlsbad.[1] The Emperor William received a naval Staff officer the same afternoon, and representatives of the Admiralty and the General Staff the following morning, between his half-past eight o'clock breakfast and his departure for Kiel, three-quarters of an hour later. These three officers were individually informed of his reception of the Austro-Hungarian Ambassador, in interviews of a few minutes each, and the Kaiser added that he " did not believe there was any prospect of great war-like developments, the Tsar would not side with the Archduke's murderers, Russia and France were not ready for war, there was no need to make special dispositions " (D, p. xiii).[2]

That is the truth with regard to the legend of the " Crown Council on the 5th or 6th of July", which originated in hotel gossip, and was quoted during the war as the best proof of Germany's will for war.[3] None of the responsible naval and military authorities were recalled from leave, no military preparations were made, and the Emperor started on his annual trip to Norway on the appointed day.

3. POINCARÉ'S VISIT TO ST. PETERSBURG.

Poincaré was anxious to pay his respects to the Russian Tsar as President of the French Republic, in the summer of 1914, as he had done in 1912 as Premier. In 1912 he had severely criticized the Serbo-Bulgarian "war treaty", and made reservations as to the obligations of the alliance in Balkan questions. Now he had come to look on every territorial aggrandizement of Austria, in the south-eastern peninsular, as a disturbance of the European balance of power which would be injurious to French as well as other

[1] Vide App. I. No. 19, p. 237.
[2] The hours are taken from notes made by the responsible Court official and the railway authorities at Potsdam.
[3] Vide Part IV. sect. 2, p. 207.

interests. But he welcomed a disturbance of this balance by the aggrandizement of Russia's protégés.

On the 20th of July the armed cruiser *France* anchored off Peterhof. Paléologue, the French Ambassador, had been a schoolfellow and friend of the President's youth. His heart beat with joy. He was a fatalist, confident that war would soon break out. He had threatened to resign if the French Chamber rejected the three years' service, and had just contradicted the Tsar, who insisted that William II. was a lover of peace. He now noted with satisfaction that Poincaré did most of the talking in the first interview between the two heads of States.

The first toasts were exchanged at the dinner given in the Empress Elizabeth's banqueting hall in the evening, on a scale of magnificence only known at the St. Petersburg Court. Paléologue thought it must have occurred to many of the Russian dignitaries who heard Poincaré's speech, that this was "how an autocrat ought to speak". The Russian people were less interested in the visit. Working men on strike came into conflict with the police. French agents reported that this was due to German machinations.

At the reception of the Diplomatic Corps the next day Poincaré told the Japanese Minister how necessary it was that his country should join the Triple Entente ; he assured the British Ambassador that Russia would do her utmost to meet England in the Persian question, and laid stress on the necessity of changing the Dual Entente into a Triple Alliance ; whilst, in a lengthy and tactless dissertation, which sounded like a threat, he explained to the Austrian Ambassador that Serbia had "friends"—the plural is significant. Thus Poincaré spoke in the name of Russia, as well as of France, both to Japan, Great Britain, and Austria-Hungary. He then said to the friend of his youth : "Sazonov must be firm, and we must support him". The leader of the Franco-Russian alliance merely shook hands cursorily with the Ministers of the smaller States. The representative of Serbia was the only one honoured with a few words of sympathy. The disturbances in the capital continued. But the police had taken care that when the President went out driving, "a handful of poor devils,

under their supervision, should cheer him at every street
corner ".

On the third day a gala dinner was given by the Grand
Duke Nicholas, the head of the Russian war party, at the
camp of Krasnoe Selo. His wife, the Grand Duchess
Anastasia, and her sister Militza, daughters of the King of
Montenegro, received the French Ambassador with enthu-
siasm. The Grand Duchess spoke of historic days. Her
father had telegraphed that war would break out before
the end of the month. She produced a *bonbonnière* that
she always carried about with her, full of earth she had
brought from the Lorraine manœuvres two years before.
The table was decorated entirely with thistles, the Lorraine
flower. " There will be war . . . there will be nothing left
of Austria . . . you will recover Alsace and Lorraine . . .
our armies will meet in Berlin . . . Germany will be
overthrown. . . ." That was the conversation at dinner,
which was silenced by a stern glance from the Tsar.

On the last day, the 23rd of July, after a brilliant review
of the troops at Krasnoe Selo, a farewell dinner was given
on board the *France*. The French President's speech concluded with the words : " *Les deux pays out le même idéal
de paix dans la force, l'honneur, et la dignité* ". The guns
thundered applause. The Grand Duke Nicholas and his
wife looked at the French Ambassador with glowing eyes.
They had understood what the words " peace with strength,
honour, and dignity " signified. " These words will form
a landmark in the history of the world ", prophesied the
daughter of the Black Mountains. On the way back to
St. Petersburg the Tsar said to the French Ambassador :
" We must be the more united and firm, the more difficult
the position becomes ".[1]

Less is known of the private conversations that took place
during the visit than of the public doings.[2] It is probable,
although it cannot be absolutely proved, that, while they
were still in St. Petersburg, the Frenchmen received the

---

[1] The above description of the visit is given by Paléologue in the *Revue
des deux Mondes* of January 13, 1922, pp. 232–47 ; vide also *La Russie
des Tsars pendant la grande Guerre*, and Szápáry's Report, A, I. No. 45.

[2] According to the index, E 6 ought to throw light on the result of
Poincaré's visit, but this part of the text has been carefully suppressed.

consular report of July 20 from Vienna (F 14), informing them of four essential points of the Austrian Note, and of its general tendency. One thing certain is that, on the 22nd of July, Sazonov already knew, ostensibly from hearsay, that Austria was preparing a *démarche* in Belgrade, and had learnt from his conversations with Viviani that "France was also very much concerned as to the turn the Austro-Serbian relations might take, and was not inclined to permit a humiliation of Serbia which was not justified by the circumstances." [1]

The Russian and French statesmen had further agreed, not only to try for their part to induce Austria not to make any demands that might be regarded as interference in Serbia's internal affairs, but also to request England to take similar action in Vienna (F 22). Thus it will be seen that steps were taken to de-localize the Austro-Serbian conflict, and make it a European question, even before anything definite was known as to the Austrian *démarche*. Further evidence that Poincaré was the presiding genius of the negotiations is supplied by what Nicholas II. said to the former French Minister, Cruppi, in 1915 :

I never for a moment forget the firmness with which the President of the French Republic spoke when leaving Russia on the 22nd of July, 1914.[2]

4. The Austrian Ultimatum.

The German Government did not take any part in drawing up the demands to be made of Serbia. A marginal note of July 4 (D 7), made by the Kaiser, that " what Austria proposed doing was entirely her own affair, because otherwise, if things went wrong, it would be said afterwards that it was Germany's fault", gives one of the reasons for this. The Berlin Cabinet knew that the Austrians were very sensitive, and did not want to be reproached later on with having again put a spoke in their allies' wheel. But a reason of greater importance was, that, in case of a serious diplomatic conflict with Russia, they wanted Germany to

[1] *Livre Noir*, Vol. II. p. 275.
[2] *Matin*, August 26, 1915. July 22nd should read July 23rd.

be in a position to mediate as a hitherto disinterested party. It is true that the confidence in the Austrian diplomats, shown by this non-interference, afterwards proved misplaced. The Berlin Government not only gave no advice, but when sounded as to what demands should be made of Serbia, expressed no opinion. On the other hand, no clear explanation of what was proposed came from the Ballplatz. There is no proof that the Ambassador, von Tschirschky, received instructions to urge action being taken against Serbia.[1]

The only influence the Wilhelmstrasse tried to exert on Vienna was to induce her to act quickly, and in case of military action, not to take any steps to mobilize in Galicia.[2] It seemed advisable to expedite matters, so that the action taken should be at a time when the impression made on public opinion by the murder was still fresh. The advice was given from precisely the point of view expressed by Viviani (p. 113). On the other hand, when once a good deal of time had been lost, Vienna's decision not to let the Note be handed to the Belgrade Government just as the French visit to St. Petersburg was being celebrated in a spirit of wild Chauvinism, was equally justifiable, for, had this been done, it might easily have caused the enemy to come to too hasty a decision. It is extraordinarily illogical to blame Germany for having urged rapid action, and at the same time for the delay which was not even due to her initiative. The reason for advising Austria not to mobilize in Galicia was that Germany knew, from what the Russian military plenipotentiary, Tatischev, said, that, during the crisis of 1912-13, it was the reinforcement of the Austrian armies north of the Carpathians that caused Russia anxiety ; the fact of the armies on the south-east frontiers of the Monarchy having been strengthened did not trouble her at all.[3]

In reality, what was known in Berlin of the Austrian Note was its general tenor, which was calculated to lead to its rejection : the forty-eight hours' time-limit, Serbia

[1] Vide Part IV., sect. 3, p. 208.
[2] A I. 15 ; D. App. IV. 2 ; Jagow, Reichstag Committee of Enquiry, Part I, p. 29.
[3] *Süddeutsche Monatshefte*, May 1922, p. 69.

being required to issue a proclamation, and the following conditions : societies to be dissolved, officers and officials implicated to be dismissed, Pan-Serbian intrigues to be supervised by Austrian officials, a judicial enquiry to be held, and Austrian delegates to take part in the preliminary investigations (points 2, 4, 5, and 6 of the ultimatum).[1] In all probability the Quai d'Orsay was just as well informed, even before the 23rd of July, by the consular report of the 20th of July (F 14), to which reference has already been made, for it mentions : substantial security for rejection of the ultimatum, to be followed by military action, a short time-limit, and further: repression of nationalism, dissolution of societies, strict supervision over school teaching, and the co-operation of Austrian officials in guarding the frontier (points 1, 2, 3, and 8). No doubt just as much was known in St. Petersburg as in Paris. A telegram respecting the Austrian intentions had reached London as early as on the 16th (E 161). But how much information this gave is still the secret of the English archives. Consequently the Entente Powers are not doing justice to the truth when they assert that the Austrian Note took them completely by surprise. The statement made by Sir Edward Grey to Prince Lichnowsky, on the 20th of July, that all he had recently heard from Vienna was that Count Berchtold deprecated the suggestion that the situation was grave (E 1 [2]), was particularly incorrect.

The ultimatum was handed to the Belgrade Government on the evening of the day Poincaré left St. Petersburg, the 23rd of July. The Austrian Ambassador had transmitted the Note to Berlin exactly twenty-four hours earlier. I have no intention of defending either the tone or the purport of the document ; it made demands which were not compatible with the dignity of an independent State. But in justice I must point out that Austria's demands were recognized as legitimate by English newspapers, even those closely connected with the Government.[3] It is a mistake

---

[1] D 29, and App. IV. 2 ; private letter of July 11th from Tschirschky, Reichstag Committee of Enquiry, Part 1, p. 119.

[2] E 161 was subsequently added to the Blue Book. The editor apparently overlooked its inconsistency with E 1.

[3] Vide App. I. No. 20, p. 238.

to suppose that Germany could have influenced Vienna to modify the Note, or even have prevented its being handed to the Belgrade Government, in the time available. Austria was not a vassal State of Germany, but a very sensitive ally, on an equality, who had her own opinion, and was not inclined to take her orders from Germany.[1] The Vienna Cabinet would have been quite justified in pointing out that they had been left a free hand.

The assertion that similar conditions had never been proposed to an independent State in modern times is quite untenable. Apart from the many far more drastic demands made of Greece by the Triple Entente in 1916 and 1917, Notes with a time-limit, and accompanied by threats of war, were addressed by England and France to Egypt in 1882, by England to Portugal in 1890, by the United States to Spain in 1898, by England to France the same year, by England to Turkey in 1906, and by Italy to Turkey in 1911. In comparison with the extraordinarily humiliating Notes Germany has had to accept since 1918, the Austrian ultimatum to Serbia may even be described as a considerate document.

No military measures were taken either in Germany or Austria between the 5th and 23rd of July.[2] As far as Germany in particular is concerned, it would be difficult to explain the following arrangements having been made, if the military authorities had been working to bring about an early outbreak of war:

On the 27th of July the Finance Branch of the Prussian War Office decided to strike off three and a half million marks from the amount it had been estimated would be required for munitions in 1915, in a report submitted on the 5th of July. On the 9th of July a proposal to postpone the date for provisioning the fortress of Strasburg from the twelfth to the twentieth day of mobilization, and the fortress of Neubreisach from the eighth to the fifteenth day, was approved, and instructions were given to report

---

[1] The Chancellor, who was at Hohenfinow, was not aware of the text of the Note at midnight (D 116) ; the Kaiser first learnt it through the newspapers (D 231).

[2] Vide App. I. No. 21, p. 239.

again on this question on the 1st of April, 1915.[1] No steps
were taken to expedite the annual work of collecting information, and revising the lists of men available in case
of mobilization, which fell due between the 10th and 27th
of July. On the 21st of July the Prussian War Ministry
fixed the end of August for further discussion of the annual
mobilization work of the 21st Army Corps (Saarbrück
Corps). On the 22nd of July the reservists who had been
called up for training at Arys were dismissed and sent home.[2]
The High Seas Fleet left for Norway on the 15th of
July, although it was known that the British Fleet
with 460 ships[3] would be assembled off Portland for a
trial mobilization and manœuvres the next day. The
Emperor William's order of the 19th to the Fleet not
to disperse till the 25th, so that orders to return home
could be carried out quickly (D 82), was a precautionary
measure taken as a matter of course. The Fleet was even
allowed to enter a Norwegian port as lately as on the 24th
(D 175), and was only recalled the following evening, on
information being received of the Serbian mobilization
(D 182).

No effort was made to secure fresh allies. The conclusion
of a treaty with Bulgaria was postponed (D 19, 21, 22 ;
A I. 11), and the matter was only taken up again on the
1st of August, when war had become inevitable (D 549).
The question of Turkey's joining the Triple Alliance was
negatived (D 45), and it was only on her expressing a strong
wish to do so, and stating that, in the event of a refusal,
she would be reluctantly compelled to conclude a pact
with the Triple Entente, that steps were taken, on the 24th
of July, to fall in with this wish (D 117, 144). Rumania
was not approached, and Greece was not invited to enter
into an alliance, as has been asserted, amongst other things,
but was merely advised to dissociate herself from Serbia

---

[1] The French occupied Mühlhausen, only a good day's march from
Neubreisach, which was not yet fully provisioned, on the 8th of August
(the seventh day of German mobilization).

[2] Communication from the Imperial archives, May 12, 1923, No. 5736.

[3] The word used in the German edition is " *Wimpeln* " (" pennants "),
so that presumably the author meant " war-ships," but the figure 460,
if correct, would obviously include all auxiliaries, such as colliers, trawlers,
etc.—[TR.]

in good time, so as not to be drawn into a conflict with Austria (D 122). On the 27th of July King Constantine did not refuse a hypothetical invitation to take part in war against Serbia, he merely protested against the accusation that he was arming against Turkey (D 243). The only exception was a telegram sent on the 23rd of July to Sweden, pointing out that the country must realize how serious the position would be in the event of Germany's earnest wish to localize the war being frustrated (D 123).

5. LOCALIZATION OR WORLD WAR ?

Germany's desire to localize the Austro-Serbian conflict was communicated to St. Petersburg, London, and Paris, in a Note which contained the sentence :

We earnestly desire to localize the dispute, because any interference by another Power would have incalculable consequences, owing to the natural play of the alliances.—D 100 (F 28).

It is true that, according to the original minutes, Count Berchtold had said, at a Cabinet Council held on the 7th of July, in Vienna, that he thought war with Russia " very probable " in the event of Austria's marching on Serbia,[1] but when looking through the minutes he corrected this, and substituted " realized that an armed conflict with Serbia might lead to war with Russia ". Naturally his wish was to arrange matters with Serbia without interference from Russia or any other Power.

The following official communiqué had been issued in St. Petersburg on the evening of the 24th of July, after a Ministerial Council which lasted five hours :

The Russian Government are closely following the course of the Austro-Serbian dispute, to which Russia cannot remain indifferent.—R 10.

In London, as is well known, the opinion was that Austria had received provocation (p. 113). Grey consequently took the view he had expressed to the German Ambassador on the 24th and 25th (E 11, 25 ; D 157 and 180), and which

[1] Gooss, p. 52, note 1.

is repeated in the preamble to the Blue Book, that the Austro-Serbian dispute

did not concern him, and that he had no title to intervene between Austria and Serbia, but that it would be a different matter if " the dispute became one between Austria and Russia, and thus affected the peace of Europe ".—E p. 5.

Even after seeing the Serbian answer, the British Foreign Secretary said to the Austrian Ambassador, on the 27th of July :

If they (the Austrian Government) could make war on Serbia, and at the same time satisfy Russia, well and good.—E 48.

And again, on the very day after the Austrian declaration of war on Serbia, he said :

There must, of course, be some humiliation of Serbia.—E 90.

Sazonov even believed, on the strength of the reports he had received, that

up to the last moment before her *démarche* in Belgrade, Austria had thought herself justified in hoping that England would make no objections to what she demanded, and that her decision was, to a certain extent, based on this belief.[1]

On the 24th of July the German Ambassador in Paris reported that the Minister of Justice, Bienvenu Martin, who was acting for Viviani during his absence in St. Petersburg, seemed " obviously relieved " on being informed of the view taken by Germany. It is true that he pointed out how difficult it was for Russia to be entirely disinterested, but he stated, on behalf of the French Government, that they

honestly shared the wish that the conflict should remain localized, and would exert themselves to that end, with a view to the maintenance of European peace.—D 154.

A more favourable report of the feeling in Paris was also sent on the 25th :

Our statement with regard to localizing the conflict has made a great impression.—D 169.

[1] *Livre Noir*, Vol. II. p. 276.

On the 26th the French Minister of Justice admitted in confidence that

Sazonov's view that only the Powers as a whole could pronounce upon Serbia's conduct could hardly be legally upheld.—D 235.

The reports of the interviews with the German Ambassador, on the 24th and 25th of July, have been falsified in the French Yellow book by the suppression of important passages.[1]

It will be seen that the Russian view of the impossibility of localizing the conflict was not shared in London. As lately as on the 26th King George believed that it was possible (D 374). As equally satisfactory news from Paris was received at the Wilhelmstrasse, and nothing was known of Poincaré's conversations with Sazonov, there was no reason for giving up the original plan at once. The opinion that it was an illusion bordering on madness, to believe for a moment in the possibility of localizing the conflict, cannot be upheld in the face of all this evidence. It is still more effectively refuted by the fact that, thanks to German mediation, there was finally a prospect of reaching an understanding, which was only frustrated by the efforts of the Russian military party, secretly supported by France.

6. Six Days of Anglo-German Mediation.[2]

Saturday, July 25.

The first English suggestion of mediation (D 157, E 11), which reached Berlin early in the morning of the 25th of July, made two proposals :

1. Extension of the time limit for the Serbian reply, which expired at six o'clock the same evening.

2. In case of serious Austro-Russian tension, mediation in Vienna and St. Petersburg by the four Powers not directly concerned, England, France, Germany, and Italy.

[1] Comparison of the French reports with the telegrams from the Russian Chargé d'Affaires in Paris, No. 184 of the 24th, and No. 188 of the 26th of July (*Livre Noir*, Vol. II. pp. 275–6 and 278–9), shows what passages have been suppressed.

[2] For a detailed account of the diplomatic negotiations, vide B. W. von Bülow, *Die Krisis* and *Die ersten Stundenschläge des Weltkrieges.*

The proposal to extend the time limit was not supported by Germany, it was merely communicated to the Ambassador in Vienna (D 171). The German attitude did not influence the course of events, as the Austrian Government had already rejected a similar Russian proposal that the time limit should be extended, in order to give the Powers time to examine the Austrian *dossier*, in the morning, before a request from Germany could reach the Ballplatz (A II. 29).

The British Chargé d'Affaires was immediately informed personally that Germany would agree to mediate between Austria and Russia (E 18). When Grey suggested, in the course of the day, that the moment for mediation should be if " the Russian were followed by Austrian mobilization " (D 180, 179 ; E 24, 25), Germany repeated her consent to this third proposal, subject to the obligations of her alliance (D 192). The " Russian mobilization " referred to was Russia's partial mobilization against Austria. It will thus be seen that, on that day, a distinction was made both in Downing Street and the Wilhelmstrasse, between an Austro-Serbian and an Austro-Russian conflict, and mediation was only considered necessary in the latter case.

On the strength of reports to hand from Paris and London, the Chancellor informed the Kaiser that " strenuous efforts were being made in both capitals to localize the conflict " (D 191).

A fourth English proposal, received in the evening, suggesting that Germany should try to induce Vienna to look upon the Serbian answer—which was not known either in London or Berlin—as satisfactory, was outstripped by events, as the Austrian Minister in Belgrade considered it unsatisfactory, and had left Belgrade. Serbia had mobilized at 3 p.m., and Austria ordered partial mobilization (eight Army Corps) against Serbia in the evening. In spite of that, the proposal Grey had made, on the strength of a far too optimistic report as to the probable purport of the Serbian reply (D 191a, E 21), was forwarded to the Ambassador in Vienna, who transmitted the English wish to the Ballplatz, " as instructed " (A II. 5).

Sunday, July 26.

The early morning hours of the 26th brought alarming news from Russia of the manœuvres having been suddenly interrupted, the troops being all sent back to their garrisons, military cadets being prematurely raised to the rank of officers, and preparations made to mobilize against Austria (D 194). Herr von Bethmann worked all the more zealously in a conciliatory sense. He not only hastened to pass on a communication from Vienna, stating that the Monarchy would not claim any Serbian territory, to the Entente capitals, but, at the same time, he appealed to Russia's love of peace, and asked France to exercise a moderating influence in St. Petersburg, and England to endeavour to dissuade Russia from mobilizing (D 198, 199, 200). This was followed in the evening by a second appeal to Russia, again laying great stress on Austria's not desiring to annex territory, and warning her that preparatory military measures on the part of Russia against Germany would compel Germany to mobilize, which would " mean war " (D 219). Both telegrams made a " very good impression " in St. Petersburg (D 282) ; the step caused " immense relief " in Paris, certainly, but no promise was given to endeavour to exert a moderating influence in St. Petersburg (D 235). The message could not be delivered in London at once, on account of its being Sunday (D 218), but even later the effort requested was not made.

In the middle of the day the Chancellor sent the Kaiser a report which sounded hopeful ; it was to the effect that there was only one authentic piece of news from Russia which gave cause for anxiety : in case of an Austro-Russian conflict, England would mediate, and she counted on being supported by France ; consequently Germany must keep quiet ; the General Staff agreed as to this (D 197). In the evening, Bethmann Hollweg felt so confident of peace that, on the strength of incorrect information that the naval reservists, who had been called up for a trial mobilization of the British Fleet, had been dismissed, he suggested to the Emperor that the High Seas Fleet should remain off Norway. This proposal was very rightly rejected

(D 221). A report from Vienna stated that the impression there was that Russia would not go beyond taking diplomatic steps (D 222).

In the course of this Sunday the view taken in London had entirely changed. Instead of four Powers mediating between Austria and Russia, in Vienna and St. Petersburg, Sir Edward Grey now made a fifth proposal, namely, that a conference of delegates representing the four Powers not directly concerned should be held in London ; and that, until it ended, all military operations should be suspended in Serbia, Austria, and Russia (E 36 ; D 236, 304). It will be seen that this meant mediation between Austria and Serbia. The change was perhaps due to a wish to expedite a settlement of the conflict, but anyhow it was a concession to what the French wished. As far back as on the occasion of the first interview between Cambon and Grey, the French Ambassador had advocated mediation between Austria and Serbia, in contradistinction to the view taken at that time by the British Foreign Secretary.[1]

It is true that even then the Russian Ambassador was not satisfied with Grey's attitude. He had not succeeded in getting the Foreign Secretary to commit himself to anything further. He was afraid that Grey " was not quite sure of public opinion, and that he feared he might not be supported if he pledged himself too soon ".[2]

Monday, July 27.

The surprising news that a Conference in London was proposed reached Berlin in the early morning of the 27th of July (D 236). It was immediately followed by a far better proposal from St. Petersburg : a telegram from the Ambassador announced that direct conversations were to be started between the Austrian and Russian Governments. Count Pourtalès had suggested to Sazonov that he should " try to get into touch with Austria-Hungary without delay, for this purpose ", in the event of the Vienna Government agreeing to modify the form of their demands to some

---

[1] The accounts of the Grey-Cambon interview of July 24th differ completely in E 10 and F 32.

[2] *Livre Noir*, Vol. II. p. 329.

extent. The Russian Minister had willingly consented to do so, and intended telegraphing at once to his Ambassador in Vienna accordingly (D 238).

Naturally the Russo-German proposal met with more favour in Berlin than the one made by Grey. Prince Lichnowsky was instructed to reply that Germany could not take part in a conference, she must restrict her mediation to a possible Austro-Russian conflict ; as regards the Austro-Serbian conflict, there seemed to be no difficulty in the way of direct understanding between St. Petersburg and Vienna (D 248, E 43).

Like the German Chancellor, Sazonov also rejected the idea of a conference at first. He agreed to it in principle, it is true, but he gave preference to the direct conversations which had already been started (R 32, E 53). Grey himself said, on hearing that Germany would not agree to it, that, although it had not been intended that the conference should arbitrate, as was assumed in Berlin, still, as long as there was any prospect of a direct exchange of views between Russia and Austria, he would suspend every other suggestion, as he considered the direct way " the most preferable method of all " (E 67). Sir Edward had already spoken of the desirability of direct discussion in a telegram of July 20 to St. Petersburg, and again to the Austro-Hungarian Ambassador three days later.[1]

Germany's refusal to take part in a conference may be regarded as a political error, but it cannot be said that this proposal was the first and best, indeed the only possibility of maintaining peace. Above all, she cannot be accused of having rejected " all " proposals of mediation, because she would not agree to this. The Berlin Cabinet had already fallen in with the suggestion that four Powers should mediate ; before this proposal was made, they had welcomed the idea of direct conversations, and, later on, as will be seen, they not only supported other methods of mediation, but advised such methods on their own initiative.

In the early afternoon the Chancellor reported to the Emperor, who had returned from Norway. He had described the position very hopefully in a preliminary telegram,

[1] Oman, *The Outbreak of the War*, 1914–1918, p. 18; A I. 59; E 3.

stating that Austria could not undertake any military
action before the 12th of August; the Serbian answer
apparently accepted all the conditions (probably according
to press information); England and France wished for
peace; Russia did not yet appear to be mobilizing (D 245).
On returning to the Foreign Office, von Bethmann found
the Belgrade answer, so often demanded in vain. It had
been held back in Vienna, and finally handed to the Berlin
Foreign Office by the Serbian Chargé d'Affaires personally
(D 271). He also found a telegram from London, in which
Grey, on the strength of the Serbian answer he too had
only just seen, begged Germany to use her influence to
induce Vienna " either to regard it as satisfactory, or as
a basis for discussion " (D 258). Lichnowsky's telegram
hinted plainly, and the hint was repeated in two telegrams
which followed, that, in case of Austria's adopting an
intransigent attitude, and its leading to a European conflagration, Germany " could no longer reckon on English
sympathy or British support." The full text of the first
report from England was telegraphed to the Embassy in
Vienna, with the addition :

Having already refused the English proposal of a conference,
it is impossible for us to reject this suggestion *a limine* as well.
If we refused to mediate in any way, the whole world would hold
us responsible for the conflagration, and it would be said that we
were the real instigators of the war. That would also make our
own position impossible in the country, where it must be made
clear that we were forced into war. Our position is the more
difficult, as Serbia appears to have conceded a great deal. Consequently we cannot refuse to act as intermediaries, and must submit the English proposal for consideration by the Vienna Cabinet,
particularly as London and Paris are unremitting in their efforts
to influence St. Petersburg. Request Count Berchtold's opinion
of the English suggestion, and of Russia's wish to negotiate directly
with Vienna.—D 277.

The fixed principle of non-interference in the Austro-
Serbian conflict was thus abandoned by Germany. For an
attempt to influence the attitude of the Vienna Government
towards the Serbian answer was equivalent to mediating
between Austria and Serbia. London was immediately
informed of the step that had been taken (D 278, 279).

The military authorities also acted with great moderation on the 27th. Although several reports of exceptional
military measures had come from Russia, the General
Staff telegraphed to the military attaché in St. Petersburg
(9.19 p.m.) :

> In view of Sazonov's statement, no military measures are con-
> templated here. But it is certain that the frontier guard is already
> mobilized, and that steps are being taken to close the frontier,
> also to protect frontier. Therefore request constant watch be
> kept on Russian military measures and report sent.[1]

The following facts could not have been known to the
General Staff at the time : Russia had already ordered
the " period of preparation for war " for the whole Empire
on the 26th ; the French had given orders for the transport
to France of all the divisions in Morocco, as far back as on
the 24th, and had further suspended all leave, discontinued
the transfer of troops from the garrisons, and ordered
non-military railway protection on the 26th, and military
protection on the 27th.[2] On the other hand, it was known
for certain that the fortified town of Kovno, close to the
German frontier, had been placed on a war footing (D 264),
and that the manœuvres in the south of France had been
broken off (D 341, note 3). The fact that the demobilization
of the British Fleet had been postponed had been made
public (F 66). Consequently, the German decision to
refrain from taking any military measures went beyond
the degree of moderation permissible. The men of the
Bavarian regiments quartered in Metz, who were on leave
getting in the harvest, were the only ones recalled, even
there, and none were recalled elsewhere.[3] The following
letter, written by General von Moltke to his wife, in the
afternoon, after a long interview with the Chancellor, shows
how extraordinarily calmly he viewed the situation :

> The position continues to be most obscure. It is not likely to
> be cleared up very quickly, it may be perhaps a fortnight before

---

[1] Reichstag Committee of Enquiry, Part 2, p. 59.
[2] *Victoire* of March 23, 1918 ; Belgian Grey Book, Vol. II. p. 118,
App. I. ; Messimy in the *Revue de France*, August 1, 1921.
[3] Despatch from the XVIth Army Corps Headquarters (Metz), Ia,
No. 1203 g.

we can know or say anything definite. You can stay on quietly at Bayreuth till then.[1]

Count Benckendorff was very much better pleased with Grey on the 27th than the day before. He wrote to Sazonov :

Grey speaks far more clearly, and distinctly more firmly to-day than hitherto. He counts very much on the impression that would be made by the measures taken with regard to the Fleet, which were decided upon on Sunday evening (the 25th) and published to-day. Buchanan's telegram, which arrived yesterday, seems to have made a very useful impression. Anyhow Berlin and Vienna will have no further reason to rely on England's neutrality.[2]

Buchanan's interesting telegram of the 26th of July is unfortunately not to be found in the English Blue Book, or can the reference be to the telegram of the 25th, which quotes Sazonov as having said that " if Russia were sure of being supported by France, she would face all the risks of war " (E 17).

Tuesday, July 28.

There were, and are still, various opinions as to the Serbian answer. Some regard it as an acceptance of all the Austrian demands except points 5 and 6 (collaboration of Austrian officials in suppressing the Greater-Serbian movement, and in the investigations prior to judicial proceedings against the instigators of the murder), whilst others consider the reservations made here and there, artful evasions. At any rate, the Emperor William formed a very favourable opinion of it, for, after reading the Note on the morning of the 28th, he wrote under it :

A brilliant performance indeed for a time limit of only 48 hours ! That is more than could have been expected. A great moral success for Vienna ! But it does away with every reason for war, and Giesl ought to have remained quietly in Belgrade. *I* should never have ordered mobilization upon that.—D 271.

If the Emperor had been anxious for a European war, the remarks, which were not intended to go beyond a small circle of persons bound to observe the greatest discretion,

---

[1] Moltke, *Errinnerungen, Briefe, Dokumente*, p. 381.
[2] *Pravda*, No. 7 of March 9, 1919.

would have been very differently worded, and would have expressed his disappointment at Austria's being deprived of the opportunity of going to war. But in addition to making these comments on the Note, he wrote to the Foreign Secretary, von Jagow (at 10 a.m.), that there was no further reason for war, and proposed his saying to Austria :

Serbia has been compelled to beat a humiliating retreat, and this is a matter for congratulation. Of course it means that there is no further reason for war. But it is certainly necessary to have a guarantee that the promises will be carried out. That could probably be achieved by temporary military occupation of part of Serbia. Just as we left troops in France, in 1871, till the milliards were paid. On this basis I am prepared to mediate in Austria with a view to peace.—D 293.

This opinion was also communicated to the Chief of the General Staff at once.[1]

The Foreign Office may not perhaps have formed quite such a favourable opinion of the Serbian answer, but it was at all events considered a basis for negotiations. A very long Note to Vienna was drafted, and in the meantime two reassuring telegrams were sent. The one stated that there was no confirmation of the military news about Russia—a very optimistic view— consequently the moment did not seem to have come to make a categorical statement in St. Petersburg, such as the Austrian Government wished, and Moltke agreed as to this (D 281, 299) ; the other transmitted peaceable assurances from Sazonov (D 282, 309).

Before the instruction to Tschirschky could be sent off, news came (towards 7 p.m.) of the Austrian declaration of war on Serbia,[2] followed soon afterwards by the announcement that Vienna considered the English proposal (that the Serbian answer should be accepted as satisfactory, or as a basis for negotiations), which had been transmitted and recommended to them the day before, had come " too late " (D 311, 313). In order to counteract the disastrous effect of this decision with as little delay as possible, not only St. Petersburg, but also London, Paris, and even Vienna,

---

[1] Letter to Moltke, vide *Deutsche Politik* of July 18, 1919.
[2] It had been known in Berlin since the 27th that Austria-Hungary intended making the declaration of war on the 28th or 29th (D 257).

were immediately advised that efforts were still being
made in Berlin to induce Austria to enter into frank *pourparlers* with Russia, and that the Austrian declaration of
war made no difference to this (D 315 and footnote 2).
The full Note finally sent to Vienna at 10.15 p.m. was on
the lines indicated by the Kaiser, and urged the Austrian
Government to repeat the definite assurance already given
to St. Petersburg, that

they were far from desiring to annex Serbian territory, and that
the military measures were only with a view to the temporary
occupation of Belgrade, and other clearly specified parts of Serbia,
in order to compel the Serbian Government to comply with the
demands in full, and establish guarantees for future good
behaviour. . . .

Von Tschirschky was instructed to speak strongly to
this effect without delay, and to suggest steps being taken
accordingly in St. Petersburg. Care was to be taken to
avoid giving the impression that Germany wished to hold
Austria back. It was merely a question of

finding a method of enabling Austria-Hungary to achieve the
object of putting a stop to the Pan-Serbian propaganda, without
at the same time causing a general war, and improving the conditions under which Germany would have to fight if this could
not be avoided.—D 323.

Seeing that Austria was very touchy, and had declared
war too hastily, this proposal not to go beyond Belgrade,
made by Germany, was very wise, and more calculated to
indicate a way out of the difficult position than almost
any other that could have been made.

After signing the draft of the Note, the Chancellor glanced
through the newspaper cuttings submitted to him, and saw
the premature announcement that Russia had mobilized
fourteen Army Corps in the south. He immediately sent
a message asking the British Ambassador to call on him,
and explained to him Germany's reasons for not having
agreed to the proposal of a conference. He spoke of his
efforts to bring about direct conversations between Vienna
and St. Petersburg, pointed out the danger of a Russian
mobilization against Austria, and assured the Ambassador

of his firm intention of co-operating with England in the interest of peace. He concluded by saying : "A war between the Great Powers must be avoided" (E 71).

This was not the last effort made by Germany to mediate in the course of that day. Half an hour after the instructions to Tschirschky had been despatched, the Emperor had the draft of a telegram to Nicholas II. in his hands, which expressed a hope that the Tsar would co-operate with Germany in endeavouring to smooth over difficulties that might still arise (D 335). The message crossed one from the Tsar, who begged Germany to exert a moderating influence on Austria, but said he feared he would soon have to yield to the pressure put on him, and be compelled " to take extreme measures, which would lead to war " (D 332). The fear was destined to be fulfilled.

Early in the afternoon the General Staff had heard that the " period of preparation for war " had probably been proclaimed for the whole of Russia ; it was fairly certain that mobilization had been ordered in Odessa and Kiev, but doubtful whether it had been ordered in Moscow and Warsaw. There was no doubt that certain preparations for war had also been ordered opposite the German frontier. All troops had been sent back to their garrisons. Frontier guards everywhere had been equipped for war and were ready to march. In France officers had been recalled from leave, troops sent back to their garrisons, railway bridges and tunnels, etc., in the frontier districts guarded, and Belfort put in readiness for action.[1] Although all this was known, the only steps taken by Germany were to recall the troops intended for " immediate " or " accelerated " mobilization to their garrisons, and have the railways guarded by railway officials.[2]

Wednesday, July 29.

On the morning of the 29th, telegram after telegram arrived describing the Russian preparations for war. By midday eighteen official communications, relating to Russian

[1] General Staff report of July 28th, 4 p.m., to the Foreign Office (not given in *Die Deutschen Dokumenten*).
[2] Former Prussian War Ministry, No. 12gg, A. 1, and letter from the Imperial Chancellor of July 27th, No. 3339.

mobilization measures, had been received since the morning of the 26th, ten of them being with reference to the German front.[1] Many of the reports were doubtful, and one or two were retracted. It was difficult for even an expert to form a clear idea of what was going on, on the other side of the frontier. Further reports also came from France, amongst them one which said that the French General Staff were surprised at Germany's taking so few protective measures (D 372). The German General Staff then really became rather uneasy, and sent the Imperial Chancellor a memorandum, which may be summed up as follows : " Russia is preparing to mobilize twelve Army Corps, is also making military dispositions on the German frontier, and threatens to mobilize the twelve Corps, if Austria marches on Serbia. Austria, who has only so far called out eight Army Corps against Serbia, will then be compelled to mobilize the other half of her army. This will make a collision inevitable, and the *casus fœderis* will arise for Germany. Russia will then say that Austria was the first to mobilize, and that she thereby proclaimed her intention of attacking. It is therefore of the utmost importance to ascertain, as soon as possible, whether Russia and France wish it to come to war " (D 349).[2] It will be seen that the possibility of Russia's ordering general mobilization *before* Austria was never even considered. But it was clear that the restraint which had hitherto been observed by the military authorities ought not to continue ; nevertheless, for the time being, they did not go beyond recalling all troops to their garrisons, guarding the airship sheds, and holding up war material for Russia and Serbia.[3]

Early in the afternoon, however, the Chancellor made urgent appeals to Paris and St. Petersburg. Herr von Schoen was instructed to call attention to the French preparations for war, and the necessity for German counter-measures :

[1] D 194, 216, 230, 242, 264, 274, 275, 276, 281, 291, 294, 295, 296, 327, 330, 331, 333, 335a. There were a number of further reports at the General Staff and Admiralty Offices, which were only verbally transmitted to the Foreign Office.

[2] D 349 must have been drafted in the morning, and ought to be inserted earlier in *Die Deutschen Dokumenten*.

[3] Reichstag Committee of Enquiry, Part 2, p. 10.

We should have to proclaim "danger of war" (*Kriegsgefahr*), which would not mean mobilization, or calling out any reserves yet, but it would increase the tension.—D 341.

Count Pourtalès was instructed to

point out very seriously (to Sazonov) that any further steps taken by Russia to mobilize would compel us to mobilize, and that it would then hardly be possible to avert a European war.—D 342.

Not satisfied with giving these warnings, Herr von Bethmann again sent to ask the British Ambassador to call on him, in order to express his regret that the Austrian Government had rejected the proposal Berlin had supported, namely, to regard the Serbian answer as a basis for negotiations (p. 135). He further informed Sir Edward Goschen of the appeal made to Vienna the day before, not to go beyond Belgrade, adding a hope that his giving him this strictly confidential information, which had not even been communicated to Prince Lichnowsky, would be regarded in London as a proof of his honest efforts to maintain peace (E 75).[1] Grey replied at once thanking him warmly (D 353, E 77).

A telegram was then drafted in reply to the Tsar. It protested against the assertion that Austria was waging an "ignominious" war against Serbia, and said in conclusion :

I consider a direct understanding between your Government and Vienna possible and desirable, and, as I already telegraphed to you, my Government is continuing its exertions to promote it. Of course, military measures on the part of Russia, which would be looked upon by Austria as threatening, would precipitate a calamity we both wish to avoid, and would jeopardize my position as mediator, which I readily accepted on your appeal to my friendship and my help.—D 359 (sent at 6.30 p.m.).

Three hours before this conciliatory message was despatched, Count Pourtalès had reported that Russia would mobilize the military districts on the Austrian frontier that very day (D 343). It was no longer possible to doubt the gravity of the position. The Kaiser, to whom the text of Pourtalès' telegram was only submitted on the morning of the 30th (D 399), had already summoned the

[1] According to Oman, p. 54–5, the statement that the matter had not been mentioned to Prince Lichnowsky should be inserted in E 75.

Chancellor and the military authorities to report to him at Potsdam on the evening of the 29th, on account of the disquieting nature of the news previously received. On this occasion Moltke proposed that " suitable counter-measures " should be taken in reply to the Russian and French preparations for war (D App. IV, 15), probably meaning the declaration of a " state of imminent danger of war " (*Zustand drohender Kriegsgefahr*), but he was unable to carry his point, in the face of Bethmann's opposition. No " Crown Council " took place on the 29th, nor were arrangements made to mobilize.[1] The following ordinary precautionary measures were decided upon late in the evening : the railways to be placed under military protection, men on leave to be recalled, fortress defences to be strengthened, and the garrison of the island of Borkum reinforced ; nothing more.[2]

Provision for the worst was made by sending the ultimatum to Belgium to the Legation in Brussels by special courier (D 375, 376). It was enclosed in a sealed envelope, only to be opened on receipt of a special order. In connection with this, the Chancellor again sent to ask the British Ambassador to come round to see him, on his return from Potsdam, late in the evening. He expressed a hope that England would remain neutral, if a Russian offensive against Austria should compel Germany to carry out the obligations of her alliance. Germany did not meditate crushing France ; in case of victory, she would not require France to cede any European territory. Holland's neutrality and integrity would be respected, so long as they were respected by the other side. As regards Belgium, the measures it would be necessary to take depended on the French operations. In any case, the integrity of the Kingdom would not be infringed, if it did not take part against Germany. England's neutrality in a possible conflict would constitute a basis for a permanent Anglo-German understanding. In reply to a question the Ambassador asked about the French colonies, the Chancellor declined to give any undertaking (D 373, E 85).

[1] *Die Kriegsschuldfrage*, July 1923, p. 8.
[2] Reichstag Committee of Enquiry, Part 2, p. 12.

It is true that the Minister in Copenhagen was instructed to call the attention of Denmark to the gravity of the position, " in case of an outbreak of war ", but this country was not expected to do more than remain neutral (D 371, 494).

When the Potsdam meeting was over, the Tsar's answer to the 6.30 p.m. telegram was handed to the Kaiser :

Thanks for your conciliatory and friendly telegram. The official message presented to-day by your Ambassador to my Minister was conveyed in a very different tone. I beg you to explain this divergency. It would be right to give over the Austro-Serbian problem to the Hague Conference. I trust in your wisdom and friendship.—D 366 (received at the Neue Palais at 8.42 p.m.).

But about this time, if not earlier, the Russian Ambassador informed the Foreign Office officially of the mobilization of four districts, Kiev, Odessa, Moscow, and Kazan, at the same time insisting that this measure " was not in any way directed against Germany " (D 380, footnote 3) [1]. Practically simultaneously (at 9.45 p.m.) a report came from the military attaché in St. Petersburg, stating that the War Minister had given him his word of honour that, up to three o'clock that afternoon, not a single man had been called up, or a single horse requisitioned (D 370). In reality the Kaiser's telegram to the Tsar had had an excellent effect. It had induced the Tsar to change the general mobilization, which had already been decided upon, into partial mobilization against Austria.[2]   But Berlin did not know this. There was, on the other hand, the official communication from the Russian Government respecting the mobilization of a Russian army far superior in strength to the Austro-Hungarian (fifty-five Russian to twenty-eight Austro-Hungarian infantry divisions, as twenty-two out of a total of fifty were detailed for service against Serbia), which showed that the Russian War Minister's word of honour was a device to gain time.   Numerous reports made it doubtful whether the present assurance that they were

[1] Vide also Swerbeiev's telegram, No. 140, of July 29, in the Red Archives, p. 177, according to which the information as to Russia's mobilization arrived in the absence of the Chancellor at Potsdam.
[2] Dobrorolsky, p. 26.

not mobilizing against Germany was honest, and finally there was a proposal of arbitration, which would take weeks, and might give the Russian hordes ample time to assemble on the German frontier. It was, therefore, most important to stop the mobilization, if not too late, and for this reason the Chancellor ordered the following telegram to be sent to St. Petersburg :

I assume that Russian mobilization on the Austrian frontier will be followed by corresponding Austrian measures. It is difficult to say how far it will then be possible to stop the rolling stones. . . . In order to avert the impending catastrophe, if possible, we are trying to induce the Austro-Hungarian Government to confirm their former assertion, by once more giving Russia a formal assurance that they are far from aiming at territorial aggrandizement at Serbia's expense, and that the only object of their military measures is a temporary occupation, to compel Serbia to give guarantees for future good behaviour. . . . We therefore look to Russia not to bring about an armed conflict with Austria, in case of the step we are taking in Vienna being successful. . . . —D 380.

Enemy propaganda has chosen to regard the " Council " at Potsdam, and the Chancellor's interview with the British Ambassador, as evidence of Germany's wish for war. The fact that the Chancellor redoubled his efforts to maintain peace just at that time shows how mistaken this conclusion was. Bethmann had been worried all day by the fact that no answer had come from Vienna to the proposal of a " halt in Belgrade ". He was justly impatient, and therefore communicated twice with Tschirschky between ten and eleven o'clock that night (D 377 and note 3).

Then he had to consider important reports that had come from St. Petersburg and London in the afternoon. Pourtalès had telegraphed that Sazonov was complaining of there being no sign of a direct exchange of views beginning either in St. Petersburg or Vienna (D 343). Lichnowsky had made the same complaint, and transmitted a statement made by the Serbian Chargé d'Affaires in Rome, that Serbia would accept the two points regarding the collaboration of Austrian officials, if the method of collaboration were explained (D 357).

The telegram did not make it very clear that, at this

interview, Grey had again referred to the question of mediation *à quatre* (E 84). But this was not of any great importance, for, in consequence of Russia's mobilization against Austria, the Austro-Serbian had now become an Austro-Russian conflict, and Germany had agreed that the four Powers should mediate in this event.

On account of the reports from the two Ambassadors, three telegrams were despatched to Vienna towards midnight (D 383, 384, 385). The first transmitted the telegrams exchanged the day before between the Kaiser and the Tsar, to be " turned to account " with Count Berchtold. The second recommended the proposal just telegraphed from Rome. It was the fifth method of mediation undertaken by Germany, for she had agreed to mediation *à quatre*, direct discussions, acceptance of the Serbian reply as a basis for negotiations, and had proposed a " halt in Belgrade ". The third telegram to Tschirschky notified Russia's mobilization against Austria, and, in view of Sazonov's complaint, repeated an urgent desire that direct discussions should be started and continued.

When this batch of telegrams was disposed of, still graver news from Downing Street and the Nevsky Prospekt was submitted to the Chancellor. Lichnowsky had had a second interview with Grey (D 368, E 88, 89). On this occasion the Foreign Secretary had suggested, as a suitable basis for mediation by the four Powers, that " Austria should state her conditions, possibly after occupying Belgrade, or other Serbian territory ". That was very like the German proposal, which Goschen had transmitted (p. 142). Lichnowsky's not having been informed of it at the time now proved a disadvantage, for he was not in a position to reply that his Government had made a similar suggestion twenty-four hours earlier. Following this proposal, however, there was Grey's unmistakable warning that England might indeed stand aside in a Russo-Austrian conflict, but not if Germany and France were involved. In this case the British Government might be compelled to take rapid decisions (D 368). That was a heavy blow, doubly heavy after the conversation the Chancellor had just had with Goschen respecting English neutrality. At the same time, it was an incentive to work still harder to maintain peace. The full text of Lichnowsky's report was sent to Vienna with the addition :

Consequently, if Austria rejects all mediation, we are faced with a conflagration in which England would be against us, and there is every indication that Italy and Rumania would not side with us, and that we two should be opposed by four Powers. England being our enemy would throw the brunt of the fighting on to Germany. Austria's political prestige, and the honour and glory of her army, as well as her just claims against Serbia, could be amply upheld by the occupation of Belgrade, or other places. By humiliating Serbia she would recover the strength of her position in the Balkans, and towards Russia. In these circumstances, we must strongly urge the Vienna Cabinet to accept mediation on the honourable conditions suggested. The responsibility that would rest both upon us and Austria for the consequences that must otherwise ensue would be very heavy.—D 395.

This was a strong recommendation of the proposal of mediation by four Powers, of which the Berlin Cabinet had hitherto only signified their approval in communicating with London. There was another matter to be settled with the Ballplatz at the same time. As above stated, a message had been received at three o'clock in the afternoon saying that Sazonov complained of Austria's refusal to exchange views directly with Russia. But two hours later Tschirschky had reported a conversation having taken place between Schebeko and Berchtold (D 356). After another three and a half hours a fresh, still stronger complaint came from Sazonov, that Vienna had " positively refused " to exchange views directly (D 365). These reports could not be reconciled—could there be a misunderstanding ? Apart from that, the Chancellor was very much annoyed with Germany's obstinate ally, on account of there being no answer to the last proposal, and also on account of the Austrian diplomats in London having talked in an unwarrantable way of " wiping out and dividing up " Serbia (D 301, 361), and he now went so far as to threaten to break off the alliance. The telegram from Pourtalès was sent on to Vienna with the comment :

This report is not consistent with what Your Excellency reported as to the interview with Schebeko. Apparently there is some misunderstanding, which please explain. We cannot ask Austria-Hungary to negotiate with Serbia, with whom she is at war. But it would be a great mistake to refuse all discussion with St. Petersburg, as this is almost a provocation to Russia to go to war, the very thing it is most in Austria-Hungary's interest to avoid.

We are prepared to fulfil the obligations of our alliance, but we cannot allow Vienna to draw us lightly, and without regard to our advice, into a world-wide conflagration. Vienna appears also to ignore our advice with regard to Italy.

Please speak very firmly and seriously to Count Berchtold at once.—D 396.

Whilst the two long Notes to Vienna were being put into cipher, the Chancellor signed two further reassuring telegrams to St. Petersburg, stating that Germany would continue to mediate, so long as Russia refrained from any hostile act against Austria, and that the refusal by Vienna of direct discussion must have been before the last German *démarche* (D 392, 397). It is true that the Hague Conference idea was rejected (D 391). This suggestion of the Tsar's will be dealt with separately [1]; for the moment it need only be said that it was never mentioned between Sazonov and Pourtalès, nor has any reference at all been made to its rejection by the German Ambassador, so it could not have had any influence on the course of events. A telegram was also sent to London, to the effect that Germany was still mediating in Vienna, and strongly urging the acceptance of Grey's proposal (D 393). It was carrying modesty too far not to point out that a similar idea had been suggested and recommended before Grey made the proposal.

Five admonitory telegrams had been sent from the Wilhelmstrasse within the three hours after midnight, all advising Vienna to give in. In the meantime a telegram had at last come from Tschirschky, but it was not at all satisfactory. Berchtold was willing to repeat the assurance of territorial *désintéressement*, certainly, but was unable to give any answer yet as to not carrying the military operations beyond Belgrade (D 388). This disappointing telegram seems not to have been submitted to the Chancellor till the morning of the 30th.

[1] Vide Part IV. sect. 6, p. 214.

Thursday, July 30th.

The Chancellor began the day at an early hour by reading the belated telegram above mentioned. Then a telegram came from Pourtalès, saying that the Kaiser's telegram had had the desired effect, but that he feared Sazonov " was doing his utmost to induce the Tsar to be firm " (D 401). This was followed by reports as to the advance of Russian troops from Kovno towards the German frontier, and the extent of the Russian mobilization, with confirmation of the news that, in the northern Governments, sailors had been called up, who could obviously hardly be employed against Austria (D 404, 410).

Bethmann reported to the Emperor what had gone on during the night, and towards midday sent him Lichnowsky's telegram, containing the warning of England's attitude (D 407). This shows how necessary it is to be careful in estimating the value of the Emperor William's marginal notes in each individual case. The admonitory Note to Vienna had been sent off at three o'clock in the morning, but the telegram which caused its being sent was only submitted to the Emperor nine hours later, so that, in this case, his very impulsive comments could not have had the slightest influence on the decision the responsible director of Germany's policy had long since taken. The Chancellor did not, however, confine his activities to reporting ; the unfavourable news was merely an incentive to him to intensify his efforts to maintain peace. When submitting Lichnowsky's report to the Emperor, he also submitted the draft of a third telegram to the Tsar, and particularly begged him not to speak of his rôle as mediator having come to an end, as he had done in a marginal note (to D 399), but only of its being imperilled (D 408). The tone of the telegram, which was sent almost word for word as drafted, was serious, certainly, but very conciliatory, although no reference was made to the Hague proposal :

Best thanks for Your telegram. It is quite out of the question that my Ambassador's language could have been in contradiction with the tenor of my telegram. Count Pourtalès was instructed to draw the attention of Your Government to the danger and grave consequences involved by a mobilization. I said the same in my telegram to You. Austria has only mobilized against Serbia, and only part of her army. If, as is now the case, according to the communication by You and Your Government, Russia mobilizes against Austria, my rôle as mediator, you kindly entrusted me with, and which I accepted at Your express prayer, will be endangered, if not ruined. The whole weight of the decision lies solely on Your shoulders now, who have to bear the responsibility for War or Peace.—D 420 (3.30 p.m. from the Central Telegraph Office).

The Chancellor tried to work through the Foreign Office in London, as he had done through the Kaiser in St. Petersburg. Lichnowsky was instructed to say that Russia's mobilization and France's preparations for war made it doubtful whether mediation would be of any avail, and to beg Grey to persuade France to suspend her military measures at once, and prevent Russia from assembling her troops on the Austrian frontier (D 409). Von Jagow spoke to the British Ambassador in the same sense (E 98).

Half the day went by, and there was still no answer from Vienna.

As the position was becoming more and more serious, a Prussian Ministerial Council was summoned.[1] The Chancellor, as Prime Minister, reviewed the political situation, and the events which had led up to it, and at the close of his speech he declared that he would not give up hope, or abandon his efforts to maintain peace, so long as his *démarche* in Vienna was not absolutely rejected. The meeting decided that

1. Germany would neither mobilize nor declare a state of "imminent danger of war" (*Zustand drohender Kriegsgefahr*), although Russia had mobilized against Austria. The only measure to be taken was a measure of "precaution" (*Sicherung*), which applied to the navy (not to the army).

2. At the conference held the evening before at Potsdam, the General Staff had only proposed the proclamation of "imminent danger of war", not of mobilization.

All sorts of rumours were flying about that morning in the European capitals. A Paris newspaper (*Paris du Midi*)

[1] The Ministerial Council was probably held about midday, vide App. I. No. 22, p. 240.

reported partial French mobilization. In Berlin a special
edition of the *Lokalanzeiger* was published at one o'clock,
incorrectly announcing that the Kaiser had decided to
mobilize. The incident was adjusted by telephoning at once
to the three Entente Ambassadors, to inform them of the
mistake, and it did not affect the course of events.[1]

A few rays of light appeared in the course of the afternoon. Prince Lichnowsky reported that he had at once
informed Grey that Germany was still trying to induce
Vienna to accept the English proposals, and he added that
he did not personally think London a suitable place for a
conference (D 418). From this it may be concluded that
the idea found less and less favour in the English capital.
Grey himself had abandoned it on the 28th (E 67). Later
on came Grey's promise with regard to the Russian military
preparations. He said he would try to influence Russia
in the sense desired, through Count Benckendorff, that very
day (D 435). He questioned there being any French preparations for war, because he relied on the false reports
from Paris. The news that the British Fleet had steamed
up the east coast to the Scottish harbours (its war stations)
was less pleasant (D 438).

A proposal formulated by Sazonov, at the request of the
German Ambassador, was transmitted from St. Petersburg
—the first Sazonov formula :

> If Austria, recognizing that her conflict with Serbia has assumed
> the character of a question of European interest, declares herself
> ready to eliminate from her ultimatum the points which violate
> principle of the sovereignty of Serbia, Russia engages to stop all
> military preparations.—D 421.

The Chancellor was so anxious to be conciliatory, that he
seems not to have taken any exception to this wording,
but when it was discussed, the conclusion reached was that
Austria would never consent to withdraw anything from
the Note she had delivered a week earlier.[2] Herr von Jagow
told the Russian Ambassador, who came to see him, that
he thought the formula would be unacceptable to Austria,

---

[1] Vide Part IV. sect. 7, p. 215.
[2] Vide the Chancellor's marginal notes and Zimmermann's memoranda
(D 421, note 2).

but added that Szápáry was instructed to carry on nogotia-
tions with Sazonov, and that another proposal had been
made by Grey, which had probably already been communicated to St. Petersburg. Thus the Foreign Secretary did
not by any means bar the way to further negotiations, on
the contrary, he pointed out how they could be continued.
The defenders of the Tsarist régime tried for a long time
to represent that Russia mobilized in consequence of the
formula having been rejected, but this effort has failed.
When the report sent by Pourtalès reached Berlin, towards
half-past three (half-past four by Russian time), Sazonov
had induced the Tsar to decide on general mobilization,
for the second time, and this time the decision was
irrevocable.[1]

Sazonov's proposal found as little favour in London as
in Berlin. About the time when Swerbeiev was talking to
von Jagow, Grey suggested to St. Petersburg that the
formula should in so far be altered as to state that if
Austria would agree not to advance beyond Belgrade, the
Powers should examine the question of what satisfaction
Serbia could give Austria without prejudice to her sovereign
rights and independence. He further expressed a hope that
if Austria limited her operations in this way, Russia would
also suspend her military preparations. The vexed question
of modifying the ultimatum was omitted from the amended
formula, at Lichnowsky's wish (E 103, D 439, 460).

Poincaré was also of opinion that Austria would not
consent to submit certain demands of the Note, which
Serbia had not accepted, to international discussion (E 99).

Vienna's rejection of the suggestion made by the Serbian
Minister in Rome (see p. 145) arrived two hours after the
Russian proposal (towards half-past five) (D 432). But
a few minutes later a fairly satisfactory message was at
last received. Tschirschky telegraphed that instructions
had been sent to Szápáry to begin conversations with

---

[1] According to Paléologue, at four o'clock ; according to Dobrorolsky,
two o'clock at latest. The interview between Jagow and Swerbeiev
cannot have taken place till after six o'clock, as reference was made to
the instruction to Szápáry, which was only known in Berlin towards six
o'clock. For Swerbeiev's telegram reporting the interview, vide App. I.
No. 23, p. 240.

Sazonov. He further stated that Berchtold would see Schebeko, and tell him that Austria-Hungary was far from desiring to annex territory, and only contemplated temporary occupation of parts of Serbia " after the conclusion of peace " (D 433). This was an acceptance of the proposal of direct discussions. In reality they had never been suspended, as Sazonov had asserted, and it was also a repetition of the assurance already given, that Austria did not aim at territorial aggrandizement, but there was no mention of limiting the military operations to Belgrade and the surrounding country. After a further quarter of an hour, a report came in, which stated that Berchtold could not give an answer to this " till he had obtained the Emperor Francis Joseph's commands " (D 434). A telephone message followed saying that the answer might be expected at noon the next day, at the earliest (D 440).

William II. had also become impatient at Vienna's long hesitation, so he decided to make a personal appeal to the Emperor Francis Joseph. The text of the telegram the Chancellor drafted at his command, which was very little altered, was as follows :

I could not see my way to refuse the Tsar's personal request that I should undertake to mediate, with a view to averting a general conflagration and maintaining peace, and I submitted proposals to your Government through my Ambassador yesterday and to-day. Amongst other things it is proposed that Austria should state her conditions, after occupying Belgrade or other places. I should be sincerely grateful if you would let me know your decision as soon as possible.—D 437 (sent at 7.15 p.m.).

The Chancellor was so annoyed at the endless delay that he sent yet another, and this time very strongly worded instruction to Tschirschky, which he drafted with his own hand (D 441). On account of threatening news from Russia, however, Tschirschky was first told not to act upon the instruction (D 451), and then less strong, but perhaps more effective, pressure was brought to bear, by transmitting a telegram from the King of England to Prince Henry of Prussia, in which the proposal to " halt in Belgrade " was warmly recommended. The Ambassador was commissioned to take the telegram to Count Berchtold without delay, and

to leave him a copy of it, to be eventually shown to the
Emperor Francis Joseph, if he wished to have one (D 464).
Both the Kaiser and the Chancellor were now appealing
from the vacillating Minister to the ruler of the Habsburg
Empire.

On the other hand, Austria's compliance with the request
for a direct exchange of opinions was not ignored as though
it were of no value. Jagow had already taken advantage
of it in his conversation with Swerbeiev, as mentioned
above. Tschirschky's report with regard to this was trans-
mited to London and St. Petersburg, with the following
addition to the message sent to the former :

> The telegram refers to our former suggestion of direct conversa-
> tions between Vienna and St. Petersburg, and shows so much
> willingness to meet us, on the part of Austria, that we hope
> England will try to induce Russia to be equally conciliatory,
> particularly in the matter of suspending her military measures.—
> D 444 and note 3.

Everything now depended, at least so it was thought in
Berlin, on whether Grey would act up to his word, and urge
the suspension of Russia's preparations for war. If he
only did so as mildly as he urged a modification of the
Sazonov formula, success was unthinkable. Would he rise
to the occasion and speak as strongly as Germany had been
speaking to Vienna for the last three days ? All speculation
of this kind was of course built upon sand, for whilst Berlin
was sending one exhortation after another to Vienna, and
besieging London with requests, the die had already been
cast in St. Petersburg.

What could have been the reasons for the delay in Vienna,
which seemed so incomprehensible ? The precaution of
asking what the Emperor wished was a matter of course,
but the Ballplatz is not far from the Hofburg, where Francis
Joseph had returned from Ischl on the 30th. The real
causes must surely have been different. In the first place
Tisza had to be consulted (D 440). It was the curse of
the Dual Monarchy that its foreign policy had to be decided
upon in two places at the same time. Then there was, in
all probability, a military difficulty, which has been little
discussed. It would have been easy to limit the operations

to Belgrade and the surrounding country, if the Austrian plan of campaign had provided for marching direct on the capital. But Conrad wanted to launch the offensive by a very roundabout way, from the north-west corner of the Kingdom, so that he would have had to traverse half the northern part of Serbia, with communications which might conceivably be very bad, before he could each his objective. Berlin was not aware of this, otherwise less stress might perhaps have been laid on the word Belgrade.

The same inactivity was shown in military as in political matters. Count Berchtold had heard of the Russian mobilization against Austria on the evening of the 29th (A III. 1. 18, D 386). This raised fifty-five active and reserve Infantry Divisions against Austria-Hungary, who had only twenty-eight left at her disposal, as twenty-two, out of a total of fifty, were destined for employment against Serbia.[1] " Mobilization against mobilization " is the rule, even with the strictest pacifists. But in Vienna the whole day of the 30th went by without the step being taken. Instead of this, the Austrian Minister wished that, " as a last effort to avert a European war," a joint Austro-German warning should be sent to Paris and St. Petersburg, similar to those Berlin had already given, once in the French capital (on the 29th, D 341), and three times in St. Petersburg (once on the 26th, and twice on the 29th, D 219, 342, 380). To have repeated it, without some fresh urgent reason, would have been contrary to all diplomatic usage, and have had the effect of a challenge, so the Vienna Government had to be left to take the step on their own account (D 427, 429, 442). But they could not make up their minds to this.[2] It was only in the evening that the Chief of the General Staff submitted a proposal to mobilize to the Emperor Francis Joseph (D 498, A III, 50). The order was given towards noon the following day (July 31), and was consequently a purely defensive measure, both as regards the date and the number of troops mobilized.

On the evening of the 30th, the German Chief of the Staff,

[1] Reichstag Committee of Enquiry, Part 2, p. 22.
[2] The Austro-Hungarian Ambassadors in Paris and Vienna were only to take the step if their German colleagues received similar instructions (A III. 15).

who was fully justified in feeling anxious, urged on the Austrian military attaché the advisability of immediate general mobilization. It was Moltke's duty to do so, as a matter of course. Without entirely disregarding the relative strength of the forces on either side, no one could come to the extraordinary conclusion that Austria ought to have left her remaining twenty-eight divisions immobile in the face of the Russian menace constituted by a numerical superiority of fifty-five divisions.[1] As regards her own measures, Germany again acted with the greatest moderation. A proposal made by the XVIth Army Corps (Metz) that the covering troops should be ordered out the next day, on account of the French having taken far more extensive measures, was rejected, the precaution was only taken in the case of a few corps in the east. A suggestion made by the Emperor, that the frontier corps should be reinforced by calling up reservists, was not carried out after the War Minister had reported to him. Therefore, even if Cambon's second-hand report that the military authorities in Berlin were urging mobilization (F 105) were true, at any rate they did not carry their point either with the War Office or the political leaders.

7. The Attitude of France and Russia during the Anglo-German Mediation.

During the six days of Anglo-German mediation, Germany and Austria-Hungary were agreed, certainly, on two points : that military action should be taken against Serbia, and that a European war should be avoided ; but there was a gradually increasing difference of opinion between them as to how far the first aim ought to be carried, in case of the second being achieved. Whilst Berlin more and more recognized, as time went on, that a general conflagration could only be avoided if the action against Serbia were restricted, Vienna still thought it possible to adhere to the standpoint that there was no need to set a limit to the military operations. There was far more unanimity between France and Russia. Russia was determined to extend a

---

[1] App. I. No. 24, p. 241.

protecting hand to Serbia from the first, even at the risk of a general conflagration. In France both Poincaré and Viviani, if not the Foreign Secretary's deputy as well, were prepared to support Russia unreservedly from the first, and they were the more ready to do so, the more serious the crisis became, even when Russia proceeded to " extreme measures ", which Nicholas II. had foreseen would lead to war.

At his first conference with Sazonov, after the news of the ultimatum had reached St. Petersburg on the 24th of July, Paléologue assured the Russian Minister,undoubtedly on the strength of instructions received shortly before from Poincaré, that France would fulfil all the obligations of her alliance (E 6). The Ambassador has himself explained what he meant by that, in describing how he took leave of Isvolsky the following evening, when they reached the same conclusion : *Cette fois c'est la guerre.*[1] For a long time the further attitude of the Paris and St. Petersburg Cabinets was only imperfectly understood, for in the documents both Governments published after the outbreak of war, all the passages which represented Germany's attitude in a favourable, and their own in an unfavourable light, were carefully suppressed. Gradually, however, various facts which told heavily against them were revealed. Finally, through the publication in the spring of 1922 of the true correspondence that passed between Paris and St. Petersburg, the first Russian Orange Book of 1914 was seen to be an almost unparalleled instance of falsification.[2] Out of sixty documents twenty-nine were entirely suppressed, eighteen more or less falsified, and only thirteen correctly given. A comparison shows that important passages are also left out or misrepresented in the French Yellow book.[3]

The suppression of Germany's efforts to localize the Austro-Serbian conflict was the least part of the deception. The most important facts in this connection, which have

---

[1] Paléologue, p. 251.
[2] Russian Blue Book, pp. 513–26 ; *Livre Noir*, Vol. II. pp. 275–300 ; Romberg, *Die Fälschungen des Russischen Orangebuches.*
[3] There are omissions or falsifications in F 28, 36, 54, 56, 62, 78, 80, 94, 101, 102, 103, 116, 117, 120, 125, 127. In addition to that, no reference is made in the French Yellow Book to nine important events.

hitherto been kept back by the Entente, are the following : On the 24th of July the German Ambassador in Paris had explained the attitude of the German Government in a tone from which it was evident that " there was still hope of the incident being adjusted by Austro-Serbian negotiations ". Another step taken by Herr von Schoen, on the 25th, was a relief to the French Ministry, as being " a sign that Germany was not bent upon war in any case ". On the 27th Herr von Schoen made a fresh proposal " that France and Germany should intervene between Russia and Austria-Hungary ". On the 28th he gave an assurance that " Germany was ready to work with the other Powers for the preservation of peace ". Finally, Germany's having been obliged to protest against " France's military preparations ", on the 29th of July, was suppressed.

But the revelations as to the close co-operation between St. Petersburg and Paris are of more importance than the evidence of these untruths. It is well known that the French Ambassador reported, on the 25th of July, that a Ministerial Council, presided over by the Tsar, had decided to mobilize thirteen Army Corps against Austria-Hungary, in the event of her " bringing armed pressure to bear upon Serbia " (F 50). He had learnt far more than this, however. The French military attaché's report of a conversation with the Grand Duke Nicholas and the War Minister, on the evening of the 25th,[1] still reposes in the obscurity of the French archives, it is true, but on the 26th Paléologue sent the following telegram, which is suppressed in the Yellow Book :

Yesterday (the 25th of July) the War Minister told me at Krasnoe that the Army Corps (thirteen) of the military districts of Kiev, Odessa, Kazan, and Moscow, were being mobilized. Secret instructions were also being sent to the Vilna, Warsaw, and St. Petersburg districts. Martial law is being proclaimed both in the towns and Governments of St. Petersburg and Moscow. The decree as to this gives a list of subjects the newspapers are not to mention, and which, as a matter of fact, only concern military matters.

The cadets who would have been appointed to regiments, in the ordinary course, on the 18th of August, were hastily given their

[1] Paléologue, p. 251.

commissions yesterday evening at six o'clock. Orders were given at the same time to break up the camp at Krasnoe. At this moment the troops are arriving back in their garrisons. The War Minister again told us that he intended to leave the initiative of a possible offensive to Germany.[1]

Paris consequently knew that Russia was taking military measures on the German front (St. Petersburg, Vilna, Warsaw) as well, and would also have heard that, in the opinion of the Russian General Staff, " war had been a certainty " since the 24th.[2]

This explains the exact coincidence of the first comprehensive military measures in France (p. 136) with the proclamation of the " period of preparation for war " for the whole of Russia on the 26th, which had seemed unaccountable.

It was precisely on this day that Sazonov began the conversations with Szápáry, which Pourtalès had proposed. When the Russian Minister demurred, on this occasion, to points 4 and 5 of the ultimatum (the dismissal of Serbian officers and officials, and collaboration of Austrian officials in suppressing the Greater-Serbian agitation), he was immediately told that point 5 only meant the institution of a secret *bureau de sûreté*, similar to those Russia had set up in Paris and Berlin (A II. 38, 73[3]). Sazonov suppressed this extraordinarily important admission (R 25), which disposed of one of the main points of disagreement between St. Petersburg and Vienna. His fear that Austria wanted to " swallow up " Serbia had also been allayed, in the meantime, by the assurance of her territorial *désintéressement*.

Now when the Russian Chargé d'Affaires in Paris reported, also on the 26th, that, in explaining that Austria disclaimed all idea of territorial aggrandizement, the German Ambassador had expressed a hope that France " would exert her influence in St. Petersburg in a pacific sense ", he received the following reply from Sazonov :

I deem it important to lose no time in correcting a misunderstanding which has found its way into the answer given by the

[1] Report to the French Senate, pp. 39 and 127.
[2] Dobrorolsky, p. 21.
[3] A II. 73 should be dated 26th instead of 27th.

acting Foreign Minister to the German Ambassador. If it is a question of exerting a moderating influence in St. Petersburg, we protest against that straight away, for we adopted a standpoint from the first, which we cannot modify, as we have already acceded to all Austria-Hungary's admissible demands.[1]

All mediation, however, is a question of trying to find a compromise between the different points of view ; therefore in stating that she could not modify her own standpoint, Russia rejected mediation of any kind. This churlish attitude was the more remarkable, seeing that Austria had already made the two important concessions just mentioned. Sazonov had only to frown, and an immediate regretful apology came from Paris : the acting Minister " had not for a moment admitted the possibility of exerting a moderating influence in St. Petersburg ", on the contrary, he had " refused to agree to the German proposal ".[2]

Isvolsky had judged the position correctly, when he reported, directly he returned to his post (July 27th), that he was surprised to find how well the acting Foreign Minister and his colleagues understood the position, and how firm and calm their determination was to give Russia the fullest support, and also to avoid the smallest appearance of disagreement.[3]

They were now sure at the Nevsky Prospekt that they would not be troubled with disagreeable advice to yield. The change that had come over the French spirit was also clearly shown in a circular note of the 27th (F 62). It may be left to the French people to discover what caused the change from the conciliatory attitude hitherto adopted, whether it was due to intervention from Paul Cambon, who was not in London between the 25th and 27th, or to Isvolsky's return, or to instructions from the *France,* which was bringing Poincaré and Viviani home. After the declaration of war on Serbia on the 28th, Sazonov telegraphed to London that this put an end to all idea of direct communication between Russia and Austria (E 70). But the following day he complained to Pourtalès, and also to London and Paris, that Austria declined to agree

[1] Romberg, pp. 18 and 19.　　　[2] Loc. cit., p. 26.
[3] Loc. cit., p. 23.

to direct discussions (D 343, 365, E 78, R 50). In reality these discussions had never been discontinued, for, on the 28th, conversations took place between Berchtold and Schebeko, and between Sazonov and Szápáry (A II. 95, III. 16).[1] It is true that there was a difference of opinion as to the purport of the pourparlers. Vienna would only agree to append an explanation to her note, and St. Petersburg wanted it modified. But that did not justify the Russian Minister in making such unfair accusations ; if he had been more truthful, Berlin would have been able to do more in the way of mediation.

But Sazonov did what was far worse even than this on the 28th. He pointed out the " necessity of mobilizing without further delay " to the Chief of the General Staff, and in words which General Januschkevitch interpreted as meaning that he was " astonished " at its not having begun earlier. The General Staff thereupon drew up two Ukases, one for general mobilization against Austria and Germany, the other for partial mobilization against Austria alone.[2]

Up to this time Austria had only mobilized half her army against Serbia (July 25), eight Army Corps, exclusively from the districts which did not border on Russian territory. Russia, with thirty-seven Army Corps available, could not feel she was menaced in any way. Neither can the step she took be accounted for by exaggerated accounts of the Austrian preparations, for the Russian General Staff was, on the contrary, very correctly informed.[3] The first seven measures for the period of political tension were taken in France on the 27th, the War Office was " delighted ", and General Joffre was highly gratified at all his orders having been carried out without a hitch.[4]

On the morning of the 29th Nicholas II. signed the Ukase for general mobilization against Austria and Germany, not the one for partial mobilization. The further necessary formalities occupied the afternoon, and in the evening the Director of the Mobilization Department, Colonel Dobro-

---

[1] In A III. 16, the word " yesterday " should be substituted for " to-day ".
[2] Dobrorolsky, p. 23. In reality Russian mobilization had begun on the 26th with the " period of preparation for war ".
[3] Reichstag Committee of Enquiry, Part 2, pp. 19, 89.
[4] Loc. cit., p. 75.

rolsky, was just going to dictate the order at the Central Telegraph Office, when instructions were received from the Tsar only to order partial mobilization against Austria. That was thanks to the Kaiser's telegram (p. 142). In the meantime, in accordance with instructions dated the 25th, but sent by post instead of telegraphed (A II. 42), Szápáry had already informed Sazonov, on the 28th, that " Austria had no intention of annexing Serbian territory, nor did she contemplate infringing Serbia's sovereignty " (A III. 16, 19), and had repeated the statement on the 29th, at the German Ambassador's suggestion.

This was all that Russia could legitimately ask. Sazonov, however, replied that he was satisfied as regards the territorial question, but that the Austrian conditions infringed Serbia's rights as a sovereign State. This view did not justify him in suppressing the Ambassador's statement. It was not communicated to any of the allies. If it had been published in good time, it would have very much influenced the position in favour of peace. Instead of that, the Minister worked himself up into a great state of excitement over the warning conveyed to him from Berlin by Pourtalès (p. 142). He wanted to look upon it as a contradiction of the Kaiser's telegram, and tried to influence the Tsar in that sense. The Tsar's intention of sending General Tatischev to Berlin—announced in a third telegram (D 390), was not carried out, and the following message was telegraphed to Paris instead :

As we cannot comply with Germany's wishes, we have no alternative but to hasten on our own military preparations, and to assume that war is probably inevitable.—R 58.

This communication, which could hardly be interpreted otherwise than as meaning that Russia had decided on general mobilization, was transmitted by Isvolsky at three o'clock on the morning of July 30 to the Foreign Office in Paris, where Paléologue's report as to partial mobilization had previously been received (F 100). At a conference which was held at once between Poincaré, Viviani, and the War Minister, Messimy, it was decided to advise Russia to carry out the measures which would bring about war, secretly.

No advice was given to refrain from taking them. This was what the Ambassador telegraphed :

> We are told we might declare our willingness to delay our preparations for mobilization temporarily, in the higher interests of peace, as this would not prevent our carrying on and even intensifying our preparations, at the same time we should have to refrain, as far as possible, from transporting large bodies of troops.[1]

So that there should be no doubt in Paris as to Russia's determination, Sazonov sent yet another " very urgent " telegram :

> We shall continue our preparations until we receive an absolutely satisfactory answer from Austria. You are informed of this in the strictest confidence.[2]

The Russian Minister's victory over his vacillating Sovereign was complete the following day (the 30th of July). Towards one o'clock in the afternoon, immediately after dictating his so-called peace formula to the German Ambassador, he telephoned to the Chief of the General Staff that the Tsar

> considers it right, in view of the latest news from Berlin, to proclaim general mobilization of the whole army and navy.[3]

That the execution of the order might not be frustrated again by a telegram from Berlin, the Minister added: " So now, carry out your orders, General, and then— don't show yourself again to-day ". In reply to a written enquiry as to the exact time, General Dobrorolsky has stated positively that the Tsar's order was given " not later than 2 p.m." (= 1 p.m. German time). The addition " on account of the latest news from Berlin " was entirely Sazonov's own invention, as no disquieting news of any kind had come from Berlin since the Tsar's decision to change general into partial mobilization.[4]

Six o'clock had just struck when Dobrorolsky dictated the fatal telegram to the telegraphists waiting in solemn silence at some dozen apparatuses in the large hall of the Central Telegraph Office in St. Petersburg. The apparatuses

[1] Romberg, p. 37.   [2] Loc. cit., p. 36.   [3] Dobrorolsky, p. 28.
[4] *Deutsche Rundschau,* July 1922, *Der 30 Juli in Petersburg.*

began to work. " That was the moment which ushered in the great epoch . . . there was no possibility of turning back, the prologue of the great drama had begun ".[1]

It may have been at the same time that Berchtold was reiterating to the Russian Ambassador the statement made by Szápáry some days before, as to the integrity and sovereignty of Serbia (A III. 45). Schebeko reported this conversation as having been of a " most friendly character ", and said his impression was that " Austria really wished to reach an understanding with Russia, but did not think it possible to suspend her operations against Serbia until she had obtained full satisfaction and ample guarantees for the future ".[2]

Sazonov kept this to himself too, and suppressed it in the Orange Book.

For many years no one could understand why the French Government, who were in such close touch with St. Petersburg, had not been informed of so decisive a step as general mobilization at once. We now know that at 11.35 p.m. on the 20th of July a telegram from Paléologue reached Paris, stating that on account of disquieting news received by the Russian General Staff and Admiralty, as to the German naval and military preparations, " the Russian Government had decided to take the first steps towards general mobilization secretly ".[3]

The reports issued by the Russian General Staff at that time are sufficient evidence that the mention of German naval and military preparations was merely a pretext.[4] But the telegram showed that the friendly advice given by France in the morning was being acted upon. This fact was concealed for nine years. For nine whole years the Entente peoples have been led to believe that Austria was the first to order general mobilization. Now that this lie has been exposed by French investigators, an attempt is made to plead that it was only a question of taking the " first steps ". But as it was already known in Paris that

[1] Dobrorolsky, p. 29.
[2] *Deutsche Allgemeine Zeitung* of May 20, 1919, No. 242.
[3] F 102 is doubly falsified. It is made up of two telegrams, and the above mentioned sentence is omitted.
[4] Reichstag Committee of Enquiry, Part 2, pp. 72 and 73.

the " first steps " had been taken on the 25th, no one could
have doubted that the words used in the telegram meant
nothing less than the actual beginning of general mobilization.
France made no protest. Her silence spoke volumes, and
was rightly understood in St. Petersburg.

8. The Meaning of Russian General Mobilization.

The word mobilization is used in two senses. In the
more limited sense it is understood merely to mean trans-
ferring the army from a peace to a war footing, without
the troops leaving their garrisons. Such mobilizations
took place in Austria-Hungary in 1908–9 against Serbia,
and in Austria-Hungary and Russia when the relations
between the two countries were strained in 1912–13. They
were limited to part of the army, and were gradually completed on the strength of a series of individual orders given
at intervals covering a considerable period. Mobilization
in the wider sense in which the word is generally used
now is another thing. The order for general mobilization
provides at one stroke for steps being taken, according to
a plan accurately drawn up in advance, not only to place
the establishment automatically on a war footing, but also
to assemble the troops, that is, to transport them to the
frontiers. The Russian mobilization of 1914 was of this
nature, and cannot be compared in any way with the mobilizations of 1908–9, and 1912–13. Both French and Russian
military men and politicians have long since recognized
that such a mobilization means war. The peace-loving
President of the French Republic, Jules Grévy, strongly
expressed this opinion in the spring of 1887, when he rejected
General Boulanger's proposal to mobilize against Germany
in the following words :

*C'est insensé, ce que vous proposez là, général ; ne savez-vous
pas que cela serait la guerre ?*

To which the General replied :

Eh bien, je suis prêt.[1]

The Emperor Alexander III. expressed the same opinion,

[1] *Grosse Politik*, Vol. VI. No. 1275, p. 204.

in January 1888, when he said frankly to the German Ambassador, von Schweinitz, on the latter protesting against the Russian cavalry being massed on the German frontier, and remarking that they could be on German ground within a few hours :

Yes, we must try to prevent your mobilizing.[1]

When concluding the Franco-Russian military convention of 1892, the French delegate, General Boisdeffre, told the Tsar plainly that " mobilization was a declaration of war ".[2] It is true that the General meant German or Austrian or Italian mobilization. But as Russian or French mobilization must automatically be followed by German mobilization, even according to the strictest pacifist principles, they would be equally equivalent to a declaration of war, from Boisdeffre's point of view. Alexander III. did not need to be told this after what he had said to Schweinitz, and he replied :

C'est bien comme cela que je le comprends.

The view expressed by the Russian delegate, Obrutchev, Chief of the General Staff, was that " Russian and French mobilization ought to be immediately followed by military action, in short, ought to be inseparable from an offensive ".[3]

As in 1888, so in 1892 a Russian plan of operations provided that Russian cavalry were to invade East Prussia directly mobilization was ordered.[4] In a Note of August 10 Boisdeffre clearly stamped the State which first ordered general mobilization as the aggressor :

To order general mobilization against Austria and Italy alone would mean acting as the aggressors in Europe, and being placed in a difficult position towards neutral countries ; whereas by waiting for Germany to mobilize, at the same time taking the necessary precautionary measures, the latter would be assuming the rôle of aggressor, with all its disadvantages, whilst Russia and France would have proved their anxiety to maintain peace to the last, and vouched for their intention of acting purely on the defensive.[5]

[1] Loc. cit., Vol. VI. No. 1176, p. 48.
[2] French Yellow Book, *l'Alliance Franco-Russe*, No. 71, pp. 95 f.
[3] Loc. cit., No. 42, App. p. 56.
[4] Loc. cit. No. 54, p. 76;   [5] Loc. cit., No. 53, p. 68.

The Russian decree, issued in the spring and autumn of 1912, that the proclamation of mobilization also meant the proclamation of war against Germany and Austria, went even further than the view that mobilization would make war inevitable. It provided for the commencement of military operations directly mobilization was proclaimed, that is, without any declaration of war, in flagrant defiance of the decision of the Hague Conference with regard to " opening hostilities ". It is true that this decree was rescinded at the end of 1912, for two reasons. The first was to avoid misunderstandings with Powers against whom it had not been intended to wage war from the first. No exception can be taken to that. But the second reason, quoted below, was a very obvious *ruse de guerre*.

On the other hand it may be an advantage to assemble the troops, without opening hostilities, so that the enemy may not be irreparably deprived of all hope of yet being able to avoid war. At the same time, Russia's military measures would have to be masked by skilful diplomatic negotiations, in order to allay the enemy's fears, as far as possible. If such measures make it possible to gain a few days' time, they must decidedly be adopted.[1]

It will be seen that there was no question of personally believing that war might yet be avoided, but only of leading the enemy to believe this. On the contrary, it is clear from the three sentences quoted, that the authors were convinced that war would be inevitable when once mobilization had begun. Their expectation that the enemy would be deceived did not show much discernment, but the scheme was none the less diabolical.

The minutes of the conferences between the Russian and French military experts in 1911, 1912, and 1913, also show that they reckoned on military operations automatically coinciding with mobilization.[2] Never once was there any reference to even the possibility of demobilization following mobilization in these minutes, which were submitted to the political authorities, and ratified by them.

[1] Memorandum by the German General Staff, *Die Russische Mobil-machung*, 1914, App. 5.
[2] Russian Blue Book, p. 697 ; German translation *Süddeutsche Monats-hefte*, July 1922, p. 210.

The view taken in official quarters in France and Russia was not different in 1914 to what it had been in 1887, 1892, and 1912. Sazonov, it is true, declared that mobilization took far longer in Russia than in the western countries. But that was absolutely misleading. The Minister must have been aware, from the minutes of the General Staff meetings, that mobilization in European Russia did not take longer, but was actually a more rapid process than in Austria. It was also clear that Russian mobilization must automatically bring about mobilization on the opposite side, consequently must have the same effect as in the western countries. Poincaré even went so far as to assert that mobilization was " the best means of insuring peace ".[1] But if he really believed that, why has he suppressed the truth for nine years, as to the order in which the several mobilizations succeeded one another ? Why did he not announce that France's Russian ally was the first to resort to this method of securing peace ? He knew far too well that the nations would not believe anything of that kind, and that in France, and every country in the world, the one who had first ordered general mobilization would be considered the aggressor. Misrepresentation of the order in which the various mobilizations took place, and the false accusation made against Austria of having been the first to mobilize, have actually been responsible for the main complaint made against the Central Powers.

A large number of witnesses from all countries recognize directly or indirectly that general mobilization in Russia made war inevitable.[2] The most competent judge, the Director of the Russian Mobilization Department, writes :

When the date for this (mobilization) is once fixed, everything is settled, there is no going back : it mechanically predetermines the commencement of war.[3]

Nor was Nicholas II. at all in the dark as to what he was doing when he signed the order for mobilization. He had already spoken, on the 25th of July, of the " extreme

[1] G. Demartial, *Comment on mobilisa les Consciences*, p. 128.
[2] Reichstag Committee of Enquiry, Part 2, pp. 31, 32, 37, 38.
[3] Dobrorolsky, p. 10.

measures which would lead to war ". On the 30th, when Sazonov had wrung the decisive order from him for the second time, he turned pale and said in a choking voice :

Think of the responsibility you advise me to take ! Remember that it is a question of sending thousands upon thousands to their death.[1]

9. The Decisions of July 31.

Berlin and Vienna.

Tschirschky's full report of the execution of his last commission reached the Wilhelmstrasse in the early morning hours of the 31st. Berchtold had been " pale and silent " while the German warning was twice read to him, and was profoundly impressed with its seriousness, but—he had to wait for Tisza (D 465). So there was still no decision.

The German Chief of the Staff had been very anxious since midnight. He had received " two reliable reports from independent sources, stating that mobilization of all Russia's armed forces had already been ordered ". But as he knew how difficult it would be to obtain permission to order German mobilization, he had decided to wait for confirmation from a third source. At seven o'clock in the morning, the General commanding at Allenstein reported that the Russian frontier was hermetically sealed, the Russian frontier guards were going to burn down their houses—as provided in case of mobilization—and red placards ordering mobilization were posted up in the Russian frontier districts. Moltke still hesitated. A red placard must be brought across the frontier. " Until then I cannot obtain the order to mobilize ".[2]

The third confirmation came twenty minutes before midday. A telegram from St. Petersburg reported :

General mobilization of army and navy ordered. First day of mobilization the 31st of July.—D 473 (handed in at 10.40 a.m. =9.40 German time).

[1] Paléologue, p. 260.
[2] Notes by von Haeften, at that time a Major on the General Staff, and General Hell, vide Schulthess's *Geschichtskalender* 1917, pp. 996–7 and 1000.

Thus Germany was faced with the war on two fronts, which had already weighed on Bismarck like a nightmare. That Russia would not fight alone was clear. A short respite, and then a hundred and ninety-two French and Russian divisions would advance against the German and Austrian frontiers, which were only protected by a hundred and thirty-five.[1] The number of non-European troops of which the enemy would be short, for the first few weeks, was counter-balanced on our side by the Austrian forces detailed for employment against Serbia.

Berlin was not indeed aware, at that time, of a good deal in the Franco-Russian agreements referred to in the last chapter, but the military authorities had reckoned for many years past with the probability of an immediate invasion by Russian cavalry massed on the frontier. During the Balkan crisis of 1912 they had also heard of the order issued in Russia that " mobilization would be equivalent to war against Germany and Austria ". It is true that they had also heard of its having been cancelled,[2] but it might have been renewed during the present crisis. In a report of the 31st of July on the situation, the German General Staff said : " As the period of preparation for waɪ lasts several days, Russian cavalry divisions may even now be ready to invade us " (D 524). It was advisable to start military operations with the least possible delay on the front where the decision was sought by the plan of campaign, and immediate mobilization seemed to be a duty, in self-defence. But the order issued at one o'clock to the German army only proclaimed a " state of imminent danger of war " (*Zustand drohender Kriegsgefahr*), not mobilization. Paris had already been informed, on the 29th, that this did not mean mobilization, or involve calling up reserves, nor need it necessarily be followed by mobilization.[3] Thus it will be seen that a fresh effort was made to postpone the measure, contrary to what would have been expedient from the military point of view. Perhaps at least a partially satisfactory answer might yet come from Vienna ; a tele-

[1] Reichstag Committee of Enquiry, Part 2, p. 41.
[2] Loc. cit., Part 2, pp. 30 and 58.
[3] Provisions of the German scheme of mobilization, relating to imminent danger of war, valid in 1914, vide App. I. No. 25, p. 241.

phone message gave some reason to hope for this (D 468), perhaps England might yet be able to exert a restraining influence on Russia.

William II. informed King George at once of Russia's having broken the peace (D 477,[1]) and sent the Tsar a fourth telegram, which concluded with the words :

> The peace of Europe may still be maintained by you, if Russia will agree to stop the military measures which must threaten Germany and Austria-Hungary.—D 480.

King George's answer did not come till more than twenty-four hours later, saying that he had sent an urgent telegram to Nicholas II. (D 574). The message to the Russian sovereign crossed one from him, which, after expressing his thanks for the Kaiser's communication, continued :

> It is technically impossible to suspend our military preparations, which were obligatory *owing to Austria's mobilization*.[2] We are far from wishing for war. As long as the negotiations with Austria on Serbia's account are taking place, my troops shall not take any provocative action. I give you my solemn word for this.— D 487.

The exact hour of the Russian mobilization was not known in Berlin in 1914, but Count Pourtalès' telegram had made it clear that it took place before the order to mobilize was given in Austria, and that mobilization against Austria and Germany could not be justified by Austrian measures. How could the Tsar have come to make such untrue statements ? Was he deceived by his *entourage*, or did he himself wish to deceive ? In either case his " solemn word " was worthless. Nor was any security given in case of the negotiations respecting Serbia breaking down, which might be brought about by Russia at any time.

The Chancellor for his part telegraphed first to Vienna (D 479). His appeal to Austria to be loyal to the alliance, in view of the Russian menace, crossed a telegram from the Emperor Francis Joseph to the Kaiser :

---

[1] In this telegram, as in D 474 and several marginal notes which, strange to say, appear not to have been read at the German Foreign Office, Vienna's acceptance of direct discussions was mistakenly regarded as acceptance of the proposal not to go beyond Belgrade.

[2] The italics are the author's.

. . . The official report from my Ambassador in St. Petersburg, stating that the Emperor of Russia had ordered mobilization of all the military districts on my frontiers, reached me yesterday, just after your Ambassador had conveyed Sir Edward Grey's proposal of mediation to my Government. . . . Conscious of my serious responsibility for the future of my Empire, I have ordered the mobilization of all my armed forces. The action in which my army is engaged against Serbia cannot be interrupted by Russia's menacing and defiant attitude. A fresh rescue of Serbia, through Russia's intervention, would have the most serious consequences for my countries, therefore I cannot possibly allow such intervention. I am fully aware of the importance of my decisions, and have made them, relying on God's justice, and confident that your army will loyally support my Empire and the Triple Alliance.—D 482.

This request for armed help against the Russian offensive, to repel which, mobilization of the second half of the Austro-Hungarian army had been ordered,[1] was at the same time a definite rejection of the English proposal to call a " halt in Belgrade ". A joint Cabinet Council held in Vienna in the morning, after Tisza's arrival, had decided to say, in reply to the English proposal submitted by the German Ambassador, that Austria

was not disinclined to consider the proposal, but *this must not be allowed to interrupt her military operations against Serbia*, and she must also make her acceptance of the proposal of mediation dependent on Russia's immediately suspending all mobilization measures, and dismissing her reserves.—A III. 80.[2]

In spite of the Austrian Emperor's appeal, Berlin adhered to the decision not to mobilize yet. German mobilization, however, could only be postponed for quite a short time, if Russia continued hers. It was in consequence of this that the ultimatum was sent to St. Petersburg at 3.30, stating that Germany was compelled by the Russian mobilization to proclaim a " state of imminent danger of war ", but that this did not mean mobilization as yet.

Mobilization must follow, however, unless Russia suspends all military measures against us and Austria-Hungary within twelve hours, and notifies us definitely to that effect.—D 490.

[1] Reichstag Committee of Enquiry, Part 2, p. 23.
[2] The italics are the author's.

In order to avoid making the Note unnecessarily peremptory, the statement that mobilization meant war, which had already been made three times, was not repeated. The German ultimatum, and the demands made by the Austrian Ministerial Council, were in complete harmony, although they had been decided upon independently. Of course it was understood that Austria would put a stop to her mobilization against Russia, if the latter restored her troops to a peace footing.

With a view to ascertaining France's attitude, Herr von Schoen was informed of the Note which had been addressed to St. Petersburg, and instructed to ask the French Government whether France would remain neutral in a Russo-German war. An answer within eighteen hours was requested. He might very well have been merely instructed to ask the question; it was hardly expedient to inform Paris of the ultimatum addressed to Russia.[1] Although there could be no doubt that the French General Staff quite understood the meaning of the words " state of imminent danger of war ", it was thoroughly explained to the French Ambassador in Berlin, both by the Foreign Secretary and the Imperial Chancellor. London was advised of all that went on, by verbal communications to Goschen, and telegraphic instructions to Lichnowsky.[2]

London.

It was on this day that Downing Street decided not to make strong representations just then in St. Petersburg, with regard to the preparations for war. Grey had indeed promised the German Ambassador that he would " try to exert influence to that effect ", when he was informed of Austria's having agreed to direct conversations (D 489). But when telegraphing to Buchanan to express his satisfaction at their resumption, he said :

I informed the German Ambassador that, with regard to the military preparations, I did not see how Russia could be urged to suspend them, unless some limit were fixed by Austria to the advance of her troops in Serbia.—E 110.

[1] Secret supplement to this telegram, vide App. No. 26, p. 242.
[2] F 116 ; Report to the French Senate, p. 125 ; E 108, D 488.

That could not be understood otherwise in St. Petersburg than as consent to the measures taken there, all the more as the Austrian advance had not even begun. Grey further told Lichnowsky that everything depended on Austria's making " such a concession as to put Russia in the wrong ", and that, in case of need, he must be in a position to justify an attitude of reserve on the part of England, by " some palpable wrong on the Russian side " (D 489). Goschen then transmitted a fresh English proposal of mediation (D 496, E III) :

1. That Germany should sound Vienna, and England would sound St. Petersburg, as to whether the four Powers not directly interested could find some way of satisfying Austria, without impairing Serbia's sovereignty and territorial integrity.

2. Austria has already stated that she would respect both.

3. The four Powers might tell Russia that they would see that the two points mentioned were not impaired.

4. All the Powers would have to suspend their military preparations.

The second point of this proposal is remarkable, as Sazonov had not passed on the statements made by Szápáry and Berchtold to this effect.[1] But as Grey had heard of them in some other way, the first condition he had mentioned to Lichnowsky was fulfilled, namely, that Austria should "make such a concession as to put Russia in the wrong ". The point regarding putting a stop to military preparations ought, however, to have been addressed above all to Russia ; for it was far more important for the maintenance of general peace that the Russian preparations against Austria and Germany should be brought to a standstill than the Austrian preparations against Serbia. Consequently, according to Goschen, the German Foreign Secretary expressed " great sympathy " with the proposal, in a long interview with him, but insisted that he must first wait for an answer as to suspension of the Russian preparations (E 121). The suggestion Grey had made, without knowing of the Russian mobilization, must be considered to have been outstripped by events.

Reports that German mobilization might be imminent,

[1] The Austrian Ambassador in London was still of opinion, on the evening of the 30th, that no such statement had been made—A III. 42.

further led the British Foreign Secretary to take up the question of Belgian neutrality. It is highly probable that the German plan of operations had been known to experts all over the world for years past ; anyhow it had been known in London since the beginning of 1906.[1] Bethmann's question of the 29th had made it certain that the plan still existed. In case it came to war, here was a reason which would make England's intervention popular in the country. This was all the more necessary, as, according to a report sent by Benckendorff on the 31st, Grey himself " understood the position perfectly ", but was held back by a certain reaction in Parliament.[2] He therefore asked both Paris and Berlin, in the evening, whether they would pledge themselves to respect Belgium's neutrality (E 144). The German answer was evasive, the French consented, as had probably already been agreed upon in the existing secret military conventions (E 122, 125).

Paris.

Cambon's report of the proclamation of " imminent danger of war " and why it was issued, confirmed the news the French Foreign Minister had received the evening before, of general mobilization in Russia. A third announcement of total Russian mobilization had come through a Havas telegram from Berlin,[3] when the German Ambassador called on Viviani, towards 7 p.m., to put the question he had been instructed to ask. According to the French report, this was done so courteously that the demand could not for a moment have appeared to be in the nature of an ultimatum (F 117). The Minister did not give any information as to the attitude France would adopt in case of a Russo-German war, and actually said that he " had no information at all as to total Russian mobilization ". Shortly afterwards (at 8.30 p.m.) a telegram arrived from Paléologue handed in at 10.45 a.m. (= 8.45 Paris time,) which announced general mobilization in Russia for the fourth time.[4] Quite apart from all the earlier reports that had been received,

[1] German White Book, May 1915, small edition, p. 106.
[2] *Pravda*, March 9, 1919, No. 7.   [3] Romberg, p. 40.
Poincaré's statement in the *Temps*, January 19, 1923.

it would surely have been only right and honourable to lose no time now in letting the German Ambassador know that his statement had turned out to be absolutely correct, and to apologize to him for having disputed it. Instead of that, more than eight years were allowed to pass before the French Government at last admitted the truth. Viviani himself continues to deny it to the present day.

On receipt of Cambon's report, a Ministerial Council had been held at four o'clock, when it was decided to take the " fullest measures " in the case of the five frontier corps, which had already formed the first frontier line of defence the day before. According to Isvolsky's report, these measures were " not to be in the nature of mobilization ", but the Russian military attaché reported the next day that all five corps were " fully prepared for war ".[1] After the arrival of Paléologue's telegram, the Ministers held a further conference, which lasted till midnight.[2] With regard to the decisions reached, the Russian military attaché reported :

> The French War Minister informed me, in great spirits, that the Government are firmly determined on war, and begged me to endorse the hope of the French General Staff that all our efforts will be directed against Germany, and that Austria will be treated as a *quantité négligeable.*[3]

This report was sent off on the 1st of August, at one o'clock in the morning (= 3 a.m. St. Petersburg time), that is, sixteen hours before the German declaration of war on Russia, and two and a half days before the German declaration of war on France. Just as Russia was the first country to mobilize, so France was the first Power officially to notify her firm determination to go to war.

During the Ministerial Council, another event was taking place. On the evening of the 31st, Count Berchtold sent word to the Austrian Ambassador that the Monarchy had " already officially informed St. Petersburg that the action in Serbia was not undertaken with the object of territorial

[1] Messimy, in the *Revue de France*, August 1, 1921 ; *Journal Officiel*, February 1, 1919, sup. p. 353 ; Poincaré, p. 267 ; Romberg, pp. 39 and 42.
[2] Messimy, as in preceding note and Poincaré, p. 275.
[3] Romberg, p. 41.

aggrandizement, and that the sovereign rights of the State would not be violated " (A III. 62). Count Szécsen hastened to the Quai d'Orsay with this news towards midnight, and was there told by the Director of the Political Department that, in his personal opinion, " the Serbian question was quite a secondary matter, in view of the step taken by Germany that day " (A III. 64).

St. Petersburg.

Count Pourtalès presented the ultimatum in St. Petersburg at midnight on the 31st of July. Sazonov pointed out the technical impossibility of suspending military measures, and repeated his former argument that " Russian mobilization could not be compared with that of other countries " (D 536).

Shortly before this, the Russian Minister had telegraphed to the Ambassadors in the five European capitals the surprising news of Szápáry's having informed him that Austria was willing to discuss the substance of her ultimatum. Sazonov thought London would be the best place for the negotiations.[1] But it appears from Szápáry's very detailed report, that he had asked for the interview, mainly because he thought it opportune, from a tactical point of view, to have given an ostensible proof of goodwill, in order to put Russia as far as possible in the wrong, and that, throughout the conversation, he had continually referred to the discrepancy between the Austrian and Russian standpoints, Sazonov wishing that the Note should be " modified ", whilst Berchtold would only agree to its being " explained " (A III. 75, 97). The Austrian report is so clear and detailed, that a misunderstanding is inconceivable. Now how was it that Sazonov, who had formerly laid such stress on the difference between the Russian and Austrian standpoints, and had even said nothing about statements made by Szápáry, which showed a real desire to meet Russia's wishes, suddenly ignored this discrepancy, and why did he suddenly want these discussions to take place in London, instead of under his direct personal influence ? There is no other

[1] Telegram from Sazonov of July 31, 1914, No. 1592, vide Red Archives I. p. 186, Romberg, p. 39.

explanation than this : the Russian Minister had achieved his first object, which was to induce the Tsar to order general mobilization, and now he wanted " to gain time, by carrying on skilful diplomatic negotiations " as suggested by the protocol of November 1912. To begin negotiations in a fresh place, with fresh instructions to the representatives of all the Powers, would be the best means of giving the huge Russian army time to complete its preparations for war. If Sazonov had really so entirely misunderstood Szápáry's communication, and taken such a favourable view of it, it would be almost inconceivable that he should not have informed Count Pourtalès of it, when the latter handed him the German ultimatum.

There are two marginal notes made by Nicholas II. on the draft of the astonishing Russian telegram. The first says : " The one does not prevent the other—continue your conversations with the Austrian Ambassador ". That obviously meant that the negotiations in London and the interviews with Szápáry could take place at the same time. But the second remark is as follows : " it is very important to keep the secret ". The word " secret " could not have referred either to the interviews with Szápáry, or the negotiations in London, for all the Cabinets had been informed of both by telegram. The only remaining explanation is that general mobilization was to be carried out secretly, under cover of partial mobilization against Austria, and, as a matter of fact, no Russian Ambassador had been informed of the measure. Both the Tsar and the Minister seem to have thought that this deception could be kept up indefinitely.

10. The Intrigues against Germany.

(a) *The Tsar's Reply to the King of England.*

The Chancellor had followed his many appeals to England by sending another on the 31st, giving a detailed account of the crisis since the 29th of July (D 513). This at last made a great impression on Grey. At 3.30 a.m. on the 1st of August he sent instructions to Buchanan " to apply at once for an audience with the Russian Emperor, and give

him a personal message from the King of England "
message gave the full text of Bethmann's telegram
long additions, in which the King said :

> I cannot help thinking that some misunderstanding has
> this deadlock. . . . I therefore make a personal appeal to you to
> remove the misapprehension which I feel must have occurred,
> and to leave still open grounds for negotiation and possible peace. . . .

It cannot be more clearly stated than George V. states
here, on the advice of his Ministers, that the one who first
mobilizes is to blame. The Tsar's answer began by saying :

> I would gladly have accepted your proposals had not German
> Ambassador presented a Note to my Government *this afternoon* [1]
> declaring war. . . .

This was followed by the assertion that " every proposal "
had been rejected by Germany and Austria-Hungary, and
that Germany showed no inclination to mediate until the
right moment to put pressure on Austria had gone by. Then
came the further statement that Russia had finally been
compelled to order general mobilization,

in consequence of complete Austrian mobilization, of the bombardment of Belgrade, of concentration of Austrian troops in Galicia,
and of secret military preparations being made in Germany. [2]

Nicholas II. may have been deceived by his *entourage*
as regards the date of the Austrian mobilization, but he
knew that Germany had not made any secret preparations,
for he had not complained of them in any of his five telegrams to the Kaiser, not even in the last one of August
the 1st, which was sent at 2 p.m. (D 546), only a few hours
before the answer sent to King George. The Tsar must
also have known something about the German efforts to
mediate, for he had just thanked the Kaiser warmly for
the mediation, " which began to give hope that all might
yet end peaceably " (D 487). The most remarkable thing
about the reply telegram, however, is that the King's
message should only have reached the Tsar *after* the
German declaration of war. Thirteen hours elapsed

---

[1] The italics are the author's.
[2] Telegrams from George V. and Nicholas II., see *The Times*, August 5,
1914.

between 3.30 a.m. (= 5.30 a.m. Russian time), when Grey's instructions were sent, and the delivery of the German declaration of war at 7 a.m. Could such an urgent telegram really have taken so long on the road ? It looks very much as though the answer had been intentionally delayed, either because the Tsar did not know what to say in reply to the just reproof, or because Sazonov prevented the British Ambassador from having an immediate audience. This suspicion is increased to certainty by the false statement that the German declaration of war was delivered in the *afternoon*. Nothing was said about the real hour—7 p.m.—so that it should not at once be known in London that King George's message must have arrived before the German declaration of war. Paléologue's account also shows that Buchanan's request for an audience was made before the delivery of the German declaration of war.[1] Sazonov must be charged with not only having prevented Tatischev's being sent to Berlin,[2] but also of having prevented King George's message from being delivered in good time.

(b) Viviani's Circular Note of August 1, and the Influence brought to bear on the British Ambassador in Paris.

Sazonov's telegram respecting Austria's being prepared to discuss the substance of her ultimatum (E 133) does not seem to have made any special impression in Downing Street at first, probably because, on the strength of what the Russian Minister himself had told him of his conversation with Szápáry, Buchanan had sent a report far more in keeping with the Austrian Minister's sober account of it than with Sazonov's optimistic telegram (E 139). It was only later on that London also took the view that Austria had made a special concession (D 687, E p. viii).

Paléologue's report of the Sazonov–Szápáry interview, on the evening of July 31st, is suppressed in the French Yellow book, and, as already mentioned, Count Szécsen's

---

[1] Paléologue, p. 264. The suspicion expressed above is confirmed by Sir George Buchanan in *My Mission to Russia*, pp. 204 and 205. Buchanan received the telegram about 5 p.m., but Sazonov fixed the " immediate " audience five hours later.

Baron Rosen, *Forty Years of Diplomacy*, Vol. II. p. 171.

communication, late in the evening of the 31st, that Austria would respect both Serbia's integrity and her sovereign rights, was at first considered of very secondary importance at the Quai d'Orsay. When Poincaré spoke of it the next day to Isvolsky, the latter, from whom Sazonov had withheld the statements made to that effect by Szápáry, on the 28th and 29th, said Szécsen's assurance was " an entire fabrication ", to which Poincaré replied :

Statements of the same kind have been made in London too, where they might make a very dangerous impression, consequently they ought to be contradicted there at once.[1]

In these circumstances it is doubly remarkable that the French Yellow book should contain a circular Note of Viviani's, on the 1st of August, stating that " on the previous evening the Austrian Ambassador in Paris had taken a rather vague and the Ambassador in St. Petersburg a definitely conciliatory step, but that the peaceable disposition shown by Austria had been rendered useless by Germany's attitude. There was no justification for Germany's ultimatum to Russia, as Russia had accepted the English proposal, which " implied a cessation of military preparations by all the Powers " (F 120).

It will be seen that two Austrian steps were turned to account in this Note, with the object of casting an aspersion on Germany : (1) A step taken by Szápáry, which he himself only regarded as a tactical manœuvre ; (2) a communication from Szécsen respecting statements made by Szápáry on the 28th and 29th in the course of direct conversations, carried on under pressure from Germany, which Sazonov had concealed, and Poincaré had described on the 1st of August as " very dangerous ", and also wished kept secret. It was further stated that Russia had agreed to suspend her military preparations, whilst in reality she was continuing her mobilization uninterruptedly, and the French authorities were just as well informed as to this as the German General Staff (D 609). These were the methods resorted to in order to prove that Germany wanted war. Similar methods were employed the same day to influence

[1] Romberg, pp. 45–6.

the British Ambassador. Sir F. Bertie reported that both Berthelot and Poincaré had told him that general mobilization was only ordered in Russia after Austria had ordered hers. In telling him this, the President of the Republic had specified the exact date, " after a decree ordering general mobilization in Austria had been issued ", and had added that military measures had been taken in Germany which were in effect a general mobilization (E 126, 134). Such untruths, or to use the right expression, such unheard of lies were transmitted to London, although correct information as to the Russian general mobilization had been received five times, although it had been made perfectly clear what a " state of imminent danger of war " meant—apart from the knowledge of this the French General Staff would have had in any case, although Russia did not contemplate suspending her military preparations, and although the French had already notified Russia at one o'clock that morning of their firm determination to go to war.

(c) *Schebeko and Dumaine call on Berchtold.*

On the 1st of August the Austrian Minister received visits in remarkably rapid succession from the Russian and French Ambassadors, both of whom tried to represent Germany as the peace-breaker. Berchtold gave the Russian Ambassador an evasive answer, and apparently did not answer the French Ambassador at all (A III. 99). The Russian Orange Book and French Yellow Book say nothing about this fruitless *démarche* on the part of the two diplomats. The Austrian Minister, however, very loyally reported the occurrence to the German Ambassador, and von Tschirschky was able to add the following, when forwarding Berchtold's letter to Berlin :

The Russian Councillor of Embassy made a similar attempt on the 2nd of August, in the case of one of the junior members of the Foreign Office, who retorted by asking him whether, by any chance, Russia's mobilization was directed against Mongolia. The Ballplatz considers the whole thing an " infamous swindle ". The game of driving a wedge between Germany and Austria is " fully seen through " in Vienna.—D 704 (dated the 3rd, but written on the 2nd).

The false accusations made against Germany in the Tsar's telegram to King George, Viviani's remarkable Note, the lies told to the British Ambassador in Paris, and the reports spread by the Russian and French Ambassadors in Vienna, are responsible for the legend which has been circulated, and is still believed in France, that Austria was quite prepared to yield at the last moment, and was forced to go to war against her will by Germany.

11. ENGLISH MEDIATION ON THE 1ST OF AUGUST.

(a) *The Second Sazonov Formula.*

As is well known, Sir Edward Grey had not thought the first Sazonov formula suitable, and had proposed instead (p. 152) that Austria should agree not to go beyond Belgrade, on the understanding that Russia should suspend her military preparations, assuming that the other Powers did the same. Sazonov did not at all approve of this solution, and altered his earlier formula as follows :

> If Austria will agree to check the advance of her troops on Serbian territory ; if recognizing that the Austro-Serbian dispute has assumed a character of European interest, she will allow the Great Powers to look into the matter and determine whether Serbia could satisfy the Austro-Hungarian Government, without impairing her rights as a sovereign State or her independence, Russia will undertake to maintain her waiting attitude.—R 67, E 120.

On the plea that he wished to make his formula conform to the English proposal, as reported by Buchanan, Sazonov had done almost exactly the reverse. Austria was to stop her advance, which everyone knew had not even begun —it only began on the 9th of August—and was consequently not to occupy Belgrade, as proposed by Grey, whilst Russia —and this was a very considerable falling off as compared with the first Russian formula—no longer undertook to " suspend her military preparations ", but only to maintain a " waiting attitude ", that is, merely to postpone the commencement of hostilities. So that there should be no misunderstanding as to what was meant, Buchanan expressly added, in his report, that the Tsar had telegraphed to the German Emperor that "it was naturally impossible to stop a mobilization which was already in progress" (E 120, paragraph 3).

Possibly deceived by the plausible word "conform", Grey passed on this formula, sent to him on the 1st of August, to all the Cabinets without comment (E 132). Simple acceptance of the dictum of one party, which differs from one's own view, cannot be called mediation. The formula thus altered for the worse did not reach Berlin till the 2nd of August. Even had the communication been received earlier, the result would have been no better, for to consent to Russia's continuing to mobilize uninterruptedly would have been incompatible with the duty of self-preservation.

The French Government also had a hand in the Sazonov formula. In a Note to St. Petersburg of July 31, they apparently supported Grey's proposal, but at the same time they suggested substituting "arrest of the Austrian advance", for the occupation of Belgrade (F 112), and Sazonov caught at the idea. Viviani recommended the second part of the proposal, namely, suspension of the Russian military preparations. Some light is thrown on the sincerity of this advice by the fact that, the day before, Paris had urged the preparations being carried on secretly and expedited, and had received the news that the first steps towards general mobilization had been taken in Russia, without protest.

(b) Berchtold's Telegram of August 1 (Morning).

In accordance with the decision of the Joint Ministerial Council, held on the morning of July 31 (p. 172), a long Note was drafted at the Ballplatz, in which Count Szögyény was informed of Tschirschky's earnest warnings and advice, and instructed to thank the Berlin Government for the communications, and say :

In spite of the change which has since taken place in the situation, owing to Russia's mobilization, we fully appreciate England's endeavours to maintain general peace, and willingly accept Sir Edward Grey's proposal to mediate between us and Serbia.[1]

[1] As regards the view that "the Powers" should have been substituted for "Serbia," vide Gooss, pp. 236 f.

But naturally we only accept on the understanding that in the meantime our military operations against the Kingdom are continued, and that the English Cabinet will induce the Russian Government to suspend the mobilization of their troops against us, in which case of course we should also immediately cancel the defensive military counter-measures the Russian mobilization compelled us to take in Galicia.—A III. 65.

Although this Note only left the ciphering office on the 1st of August, towards four o'clock in the morning, it did not refer to the general Russian mobilization, of which news had been received in the meantime, but only to the partial mobilization against Austria; and although the proposal to limit the military operations to the occupation of Belgrade, which was so strongly recommended by London and Berlin, was not accepted, a prospect was held out that Austria would agree to mediation if this partial mobilization were cancelled. There is no evidence of when the Austrian Ambassador carried out the instructions dated the 31st of July, as it was not the custom, at the Wilhelmstrasse, to make notes of verbal communications. Anyhow, the fact that Russia had extended her partiality to general mobilization had in the meantime been known for twenty-four hours, and the Emperor Francis Joseph's telegram to the Kaiser, rejecting Grey's proposal, had also been received (p. 172). The view taken in Berlin entirely coincided with that expressed in the Vienna Note, namely, that suspension of the Russian mobilization against Austria, as well as against Germany, was an indispensable condition of Austria's acceptance of mediation.

Count Berchtold had also communicated his telegram to the Ambassadors in Paris and London, but only for their " personal information ". In spite of this, Count Mensdorff, who received it in the afternoon of August 4, decided, after talking the matter over with Prince Lichnowsky, to inform Grey of it " in confidence " (A III. 94). The Note made an impression on Sir Edward, who, like Count Mensdorff himself, did not know of the Emperor Francis Joseph's telegram to the Kaiser. Although the condition " halt in Belgrade " was not accepted, he thought the conditional acceptance of mediation showed a disposition on the part of the Austrian Minister to meet him, and he seems to have at last realized that the obstacle in the way of understanding and mediation was not Austria's advance in Serbia, or even the further unlimited advance Count Berchtold claimed her right to make in the meantime, but solely the Russian mobilization, and indeed her mobilization against Austria alone. He had given St. Petersburg to understand, only the day before, that he did not see how Russia could suspend her military preparations, if Austria did not fix a limit to her advance in Serbia (E 110), and had just informed all the Cabinets of the second Russian formula, demanding a cessation of the Austrian advance, which had not yet begun, and a continuance of the Russian mobilization, not only against Austria, but also against Germany, and now he telegraphed the text of the Vienna proposal to Buchanan, with the following addition :

You should inform Foreign Minister that if, in consideration of the acceptance of mediation by Austria, Russia can agree to stop mobilization, it appears still to be possible to preserve peace.— E 135.

This Austrian proposal, which was in direct opposition to the view taken by Sazonov, was rejected by the Russian Government. This is clearly shown by the fact that the reply is not mentioned in the English Blue Book. The first intimation Berlin had of the favourable reception of the Austrian Note in London, and of Grey's conversion to the right view of the Russian mobilization, was through the English Blue Book. The only communication received on the 2nd of August was a telegram from Lichnowsky, saying he had been told at the Foreign Office that "Austria now seemed willing to agree to her points of dispute with Serbia being discussed by a Conference of four Powers in London. But the communication had come too late to be of any practical use " (D 687). What really came too late was Grey's recognition that the suspension of Russia's mobilization was above all things necessary for the maintenance of general peace. If Mensdorff told him all that was in the Note, Grey's having not only said nothing, later on, about Germany's efforts to act as mediator, which were fully described in it, but directly denied them, is incomprehensible.

12. GERMANY AND AUSTRIA-HUNGARY DECLARE WAR ON RUSSIA.

Active progress was made with the preparations for war in France on the 1st of August. The cavalry regiments stationed on the frontier had taken up their war positions the day before, and the mounted troops brought by train from more distant garrisons arrived very early in the morning. The five frontier corps were ready for war.[1]

At eight o'clock in the morning General Joffre demanded general mobilization, and said that if it was not ordered he must resign his command. A Ministerial Council, which sat from nine o'clock till midday, decided to comply with the Commander-in-Chief's request, and to refuse to answer the German enquiry. The War Minister was authorized to hold back the order for mobilization for a few hours, but at 3.30 Joffre appeared for the second time, and was given the document he wanted. A quarter of an hour later the order was being flashed over the telegraph wires. Viviani then came to tell Messimy that on hearing from him (Viviani) that Russia had agreed to suspend her mobilization—which was incorrect—and that Austria consented to her ultimatum being discussed, the German Ambassador had said there was a " gleam of hope ". But, after telephoning an enquiry to the General Staff, the War Minister replied :

It is too late, the machinery has been set in motion.[2]

An admission which spoke volumes. So even then, if it had been true that Russia had agreed to put a stop to her mobilization, it would have been " too late," according to French evidence, because France had mobilized. The following report, telegraphed by the Russian military attaché, when Isvolsky informed Sazonov of the mobilization, is even more eloquent : Messimy wished influence to be

[1] Reichstag Committee of Enquiry, Part 2, p. 77 ; Romberg, p. 42.
[2] Messimy, in the *Revue de France*, August 1, 1921 ; further, F 125.

brought to bear to induce Serbia to be quicker in taking the offensive, and to be kept *au courant* himself as to the date when Russia would start her offensive against Germany.[1]

Those were not the unofficial utterances of irresponsible military men ; they were wishes expressed by one Government to another. An explanation was then sent to London, which was quite untrue, namely, that German mobilization was " in full swing ", consequently French mobilization was an " essential measure of protection " ; if war broke out, it would be clear from which side the aggression came (F 127). Again an admision that the one who first orders general mobilization is the aggressor.

Berlin was no more deceived than Paris as to the position on the 1st of August. It was known that the French covering troops were being assembled along the whole frontier (D 609.) At midday the Federal Council authorized the Chancellor, in the event of Russia and France refusing to make satisfactory statements, to tell both the Powers that they had brought about a state of war with the German Empire (D 553). As Count Pourtalès' report of his midnight interview was not regarded as Russia's final answer to the German ultimatum, the Note sent to St. Petersburg, shortly before 1 p.m., provided both for its rejection and for a refusal to give any answer (D 542). It is true that the German declaration of war on Russia was nothing more than public acknowledgment of a position which had become inevitable, in consequence of Russian general mobilization, but it was none the less a political error. According to the German plan of campaign, Germany had no military interest in hastening the commencement of operations in the east. It seems that the step was taken more for formal legal reasons, and it is the more to be regretted, because, according to the facts now known, if Germany had waited a little longer, France would probably have forestalled her declaration of war, just as she forestalled her mobilization.

About an hour after the document had been sent off to Pourtalès, a fifth telegram from the Tsar to the Emperor William arrived :

[1] Romberg, p. 44.

I received your telegram. Understand that you are compelled to mobilize, but wish to have the same guarantee from you as I gave you, that these measures do not mean war, and that we shall continue negotiating for the benefit of our countries, and universal peace, dear to all our hearts. Our long proved friendship must succeed, with God's help, in avoiding bloodshed. Anxiously, with confidence await your answer.

This was fresh confirmation of Germany's efforts to mediate, and at the same time the Tsar recognized that Germany's mobilization, which had not yet taken place (!), was a matter of course, and thus at last admitted that Russia had mobilized against Germany, which had been denied the day before. As to the credibility of the remaining asseverations, we need only recall the answer sent a few hours later to King George, (p. 179), containing nothing but untruths.

At five o'clock in the afternoon, when no answer had come from St. Petersburg to the ultimatum of the day before, the order for mobilization was given in Germany (D 554), the last of the four Great Powers entering on war to give this order. An hour later the answer came from Paris :

France will do what her interests demand.—D 571.

The information Viviani added, as to Russia's alleged willingness to put a stop to her mobilization, was all the more curious, as the Tsar himself had admitted the contrary four hours earlier. With the receipt of the French answer, the moment contemplated for declaring war on France had arrived, but shortly before this, Lichnowsky had telegraphed that Grey had said " if Germany did not attack France, England would remain neutral, and would guarantee France's neutrality " (D 562, 570).

With marvellous optimism, and a blindness to France's will for war, which was almost inconceivable in view of the documents now made public, the Emperor and the Chancellor grasped at the possibility of avoiding war with their western neighbour. William II. suggested concentrating the whole German army in the east, but Moltke replied that, for technical reasons, they must first be allowed to assemble on both fronts, as provided, and the troops could then be sent from west to east.[1] Both King George and his Minister were accordingly informed that Germany agreed to the proposal, if England would guarantee France's absolute neutrality till the end of the Russo-German conflict, with all her armed forces. The concentration of troops in the west, which had already begun, could not indeed be altered now, but if England gave this promise the German troops would not cross the French frontier for another forty-eight hours (7 p.m. on the 3rd of August) (D. 575, 578, 579). The order to the regiments which were not mobilized, to occupy the German railways in Luxemburg at once, was cancelled.[2]

Whilst all this was going on, Goschen had a long interview with Jagow. The Ambassador had received a telegram from Grey, saying that Russia had announced Austria's willingness for discussions—nothing was said in the telegram as to the subject to be discussed—and Russia (Austria?) had stated that she would agree to mediation which would not be open to the same objections as Sazonov's first formula. It was very easy for Jagow to reply that the credit for the continuance of direct conversations was due to Germany, and that naturally Russia must counter-order her mobilization, as a prior condition of the mediation in question (D 595, E 131, 138).[3] Grey himself telegraphed this view to St. Petersburg about the same time (E 135).

At nine o'clock in the evening there was still no answer from St. Petersburg to the ultimatum of the 31st.[4] By this time the hope of avoiding war with France, which had been raised by the news from London, seems to have extended

---

[1] Moltke, pp. 19 f.   [2] Loc. cit., p. 22.
[3] The mention of Austria in E 131, as being willing to accept mediation, is probably a mistake, as D 595 mentions Russia, and Austria knew nothing about the first Sazonov formula.*
[4] The telegram was held up by the Russian authorities, and only communicated to the Foreign Office by the Ambassador on his arrival in Berlin.

---

* D 595 quotes Sir Edward Goschen as follows :

BERLIN, *August* 1, 1914.

" Sir Edward Grey states that he hears from the Russian Government that the Austro-Hungarian Government are prepared to discuss matters with the Russian Government, and that the Russian Government are prepared to accept mediation as the basis of such discussion, a basis which is not open to the objections which were raised to the formula originally suggested by Russia."—[TR.]

to a hope that war with Russia might perhaps be avoided as well. In order to expedite matters, William II. sent an urgent telegram *en clair* to the Tsar at 10 p.m. :

> Thanks for your telegram. I yesterday pointed out to your Government the way in which alone war may be avoided. Although I requested an answer by noon to-day, no telegram from my Ambassador has reached me up to now, conveying an answer from your Government. I have therefore been obliged to mobilize my army. Immediate, affirmative, clear, and unmistakable answer from your Government is the only way to avoid endless misery. Until I have received this answer, alas, I am unable to discuss the subject of your telegram. As a matter of fact I must request you to immediately order your troops on no account to commit the slightest act of trespassing over our frontiers.—D 600.

But this hope was to be quickly dispelled. In the meantime not only had news of the French mobilization arrived (D 590), but also a long despatch from Lichnowsky. Grey had first informed him that the Cabinet considered the German answer, as regards the neutrality of Belgium, a matter of very great regret. But the Minister replied in the negative to the Ambassador's question whether he could make a definite statement as to what England's attitude would be in case Germany respected the neutrality of the Kingdom. Grey then, for his part, put the question, which has been suppressed in the English Blue Book, whether, in case of a Russian war, it would not be possible for Germany and France to remain armed without attacking one another. But he gave a hesitating answer to the counter-question whether France would agree to this, and said he would enquire (D 596, E 123). An hour later Lichnowsky reported that this conversation disposed of the English suggestion (D 603). A telegram from King George spoke of a " misunderstanding " (D 612).[1] The truth was that Grey had made his suggestion " without having communicated with France, and without being aware of the mobilization ", as he informed Lichnowsky later (D 361). That meant, therefore, that France had rejected the proposal Germany had accepted, and on the plea that, as she had already

[1] Delivered in Berlin at 11 p.m., *Deutsche Allgemeine Zeitung*, October 11, 1921, No. 477.

mobilized, it was no longer possible for her to remain passive.[1]

At 7 p.m. (= 6 p.m. German time) on the 1st of August Count Pourtalès had addressed the question contained in the ultimatum three times in succession to Sazonov, who had answered it three times in the negative, whereupon the Ambassador handed him the declaration of war (D 588). His telegram to that effect did not reach Berlin till the morning of the 2nd of August, nor did any answer come from the Tsar to the Kaiser's last suggestion. On the other hand, there were reports that small Russian detachments had crossed the frontier (D 629). Although it was unnecessary to attach too much importance to this, still, combined with the obvious fact that telegraphic communication had been cut off, there could no longer be any doubt that the Russian answer to the question of suspending mobilization had been in the negative.

Russia's decision was known earlier in Paris than in Berlin. Isvolsky had been able to convey it to Poincaré at 11 p.m. on the 1st of August. On hearing it, the President gave the Ambassador the most positive assurance that both he and the whole Cabinet were firmly determined to carry out in full the obligations imposed on them by the treaty of alliance. But this, he said,

raised a succession of extremely complicated questions, both of a political and strategical nature. In the first place, according to the French constitution, it was necessary to obtain the consent of Parliament before war could be declared, and at least two days would be required to summon a meeting of the Chamber. Although Poincaré had no doubt as to the result, he would prefer to avoid a public debate regarding the application of the treaty of alliance. On these grounds, and for reasons which mainly concerned England, it would be better if the declaration of war were made by Germany, not by France. It must further be remembered that to-day was only the first day of mobilization, and that it would be more to the advantage of both allies if France did not begin her military operations till her mobilization was further advanced. . . .[2]

A Ministerial Council concurred with Poincaré's opinion on all points, from which it is perfectly clear that France

[1] None of the telegrams sent from London to Paris on the 1st of August are to be found in the English Blue Book.
[2] Romberg, p. 45.

only refrained from immediately declaring war on Germany
mainly out of consideration for England, and also in order
to avoid a public debate regarding the application of the
Franco-Russian treaty of alliance. By the terms of this
treaty, France was only bound to mobilize if one of the
Triple Alliance Powers had previously mobilized, and, by
the alteration made in 1906, which has been concealed from
the French people till now, only if that Power were Germany.[1]
The French people are still in ignorance of the text of the
military convention which was valid in 1914, and are still
under the delusion that the mobilization ordered in 1914
was the fulfilment of an obligation of the alliance.

Austria-Hungary immediately recognized the existence
of a state of war with Russia. The day before Germany
declared war the Austrian General Staff had already notified
the concentration of the rest of the army in Galicia, and
the Emperor Francis Joseph had made an appeal for joint
action against Russia (D 498, 482). The Austrian monarch
telegraphed to the King of Italy on the 1st of August his
firm hope " that he might rely on the support of the allies "
(A III. 100A). The following day Count Berchtold asked
Italy to recognize that the *casus fœderis* had arisen under
the terms of the Triple Alliance (A III. 106), and on the
3rd of August he submitted the draft of a declaration of
war on Russia to the Emperor (A III. 124). The declaration was not sent till the 5th (D 860) purely for military
reasons, " to enable the concentration of troops in Galicia
to proceed without interruption for as long as possible "
(D 772). It had to be sent via Sweden, and was consequently only delivered on the 6th of August (A III. 161).

13. GERMANY DECLARES WAR ON FRANCE AND FRANCE ON AUSTRIA-HUNGARY.

When once France, and then Germany, had mobilized,
and a state of war existed between the German Empire and
Russia, declaration of a state of war between Germany
and France was purely a matter of form. In addition to
that, the concentration of large bodies of troops on the

[1] General Staff protocol, Russian Blue Book, pp. 697 ff.

frontier had led to slight collisions. It can easily be understood that, after forty-four years of peace, a few ambitious young officers on both sides were anxious to have the honour of striking the first blow, in spite of strict orders to the contrary. According to the German General Staff, German patrols overstepped the road frontiers about forty times, and French detachments about fifty-six times. In eleven cases the reports stated that they were fired upon.[1] As early as on the 2nd of August the French Government were considering the possibility of turning the German frontier violations to account, while suppressing their own, and informing Parliament on the 4th that " France had been attacked ", in order to avoid making " a formal declaration of war ".[2] Besides this, the agitation against subjects of the Central Powers resident in Paris had begun, and their diplomatic representatives were being treated in a manner which was contrary to international law.

From the morning of the 3rd of August onwards all the cipher telegrams that passed between the German Foreign Office and the Embassy in Paris were mutilated to such an extent that they could only be partially deciphered, or not at all.[3] The Bavarian Minister was obliged to leave his house, on account of the attitude of the people, and to take refuge with the staff of the Legation in the German Embassy, where the attitude of the crowd also became threatening in the evening.[4] German and Austro-Hungarian subjects were driven out of their homes, their business premises were plundered, and the members of the staffs of both the Embassies could hardly venture to show themselves in the streets or the public restaurants any longer (A III. 119). The newspapers found fault with the German Ambassador for not having left yet, and urged him to " hurry off ". Even at the Quai d'Orsay his remaining in Paris seemed to give dissatisfaction, for his Austrian colleague reported on the evening of August 3 :

The long delay of the German Government in recalling their Ambassador, when hostilities had begun on *both sides*,[5] made a bad impression here.—A III. 120.

[1] Vide App. I. No. 27, p. 243. [2] Romberg, p. 48.
[3] D 716, 734a, 749, 776, 809. [4] Bavarian Documents, p. 183.
[5] The italics are the author's.

In the meantime it had also occurred to the authorities in Berlin to make the French raids across the frontier a reason for declaring war. Just as in Paris, they forgot how unreliable such reports are in times of extreme tension, for troops unaccustomed to war, and, even more often, the terrified inhabitants of frontier districts are apt to see the enemy in imagination where there is none. It would have been better to do as had been originally intended, and simply say : " As France gives no assurance that she will remain neutral, Germany cannot leave her to choose the date on which to carry out the threat to the German western frontiers " (D 608). The declaration of war, sent to Herr von Schoen on the 3rd of August, to be transmitted at 6 p.m., arrived, like all the telegrams sent in cipher at that time, in such a mutilated condition that the parts relating to French violations of the frontier by ground forces, on which most stress was laid, could not be deciphered. For instance, the first sentence of the telegram read as follows : " *Deutsche Erwehrungen hatten Brennerei kel italienischer Botschafter* ". On the other hand, later passages, which dealt with air raids in general, were partially decipherable, and the sentence, " Yesterday French airmen dropped bombs on the railway at Carlsruhe and Nuremberg " was perfectly legible (D 734a). This was the origin of the legend that Germany declared war on France solely on the ground of a report that bombs had been dropped on Nuremberg, which is well known to have been based on a mistake.[1]

A state of war between Austria and the Western Powers was a matter of course, as soon as it existed between them and Germany. Count Berchtold had already instructed the Austrian Ambassador in London to state this on the 2nd of August (A III. 112). But as they were anxious about the Austrian Fleet, which had not yet been mobilized, the Vienna Government postponed declaring war till the 12th of August, with Germany's consent. They were consequently forestalled by France, who declared war on the ground that the Tirolese Army Corps had been sent to Germany. In reality it had been sent to the Galician

[1] Vide Part IV. sect. 9, p. 220.

front, without passing through Germany.[1] This was a far greater mistake than the one made by Germany with regard to the Nuremberg bombs.

14. ENGLAND DECLARES WAR ON GERMANY.

England's attitude in the crises of 1908–9 and 1911 had encouraged the war parties in France and Russia. The language of the Foreign Office was more reserved during the 1912–13 period of anxiety, although even then Poincaré asserted that " from the tone and nature of the assurances given by the British Government, he thought he could rely on England's armed support, under the present political conditions, in case of a conflict with Germany ".[2] In 1914 Grey and his colleagues showed less reserve than a year and a half before.

As far back as on the 27th of July the Under-Secretary of State, Nicolson, gave the German Ambassador to understand that, in case of a European war, England would not pledge herself to remain neutral, and he also informed the French Ambassador of this at once (F 63). On the same day it was publicly announced that the demobilization of the British Fleet had been postponed (F 66). On the 29th Grey personally repeated the hint Nicolson had given Lichnowsky, that he was " not to be misled by the friendly tone of the conversations into believing that England would stand aside ". And again Cambon was informed, this time in advance, of the warning given to Germany (E 87). The attitude the British Minister would personally adopt in case of war was consequently decided before the question of Belgian neutrality was raised.

The mobilized British Fleet proceeded to its war stations as far back as on the morning of the 29th, and in the afternoon the " warning telegram ", corresponding to the " state of imminent danger of war ", was sent out, both to the Navy and Army—two days earlier than in Germany.[3] The circumstance that the powerful British Navy had been ready for war since the middle of July, in consequence of

[1] A III. 163, 165, 166, 169, 170, 173, 175.
[2] *Livre Noir*, Vol. II. pp. 32 f.
[3] Corbett, *History of the Great War* (*Naval Operations*), pp. 26 and 28.

the test mobilization, had a very bad effect on the development of the crisis, for the hasty measures taken by the British Admiralty and the fact of the greatest battleships that had ever been launched having put to sea, made an immense impression on the Russian war party, and convinced them that Great Britain would fight on the side of Russia.[1]

On the 30th of July, the day after the Fleet had put to sea, the French Ambassador reminded Grey of the correspondence of November 1912, and, according to Cambon's report, the answer he received, which is not given in the English Blue Book, was that Grey shared his view that " the moment had come to consider and discuss together every hypothesis " (E 105, F 108). But even on the 31st of July, a day later, the Cabinet did not consider that the moment had come to assure France that England would intervene (E 119, F 110). The British Ambassador in Paris was therefore to be instructed as follows :

> No one here considers that in this dispute, so far as it has yet gone, British treaties or obligations are involved. Feeling is quite different to what it was during the Moroccan question. That crisis involved a dispute which directly concerned France, whereas France is now being drawn into a dispute which is not hers.—E 116.

Cambon, who refused to report this decision to Paris,[2] was assured by Nicolson that the question of intervention would be brought before the Cabinet again the very next day, and both Grey and the Under Secretary gave him to understand that Belgian neutrality would play an important part in the discussion (F 110). The next morning a Cabinet Council did, in fact, adopt the resolution reported by Lichnowsky in the evening, that the German answer with regard to Belgium was a matter of very great regret (p. 191). The French Ambassador was informed of this at once, and was further told that when the Cabinet met on Monday (the 3rd of August) Grey would propose that the British Fleet should oppose the passage of the Straits of Dover by the German Fleet, or any operations against the French North Sea coasts. In saying this the Foreign

[1] Reports by the St. Petersburg correspondent of *The Times*, at the end of July 1914.
[2] *Revue de France*, July 1, 1921, p. 38.

Secretary gave his personal assurance of armed naval support, although, according to reports received in London, general mobilization had been ordered in Russia some time before it was ordered in Austria (E 113, 127), and although Germany had not mobilized at all yet, to say nothing of having made no declaration of war. King George, however, gave another evasive answer to Poincaré's request of the previous day, that England should declare her solidarity with France and Russia.[1]

Contrary to all custom, the English Cabinet met on Sunday (the 2nd of August) instead of Monday. Grey was unable to carry his point at the first meeting. Then a letter came from the leader of the Conservative Party, Bonar Law, to the Prime Minister, Asquith, urging the Government to support France and Russia.[2] The Cabinet then decided, at a second meeting, to protect France against possible German naval operations, subject to the approval of Parliament (E 148, F 137). To Cambon this meant that " the game was won ". A great country, he writes in his memoirs, cannot wage war " by halves " ; once it decides to fight at sea, it must also fight on land.[3] It is evident now how very much England had tied her hands by the naval agreement concluded with France in the autumn of 1912, in consequence of which France sent the remaining portion of her fleet to the Mediterranean, leaving her northern coasts unprotected (p. 112). In a conversation with Lichnowsky, Asquith not only referred to the question of Belgian neutrality, but also to the unprotected north coasts of France, pointing out that the French had left their northern coasts exposed, in order to reinforce their Mediterranean fleet, " relying on British support " (D 676). This second reason for going to war influenced England earlier than the first, for no German soldier had put foot on Belgian soil, nor had the ultimatum been presented to the Belgian Government as yet. In the evening the Cabinet sanctioned the step the Admiralty had taken the first thing in the morning, of calling up the Naval Reserves— the last stage of mobilization.[4]

[1] Poincaré, pp. 276–7.   [2] *The Times*, December 15, 1914.
[3] *Revue de France*, July 1, 1921.   [4] Corbett, p. 29.

On the 3rd of August Germany, acting on the advice of her Ambassador in London, gave an assurance that she would not undertake naval operations of any kind against France (D 714). When Lichnowsky executed this commission, he was given the surprising information that, according to reports received from the British Ambassador in Vienna, the opinion in London [1] was that Germany was the aggressor, and that consequently Austria was not bound to recognize an obligation arising out of the alliance (D 764). The continued slanderous reports from France of premature German steps towards mobilization, and violation of French territory, had taken effect. In the meantime, under pressure from the Foreign Office, the Belgian Ambassador was trying to obtain reports from Brussels of any violation of Belgian neutrality by Germany.[2] Although these efforts were unavailing, orders were given at 11 a.m. to mobilize the British Expeditionary Force.[3]

Before the House of Commons met, on the 3rd of August, Grey told the French Ambassador that the statement with regard to British naval help might be considered binding (F 143). The Foreign Secretary then made his great speech in Parliament, the gist of it being that, in view of France having left her northern coasts unprotected, relying on England's friendship, and of her own interest in Belgium, England could not remain neutral.[4] The great majority of the House were of the same opinion. In the evening a Cabinet Council resolved to request Germany to withdraw the ultimatum handed to Belgium at 7 p.m. on the 2nd of August, with a time limit of twelve hours, and to respect Belgian neutrality.[5]

At 7 p.m. on the 4th of August Sir Edward Goschen handed England's final demands to the German Government, with a time limit of five hours for an answer, in accordance with the Cabinet's decision (D 839, E 160). At midnight the European war had become a world war.

---

[1] This is obviously a mistake. Lichnowsky's report, to which the author refers, mentions what Sir William Tyrrell had given him (Lichnowsky) to understand was the opinion in Austria (not London), according to telegrams from Sir Maurice de Bunsen.—[TR.]
[2] *Deutsche Allgemeine Zeitung*, May 22, 1919, No. 246.
[3] Haldane, p. 35.   [4] English Blue Book, II. p. 93.
[5] Poincaré, p. 280.

15. SEVENTEEN CONCLUSIONS.

1.

Germany pursued no aim either in Europe or elsewhere which could only be achieved by means of war.

Austria-Hungary's only aim was to maintain the *status quo*. Her first intention of rectifying her frontiers at Serbia's expense was immediately abandoned at Germany's instance, and even Sazonov was convinced of her territorial *désintéressement* by her definite statements (A III. 19).

France aimed at recovering Alsace Lorraine, and many leading French politicians also hoped to annex the Saar basin, whilst Russia aspired to possession of Constantinople and the Straits, both Powers knowing well that these aims could not be achieved without a European war.

2.

Germany's preparations for war were on a considerably smaller scale than those made by France, having regard to the political constellation, her geographical position, the extent of her unprotected frontiers, and the number of her population. From 1913 onwards, even her actual numerical peace strength was less, in respect of white troops, quite apart from the steadily increasing strength of the French coloured troops.

As compared with Russia's armaments, those of Austria-Hungary were absolutely inadequate.

The Franco-Russian allies were far superior to the Central Powers as regards the amount of war material, as well as of man power at their disposal.

3.

It was a political mistake to construct a German battle fleet, instead of completing the naval defences, but even in London the proportion of ten to sixteen Dreadnoughts finally proposed by Germany was not regarded as a menace.

4.

Even after Bismarck's time the German Empire repeatedly omitted to take advantage of favourable opportunities for a war of prevention.

5.

The Russian suggestion of the first Hague Conference was not based on pure love of peace. All the Great Powers, without exception, were most sceptical as regards the question of reducing armaments ; the Russian proposal of 1899 was unanimously rejected, and public opinion in France strongly opposed Campbell-Bannerman's 1907 suggestion.

Neither at the first nor the second Hague Conference was any proposal to adjust serious international conflicts, affecting the honour and vital interests of a nation, brought forward or supported by any Great Power.

6.

The world war was not decided upon at Potsdam on the 5th of July, 1914 ; Germany merely assented to Austria's going to war with Serbia.

The possibility that the Austro-Serbian war, like others— the Boer, Moroccan, Tripolitan, and Balkan wars—might lead to further complications, was well weighed, but the risk was thought very small, in view of the special provocation.

7.

After the publication of the Serbian reply, Germany no longer thought war advisable, even against Serbia, and only favoured strictly limited military operations, which were considered justifiable, even in London.

8.

It is true that Germany did not support the proposal to extend the time limit, and rejected the idea of a conference. She not only, however, accepted every other proposal of mediation which came from London, but proposed on her own initiative the two most suitable methods of negotiation, namely, direct conversations between Vienna and St. Petersburg, and the idea of not going beyond Belgrade, which was adopted by Grey.

Sazonov's first formula was considered unacceptable, even in London, and the second was far worse than the first.

9.

An understanding had almost been reached by the methods Germany had been the first to propose, namely, direct discussions between Vienna and St. Petersburg, and limiting the military operations against Serbia, when the Russian mobilization suddenly tore the threads asunder.

10.

The leading men knew just as well in Paris and St. Petersburg as in Berlin, that this mobilization must inevitably lead to war.

Viviani telegraphed to London on the 1st of August that the one who first orders general mobilization is the aggressor, and he saddled Germany with this responsibility, knowing that the accusation was false.

11.

France did not advise moderation in St. Petersburg during the crisis. Finding that the first attempt to do so had annoyed Sazonov, the French Government refrained from taking any further steps in this direction.

12.

France not only did not advise Russia against ordering general mobilization, but gave surreptitious advice as to how she could carry on her military preparations secretly without provoking Germany to take timely counter-measures.

13.

Russia was the first Power to order general mobilization. France was the first Power to inform another Power officially of her decision to take part in a European war.

14.

England was never as firm in advising moderation in St. Petersburg as Germany in giving this advice to Vienna. Unlike other British diplomats, Sir Edward Grey only

realized the meaning of the Russian mobilization when
it was too late, and St. Petersburg was no longer willing
to put a stop to it.

15.

Germany's premature declaration of war on Russia was
a political error, which can be accounted for by the immense
danger of the position on two fronts ; her declaration of
war on France was a pure formality.

The decisive event was not this or that declaration of
war, but the action which made the declaration of war
inevitable, and this action was Russia's general mobilization.

16.

England declared war on Germany because she did not
consider it compatible with her interests that France should
be defeated a second time. Belgian interests, and the
treaty of 1839, which Lord Salisbury had been prepared
to sacrifice in 1887, were the reasons adduced to make it
popular.

Over and above this, the naval agreement of 1912 with
France compelled England to abandon her neutrality
before Belgium's neutrality was violated.

17.

Greater diplomatic skill was shown by the Entente than
by the Triple Alliance Powers.

By her false statements regarding Germany's preparations for war, particularly regarding the alleged priority
of the German mobilization, by magnifying insignificant
incidents on the frontier into invasions of French territory,
and by withdrawing her covering troops to a distance of
ten kilometres from the frontier,[1] France created the prior
condition in London, which Benckendorff had indicated,
as far back as at the end of 1912, as necessary for England's
intervention. An impression was produced in London that
" the opponents of the Entente were the aggressors ".[2]

---

[1] As to this *ruse*, to deceive public opinion, vide Part IV. sect. 8, pp. 217 ff.
[2] Siebert, p. 588.

PART IV

INCIDENTS OF THE CRISIS

1. Szögyény's Telegram of July 5.

In his *Réponse au Kaiser*, Viviani speaks of a " terrible " telegram sent by the Austrian Ambassador in Berlin on the 5th of July. This telegram reports an interview with the Kaiser at midday on the 5th of July, and is as follows (A I. 6) :

When I had let the Emperor William know that I had an autograph letter to give him from His most gracious Majesty the Emperor and Apostolic King, which Count Hoyos had brought me to-day, I received an invitation from their German Majesties to lunch at the Neue Palais to-day.

I handed the letter and enclosed memorandum to His Majesty. The Emperor read both documents in my presence with the greatest attention.

First of all His Majesty assured me that he had expected us to take strong action against Serbia, but after what our most gracious Sovereign had explained, he must admit the necessity of keeping a serious European complication in view, and therefore he would not give any answer until he had conferred with the Imperial Chancellor.

After lunch, when I again pointed out, with the greatest emphasis, how serious the position was, His Majesty authorized me to inform our most gracious Sovereign that in this case, as in all others, we could rely on Germany's full support. As already stated, he must first hear the Imperial Chancellor's opinion, but he had not the slightest doubt that Herr von Bethmann Hollweg would entirely agree with him, particularly as regards action on our part against Serbia. But in his (the Emperor's) opinion, this action ought not to be delayed. Russia's attitude would be hostile in any case, he had been prepared for this for years, however, and even if it came to war between Austria-Hungary and Russia, we might be sure that Germany would stand by us with her customary loyalty to the treaty of alliance. Moreover, as things were now, Russia was not by any means ready for war, and certainly would not appeal to arms without thinking it over very carefully. But she would rouse the other Powers against us, and fan the flame in the Balkans.

He quite understood that it would be very hard for His Imperial and Royal Apostolic Majesty, whose love of peace was well known, to march upon Serbia ; but if we really had recognized the necessity of taking military action against Serbia, he (the Emperor William) would be sorry if we did not take advantage of the present moment, which was so favourable for us.

As far as Rumania was concerned, he would see that King Carol and his advisers adopted the proper attitude.

He did not at all care about entering into an alliance with Bulgaria ; he had never had the smallest confidence in King Ferdinand or in his advisers, either past or present. In spite of that, he would not make the least objection to the Monarchy's entering into a treaty of alliance with Bulgaria, but care must be taken that it was not directed against Rumania, and—as pointed out in the memorandum—Rumania must be informed of it.

The Emperor intends leaving for Kiel early to-morrow morning, and starting on his northern cruise from there ; but His Majesty will talk over the matter in question with the Imperial Chancellor before he goes, and has sent to Hohenfinow to command his attendance at the Neue Palais this evening, for that purpose.

Anyhow I shall find an opportunity of conferring with the Imperial Chancellor in the course of to-morrow.

It will be seen that the Emperor would not " give any definite answer " before lunch, and it was only afterwards that he promised Germany's full support, in case of a European complication, apparently under pressure from the Ambassador. He added, however, that Russia was " not ready for war yet " and would " certainly think over the question of appealing to arms very carefully ". In conclusion, he again said that he would consult the Chancellor. The result of this interview between the Emperor and the Chancellor in the afternoon of the 5th was the instruction sent to Tschirschky on the 6th of July (D 15), which must be regarded as the official German view.

Herr von Bethmann informed Count Szögyény the next day (July 6) of the result of the interview he had with the Emperor, after the Austrian Ambassador left, and the latter then sent a second report which exactly coincides with the instruction sent to Tschirschky (A I. 7). In adding that in the further course of the conversation he had gained the impression that both the Chancellor and the Emperor would consider " immediate action " the " most radical and the best solution " of the Austrian difficulties in the Balkans, the Ambassador meant that they wished action against Serbia to be taken quickly, while the impression made by the murder was still fresh, in which they were perfectly right.

A comparison of Szögyény's two reports of the 5th and 6th of July shows that the tone of the first is stronger, on account of the sentence " even if it came to war between Austria-Hungary and Russia, we might be sure that Germany would stand by us, with her customary loyalty to the treaty of alliance ", which does not occur in the second report. The expression " terrible " used by Viviani with regard to this telegram obviously applies to these words, which, however, ought not to be read without the qualifying sentence as to Russia's unreadiness for war. In any case, if the Vienna Government had really thought this sentence made a difference between the two telegrams, they could not, according to generally recognized principles, have regarded the first report of the 5th of July, concerning a conversation which the Emperor William expressly pointed out was not yet binding, as official, in preference to the second report, which gave the view expressed by the Chancellor, as the responsible director of Germany's policy, after consultation with the Emperor.

In his book, *Der deutsch-englische Gegensatz, und sein Einfluss auf die Balkan Politik Oesterreich-Ungarn* (p. 80), Count Hoyos says he gained the impression that the German Government were in favour of " immediate action " against Serbia, and that Bethmann " considered the present moment more favourable, from the international standpoint, than later on ". In this he is right, but he is mistaken in the conclusion he draws that their wish to expedite the action was equivalent to " unreserved " support of the Austrian " war policy ". " Under all circumstances " were just the words the Chancellor struck out of the draft of the instruction submitted to him.

2. THE LEGEND OF THE CROWN COUNCIL OF JULY 5.

In July 1917 a report was circulated by enemy propaganda in foreign countries that a Crown Council was held at Potsdam on the 5th of July, 1914, which was presided over by the Kaiser, and attended by the principal German and Austrian civil and military authorities, and that war against Russia and France was decided upon at this Council. A question having been asked in the Reichstag as to these reports, a higher official of the Ministry of the Interior wrote a letter to his Chief on the 2nd of August, 1917, giving the following report of how the legend originated (this letter is now amongst the Foreign Office documents) :

On the evening of the 5th of July, Herr Stein, the correspondent of the *Frankfurter Zeitung*, was at a well-known restaurant in Potsdam. A number of men came into the restaurant whom Stein at once recognized as officers of high rank, especially as Conrad von Hötzendorf and Moltke were among them. The officers went into a room reserved for them. After a time, the manager of the restaurant came to Herr Stein in some excitement. He said that the waiter who was serving the officers had just told him that they were talking of war with Russia, as though it were an accomplished fact, and asked what Stein thought of that.

Herr Stein was questioned about the incident by the Foreign Office, and he declared that the statement was a " pure invention ". What really happened was as follows : " He was sitting in the Kaiserhof Hotel in Berlin between ten and eleven o'clock in the evening, on the 5th of July, when one of the employees of the hotel came to his neighbour and whispered to him that a waiter, who was serving some officers of the Guards from Potsdam at an adjoining table, had heard that a meeting of Austrian and German diplomats and military men had taken place that day at Potsdam—Szögyény, Bethmann Hollweg, and Zimmermann were mentioned—and that the Emperor had given up his trip to Norway on this account ".

The " Austrian military men " were, no doubt, the members of the Austro-Hungarian Embassy who had appeared in military uniform, as reserve officers, and this hotel talk was the origin of the legend. As it is still asserted, now and then, in foreign countries, that a conference took place on the 5th of July, which was attended by most of the German Ambassadors and by the principal naval and military authorities and the directors of the great banks, in spite of the detailed statement in the preface to the *Deutschen Dokumenten zum Kriegsausbruch*, it may be explicitly stated that

1. According to the Foreign Office records, the following Ambassadors were at their posts on the 5th of July : Herr von Tschirschky in Vienna, Count Pourtalès in St. Petersburg, Freiherr von Schoen in Paris, Herr von Flotow in Rome ; Prince Lichnowsky took over the conduct of the Embassy in London again on the 6th, and was consequently on his way there on the 5th. Herr von Wangenheim (Constantinople) was on leave, but, according to the evidence of his widow, he was neither in Berlin nor in Potsdam on the 5th of July. Even the Foreign Secretary, Herr von Jagow, was on leave, and only resumed work at the Foreign Office on the 7th.

2. Of the military men, the Chief of the General Staff, Moltke, was taking the waters at Carlsbad; his deputy, Count Waldersee, had gone to the funeral of an aunt in Hanover; the First Lord of the Admiralty, von Tirpitz, and the Chief of the Admiralty Staff, von Pohl, were on leave.

3. Bank directors were never invited to attend Crown Councils in Wilhelminic Germany.

3. THE EMPEROR WILLIAM'S ALLEGED INSTRUCTION TO TSCHIRSCHKY.

On the 8th of July, 1914, Count Berchtold wrote to Count Tisza :

Tschirschky has just left me. He informed me that he had received a telegram from Berlin, in which his Imperial master commissions him to state emphatically here that Berlin expects Austria to take action against Serbia, and that if we let the right moment pass without striking a blow, it would not be understood in Germany. . . .—A I. 10.

It will be seen that the Austrian Minister does not speak of a telegram from the Emperor, but of a " telegram from Berlin ", in which the Emperor, etc. These expressions coincide exactly with the instruction the Chancellor sent Tschirschky on the 6th of July (D 15). It was telegraphed from Berlin, not from Potsdam, where the Emperor was staying, and in this telegram Bethmann spoke of the instruction as being given on behalf of the Emperor, who was mentioned no less than eight times. There are no further instructions to Tschirschky in existence, as will be seen from the following :

1. Every important document relating to the crisis found amongst the Berlin Foreign Office Papers, has been published from the 28th of June onwards. In addition to that, a list has been made of unimportant items, which were eliminated from the correspondence between Berlin and Vienna by the three editors, so that information as to their purport can be quickly given at any time. Herr von Tschirschky was given his fundamental instructions in the telegram of July 6, No. 113 (D 15). He does not appear to have been given any instruction with regard to the action against Serbia before the 6th of July. The next telegram after that date, No. 116, of the 10th of July (D 28, Note 2), only transmits a Bucharest telegram to the Vienna Embassy. Accordingly the only telegrams between the 6th and 10th of July, not given in the *Deutschen Dokumenten*, are Nos. 114 and 115, the first dealing with the Bulgarian loan, and endeavouring to allay the Austrian Government's doubts as to Bulgaria's general attitude, whilst the second related to the German armoured cruiser *Goeben*, which had been sent to the Mediterranean long before, remaining at Pola. Consequently no telegram from the Foreign Office to the Ambassador, relating to the Serbian question, is missing either before or after the 6th of July.

2. Nor is there any unpublished telegram, relating to the Serbian question, to be found in the archives of the German Embassy in Vienna. Professor Schücking and I asked for the Embassy papers, and examined them exhaustively, covering the whole period from the Sarajevo murder to the outbreak of war. It was from these documents that we noted the time when the Berlin telegrams were received at the German Embassy, which could not be ascertained in any other way. The notes made by Herr von Tschirschky of his conversations at the Ballplatz, as required by the Berlin Foreign Office, and which were

published by the Reichstag Committee of Enquiry, were also taken from amongst the Embassy papers.

3. In order to ascertain whether the Ambassador might possibly have put an instruction amongst his private papers, an enquiry was made of his family, which was answered in the negative. (The evidence given by Prince Hatzfeldt, Herr von Tschirschky's son-in-law, is in the possession of the Committee of Enquiry.)

4. Enquiry has also been made as to whether, contrary to all custom, the Emperor could have telegraphed direct to the Ambassador from on board the *Hohenzollern*, on which he embarked directly he arrived at Kiel, at three o'clock in the afternoon, having left Potsdam at 9.30 a.m. on the 6th of July. A telegram *en clair* was out of the question. As to the possibility of a cipher telegram, the ciphering clerks on board the *Hohenzollern* during the Norwegian cruise in 1914, have stated that ciphers for strictly confidential matters, such as would have been used in the case in question, were not taken on board at all. Telegrams could be sent in ordinary cipher, but even these all went through the Berlin Foreign Office, and it would consequently be possible to trace them in the records there. To verify this the *Hohenzollern's* letter book was examined, and the evidence given was found to be correct.

5. There was no possibility of the message having been sent to the naval attaché in Vienna, via Kiel, as the naval and military attachés had no cipher of their own, and could only send and receive cipher telegrams through the Embassies and Legations.

Consequently the only question is why Berchtold, in his letter to Tisza, gave the instruction to Tschirschky a stronger interpretation than is compatible with the text of D 15.

The explanation must be simply that the German Ambassador could not give him a copy of the despatch, as it was only intended " for his personal guidance ", therefore he had to convey his instructions verbally, and that the Austrian Foreign Minister made capital out of the " telegram from Berlin ", and the frequent references to the " Imperial master ", to influence the Hungarian Prime

Minister, who was still opposed to the action against Serbia.

In connection with this, reference must be made to another point of secondary importance, which has been seized upon by hypercritics, namely that Tschirschky was reproved for his original lukewarm attitude. As a matter of fact, Szögyény said in a telegram (No. 243), which is not in the Austrian Red book, but was sent from Berlin at 2.14 p.m. on the 8th of July :

The Foreign Secretary returned from leave yesterday. I have not been able to speak to him yet, but yesterday and to-day I had opportunities of hearing the Under Secretary and various influential Foreign Office officials express the view that our decisions are awaited with impatience here, as this is thought to be the right moment for taking energetic action against Serbia, so favourable a moment will not so easily occur again.

I was told at the Foreign Office that, from a report sent by Tschirschky, his attitude towards Your Excellency was considered here to have been rather " lukewarm ". He has been reproved for this. . . .

This telegram gives an insight into the nature of Szögyény's intercourse with the Wilhelmstrasse. He was in the habit of constantly obtaining information from a number of Foreign Office officials, not only from the Imperial Chancellor, the Foreign Secretary, and the Under Secretary, but also from their subordinates. As there is nothing about the " reproof " in the records, the only explanation is that one of the subordinate " influential officials " had heard something about the Emperor's marginal note on Tschirschky's report of the 30th of July (D 7), and had discussed it with the Austrian Ambassador.

4. Szögyény's Telegram of July 27.

On the 27th of July the Austrian Ambassador telegraphed (A II. 68) (handed in at 9.15 p.m.) :

The Foreign Secretary informed me, in the strictest confidence, that the German Government would shortly acquaint Your Excellency with possible English proposals of mediation.

The German Government give the most positive assurance that they do not identify themselves in any way with the proposals, they are even decidedly against their being considered, and they only forward them, in compliance with the English request.

In doing so they are guided by the view that it is of the utmost importance that England should not make common cause with Russia and France at the present moment. Consequently everything must be avoided that would break off the communications between Germany and England which have hitherto worked so well. If Germany were to tell Sir Edward Grey plainly that she would not forward the wish to Austria-Hungary, which England thinks more likely to be considered if it comes through Germany, this would lead to the very state of affairs it is so essential to avoid.

Moreover, whenever England made a request of this kind in Vienna, the German Government would state most explicitly that they did not in any way endorse such requests for intervention, and only passed them on to Austria-Hungary in compliance with England's wish.

The English Government, it appears, had already approached him (the Foreign Secretary) yesterday through the German Ambassador in London, and through their representative here, with a view to inducing him to support England's wish that we should modify the note to Serbia. He, von Jagow, replied that he would certainly comply with Sir Edward Grey's wish that he should forward England's request to Your Excellency, but he could not second it, as the Serbian dispute was a question of prestige for the Austro-Hungarian Monarchy, in which Germany had an interest.

He, the Foreign Secretary, had therefore forwarded Sir Edward Grey's Note to Herr von Tschirschky, but without instructing him to submit it to Your Excellency; he had then been able to inform the English Cabinet that he did not directly reject the English wish, and had even passed it on to Vienna.

In conclusion the Secretary of State repeated his view of the case, and begged me, in order to avoid any misunderstanding, to assure Your Excellency that his having acted as intermediary in this instance does not at all mean that he is in favour of the English proposal being considered.

The American delegation at Versailles only published the two first paragraphs of this telegram, which, taken by themselves, must give an impression of Machiavellism. But if the fourth paragraph is correctly read, it does away with this impression. In it the Berlin Government state that whenever an English proposal is made which they do not think suitable, they will inform the Cabinet in London that they do not support the proposal, and are merely forwarding it to Vienna, in compliance with England's request. This would have been a perfectly frank and honourable course, and it is what the German Government really did. With regard to the purport of the telegram, it should be noted : (1) that England never proposed that Austria should " modify the Note to Serbia " (paragraph 5 of the report). The Ambassador was probably referring to the proposal which reached Berlin on the evening of July 25, that Germany should try to induce Vienna to consider the Serbian answer satisfactory. Neither Berlin nor London knew what the answer was at that time. (See last paragraph describing the events of July 25, p. 131.) (2) This proposal was forwarded to Vienna, and at the same time the British Chargé d'Affaires was told that it had only been passed on, and that the Government did not see their way to going beyond this (E 34). (3) Both Herr von Bethmann Hollweg and Herr von Jagow have stated most positively that they never made any communication to the Austrian Ambassador, which would coincide with the two first paragraphs, published by the American delegation at Versailles. (4) The Austrian Ambassador, Count Szögyény, was to have been recalled some time before. It was only at the request of the German Emperor that the authorities in Vienna agreed to his holding his responsible post till the 18th of August, the Emperor Francis Joseph's birthday.[1]

5. THE SO-CALLED GERMAN ULTIMATUM OF JULY 29 TO RUSSIA.

At the meeting of the French Chamber on the 5th of July, 1922, and in his *Réponse au Kaiser*, Viviani asserted that Germany had sent Russia an ultimatum on the 29th of July. Towards noon on that day, when eight fresh official reports of Russian mobilization measures had been received in Berlin within twelve hours, five of them reporting mobilization on the German frontier, Count Pourtalès was instructed to " point out very seriously to Sazonov that a continuance of Russian mobilization

---

[1] The author wishes it stated that the comment on this despatch is the only point on which he has changed his opinion since the publication of the German edition of his book. (Comp. *Leitfaden zur Kriegsschuldfrage*, p. 176.)—[TR.]

measures would compel Germany to mobilize, and that it would then hardly be possible to prevent a European war " (D 342). The Ambassador carried out this instruction shortly before eight o'clock in the evening, and in doing so he emphasized the fact that " it was not a threat, but merely a friendly warning " (D 378).

Nicholas II. had already signed the Ukase ordering general mobilization on the morning of the 29th, long before Pourtalès spoke to Sazonov. At the eleventh hour a telegram from the German Emperor induced him to change the order into one for partial mobilization (p. 162). The true facts are, therefore, exactly the opposite of what Viviani stated. No German ultimatum was sent on the 29th; on the contrary, the Emperor William took a friendly step. When Sazonov tried to make out that the warning Pourtalès gave was not consistent with the Kaiser's telegram, it was because the Russian Minister was bent on war from the morning of July 29, onwards, as is proved by his having succeeded in securing the order for general mobilization that day.

6. The Tsar's Proposal regarding Arbitration.

The second volume of the *Livre Noir* (p. 283) gives the following letter written by Nicholas II. to Sazonov on the 27th of July :

> I will receive you to-morrow at six o'clock. I have had an idea, and in order not to lose time, which is gold, I will tell you what it is : Why should we not propose to Austria, after obtaining the assent of France and England, and then of Germany and Italy, to submit her dispute with Serbia to the Hague Court of Arbitration ? Perhaps it is not too late to do that before events occur which would be irreparable. In order to gain time, try to take this step to-day before making your report. I still hope for peace.

It will be seen that the Russian Minister was charged to ask England and France on the 27th, whether they agreed to the proposal that Austria should submit the dispute to the Hague. As neither the English Blue Book nor the French Yellow Book contain the slightest reference to any such *démarche*, Sazonov obviously did not carry out the command. Then, two days later, on the evening of the 29th, when the Kaiser's conciliatory telegram had effected the change from full mobilization to partial mobilization against Austria, the Tsar again took up his suggestion in a telegram to William II. But even now Sazonov evidently refused to entertain the idea, for he never mentioned it to the German Ambassador, who had, therefore, no occasion to express any opinion on the Tsar's telegram concerning it.

Obviously the Russian Minister thought his Sovereign's idea inexpedient and impracticable. In view of this attitude, it was really rather too much of a good thing that, in January 1915, he should have published the Tsar's telegram of July 29 in the *Messager Officiel*, as a proof of Germany's " will for war ". If the rejection of the Hague idea had really been a proof of that, the Minister would have been bringing it against himself. Not only that, but on the 27th of July, when the Tsar wrote to Sazonov, the idea might anyhow have been worth considering. But two days later, on the 29th, a procedure, which would have taken so long, could only have been considered if Russia at the same time suspended, not only her full mobilization, but also the partial mobilization which menaced Austria with forces double the strength of her own.

7. The Special Edition of the " Berliner Lokalanzeiger."

On the 30th of July a special edition of the *Berliner Lokalanzeiger*, published at 1 p.m., falsely reported German mobilization. The newspaper was confiscated at once, and no time was lost in telephoning to inform the three Entente Embassies that the news was incorrect. The Russian Ambassador, who had telegraphed the false report to St. Petersburg, contradicted it, first in a telegram *en clair*, and then in cipher. In the ten official announcements made between the 30th of July and the 2nd of August, neither the Tsar, nor his Ministers, nor the General Staff, ever attempted to give this false report as a reason for the Russian mobilization.

It was not till the beginning of December 1914, when the truth as to the order in which the mobilizations of the various States succeeded one another began to leak out, even in the Entente countries, that Sir Edward Grey tried to suggest to the Russian Government, as is shown by some of Benckendorff's telegrams, which were intercepted by Germany, that the special edition was responsible for Russia's mobilization, that Swerbeiev had, indeed, contradicted the report, but the German Government had held back his telegram for some time, so that the false report which had purposely been given out might do its work in the meantime, and lead Russia to order general mobilization. It is evident, however, that Sazonov was afraid to associate himself with this intrigue, and therefore nothing more was said about it, even in London, until two years later, in October 1916, when the British Foreign Secretary repeated his not very brilliant theory as to the origin of the Russian mobilization in a public speech to foreign journalists. As the Central Telegraph Office in Berlin had thoroughly investigated the matter as far back as in December 1914, in consequence of the telegrams from Benckendorff, which were intercepted at that time, Herr von Bethmann was able to prove, in his speech of November 9, 1916, that both the telegrams sent by the Russian Ambassador, to contradict the false report, were despatched without delay.

On the strength of the investigations made in December 1914, and of what has transpired in the meantime as to the exact time when the decision was reached, and the order given to mobilize the whole forces of the Russian Empire, it is now possible to state :

1. Swerbeiev's telegram giving the false report of German mobilization on the 30th of July, 1914, did not reach the Berlin Central Telegraph Office till 3.28 p.m. (= 4.28 Russian time), according to the evidence of the Director of the Mobilization Department of the Russian War Office, Dobrorolsky, more than two hours after the Tsar had

decided on general mobilization for the second time, and this time irrevocably.

2. On account of the mass of German State telegrams that had to be sent off, and the wires to St. Petersburg being occasionally blocked, as the Russian order for mobilization was just being sent out, the telegram giving the false report was not despatched till 11.20 p.m. (= twenty minutes after midnight, Russian time), more than six hours after the Russian order for mobilization was flashed over the wires.

3. In answer to an enquiry, General Dobrorolsky has stated in writing that the false report published by the *Lokalanzeiger* " did not directly influence the order for mobilization, as it only became known in St. Petersburg later ".   The news made a great impression, certainly, when it arrived, so much so that the General Staff would not believe the *démenti*, and looked upon the report as proof that the Russian Government had been right in the decision they had taken.

This ought to dispose, once for all, of the legend that a special edition of a Berlin newspaper had caused the Russian Government to order general mobilization.   (For authentic information as to the accuracy of the time mentioned in the foregoing, and as to Grey's intrigues, see the May 1922 number of the *Deutsche Rundschau, Der Zusammenbruch der Ententelegende über die russische allgemeine Mobilmachung.*)

8. The French Ten-Kilometre Imposture.

(Already published in the *Frankfurter Zeitung* of January 7, 1913, No. 15.)

The fact that the French covering troops were kept at a distance of ten kilometres from the frontier when taking up their positions on the 30th of July, is adduced by official France, and particularly by M. Viviani, who was Foreign Minister in 1914, as one of the most important proofs that, during the crisis of 1914, France pursued a policy of peace to the last.   This measure was certainly well calculated to make a great impression on anyone who was not intimately acquainted with the conditions, but it did not in any way retard France's preparations, or make her less ready for war, and cannot therefore be the slightest evidence of peaceable intentions. No less an authority than Viviani himself stated in the French Chamber, on the 31st of January, 1919 (*Journal Officiel*, p. 297), that the War Minister had not made " any technical or military objection " to the measure. After an interruption from the former War Minister, who was present, and confirmed this statement, Viviani continued : " nor did the order meet with any opposition from the General Staff ".

That the highest military authorities agreed on this point will readily be understood, when the nature of the French frontier defences against Germany is realized. Soon after 1871, France had constructed a line of frontier fortifications, beginning with Verdun in the north, and extending uninterruptedly to the Swiss frontier, with only one gap barely fifty kilometres wide, between Toul and Epinal. The northern part of this gap was protected by Fort Mannonvillers, which was only ten kilometres from the German frontier, and whose guns commanded the frontier and the territory beyond. This powerful barrier of fortifications afforded excellent cover for the concentration of the French army, no matter whether the covering troops were brought somewhat nearer or not. For placing the covering troops further back did not mean that the bulk of the troops would be assembled further back. It merely meant that the covering troops would be nearer to them. Viviani even went so far as to say, on the occasion referred to above, that the 42nd Infantry Division, which, according to the original plan, was to have been posted twenty-five kilometres from the frontier, was not moved back, in consequence of the fresh order given on the 30th of July, but was actually pushed considerably further forward. Germany was only similarly protected by fortifications on the Metz-Thionville section, therefore she could not have taken the step that was taken in France.

In his speech of January 31, 1919, Viviani not only divulged the fact that the French Ministry of War and General Staff had approved of the step, and that the

42nd Infantry Division had been pushed forward, but he also revealed the true reason for the ostensible sacrifice having been ordered. " Diplomatic considerations " were mentioned as a reason for the step, even in the order General Joffre issued to the army commanders, when giving directions as to the covering troops. A telegram sent by the War Minister to General Joffre, at 5 p.m. on the 1st of August, shortly after the order for mobilization had been given, speaks still more plainly :

In order to secure the co-operation of our English neighbours, it is still essential not to allow patrols and detachments to go beyond the general line fixed in telegram No. 129 of the 30th of July.

A third telegram sent at 10.30 p.m. on the 1st of August called attention to the fact that the ten kilometre line applied to cavalry patrols as well, and " for important diplomatic reasons ". (All the orders as quoted by Viviani are to be found in the *Journal Officiel.*)

But in spite of these repeated warnings, the order was not strictly observed (p. 243, No. 27). Nor was the French frontier by any means left entirely unprotected. On the contrary, the Customs officials and others in the service of the forestry department—in all 1,500 higher and 27,000 subordinate officials—were left at their posts. In France these organizations became part of the army on mobilization, and their duty was to assist in guarding the frontiers and coasts, collect information about the enemy, and act as guides to the troops, etc. The men were armed with army rifles, and attended drill and musketry courses even in peace time. A memorandum published by the French Foreign Office shows that, in 1914, Customs officials were posted along the frontier to the number of four to ten for every hundred to five hundred yards, and had fired on German patrols.

Whilst the frontier was thus amply guarded against attacks from weak German patrols, which were all that had to be taken into consideration, the order was liberally turned to account as a means of influencing England. Viviani at once communicated it officially to London, making at the same time a number of incorrect statements as to movements of German troops. Poincaré wrote to the King of England about it on the 31st of July. This politico-military strategy was successful. According to Viviani's statement on the 31st of January, 1919, King George replied that he " admired " the moderation shown by the French, and, later on, the American Ambassador in London told him that France had " given a clear proof of her sincerity to the whole world". Anyone who knew how matters really stood, and what Viviani said in the French Chamber, will come to a very different conclusion, which may be summed up as follows :

1. The French covering troops were ordered to their war positions on the morning of the 30th of July, although the country was not menaced by any mobilization on the part of a neighbour. The order to the German covering troops in the west was only given when a " state of imminent danger of war " was proclaimed on the 31st of July, at 1 p.m., after official news had been received of the public announcement of general mobilization in Russia. As late as 6 p.m. on the 30th of July, when the French covering troops were already in position, a proposal to give similar orders to the XVIth Army Corps (Metz) was rejected by the Prussian Ministry of War.

2. The withdrawal of the French covering troops did not involve any military disadvantage. The pickets provided by the Customs officials, organized on military lines, who remained on the frontier, were sufficient protection against German patrols.

3. In innumerable cases, the order to remain at a distance of ten kilometres from the frontier was not obeyed.

4. The order was not given for the sake of peace, but purely for diplomatic reasons, and mainly to secure England's armed help.

9. How the Report of Bombs having been dropped on Nuremberg originated.

(Already published in the morning edition of the *Berliner Tageblatt*, March 7, 1922.)

The record book kept by the *Oberquartiermeister I* of the Great General Staff contains the following entry on the

2nd of August, 1914 : " IIIrd Bavarian Army Corps reports that airmen are dropping bombs near Nuremberg ". The following facts may be gathered from unprinted records amongst the Imperial archives :

On the 2nd of August, the Chief of the Staff of the IIIrd Bavarian Army Corps (Nuremberg) received a telephone report, from the Nuremberg railway authorities, of bombs being dropped in the neighbourhood of Nuremberg, and passed on this report to the General Staff in Berlin provisionally. After the railway authorities had recognized that the report was incorrect, the Chief of the Staff informed the General Staff of this, also by telephone.

The Nuremberg railway authorities had received the information both from the Würzburg–Nuremberg and Ansbach–Nuremberg sections of the line. The Nuremberg office of the Line Commandant thereupon telegraphed the report to the Railways Department of the Great General Staff, adding that "reliable information could not be obtained ". According to the records, this report was not contradicted or supplemented. As the railway authorities sent a circular telegram to all the stations on the Würzburg–Nuremberg and Ansbach–Nuremberg sections of the line, informing them of the alleged occurrence, the news must have reached the Press in this way.

The war diaries of the IIIrd Bavarian Army Corps, the 5th Infantry Division (Nuremberg), and the 21st Infantry Regiment (Bayreuth), contain innumerable rumours and telephone reports of enemy air raids. Most of these reports were found to be untrustworthy, but precautionary measures were nevertheless taken for all eventualities, and this would equally have become known to the Press.

The incorrect report of bombs having been dropped near Nuremberg must consequently be put down to the fact that the report contradicting it, sent by the Chief of the Staff of the IIIrd Bavarian Army Corps, was not passed on to the Foreign Office, or, at all events, not in good time. The Foreign Office could also have made further enquiry into the facts, on its own account, for in the afternoon of the 3rd of August, after sending the declaration of war to France, a report was received from the Prussian Minister

in Munich, throwing doubt on the occurrence (D 758).
At the same time, it must be remembered that, in the
correct text of the declaration of war, the Nuremberg
incident plays quite a secondary part, no special attention
was paid to it, and therefore it was only mentioned lastly,
in the declaration of war, after the road frontier violations.

10. ITALY'S ATTITUDE.

In 1902, when the Triple Alliance was again renewed,
Italy at the same time virtually turned her back on it by
concluding an agreement with France, which bound the
two States mutually to observe the strictest neutrality, not
only in case of one of them " being attacked by one or more
Powers, either directly or indirectly ", but also in case of
one or other " being compelled to take the initiative in
declaring war, in consequence of direct provocation, or for
the maintenance of its honour or security ".[1] After
England had concluded the Entente with France in 1904,
and by so doing had alienated herself from Germany, Italy
no longer considered the Triple Alliance anything but a
means of achieving perfectly definite aims, for as her coast
was very much exposed to attack by the British Fleet,
she would never have taken part against England in any
serious conflict. The attitude of the Italian representative
at the Algeciras Conference in 1906 was in itself clear proof
of the change. Italy's original consent to the annexation
of Bosnia and Herzegovina by Austria, in 1908, was with-
drawn directly England showed herself strongly opposed
to it. And the Treaty of Racconigi, which followed this
in 1909, signified her unreserved approval of Russia's
ambitions regarding Constantinople and the Straits.

It is true that France's spiteful attitude towards the
occupation of Tripoli (1911), and the common Austro-
Italian interest in preventing Serbia from establishing herself
on the Adriatic, and in setting up an independent Albanian
State to counterbalance Slav expansion, led to a temporary
fresh *rapprochement* to the Central Powers ; but hardly had

[1] *Les Accords Franco-Italiens*, 1901–2, No. 7.

Albania been set up, when fresh points of dispute arose between Vienna and Rome.

The attitude of the Cabinet in Rome had no decisive influence on the course of the crisis in the summer of 1914. Berlin knew very well from the beginning that, in case of an Austro-Serbian conflict, Italy would demand compensation, and that the Trient district would be of most account in this respect. Austria, on the other hand, would not sound Italy in advance, as she had no confidence in her discretion, and was afraid the plan might leak out in Belgrade (D 87). As had been foreseen in Berlin, a claim was made in Rome for compensation, on the basis of Article 7 of the Triple Alliance, directly the Austrian ultimatum was presented, and compensation was demanded " even in case of a temporary occupation of Serbian territory ". As against this, Count Berchtold was of opinion that Italy had already been compensated by her occupation of the islands in the Ægean Sea (D 212). As Italy threatened to adopt an anti-Austrian attitude if compensation was refused, Berlin urged an understanding being reached. But the Vienna Government was only willing to discuss the matter in case of " an occupation, which would not be considered merely temporary " (D 267, 269, 328). On the 30th of July, Berchtold had still paid no attention to the advice given by Berlin (D 396). He did not tell the Italian Ambassador until the 1st of August, when Russia's general mobilization had made war inevitable, that he accepted the interpretation given to Article 7 of the Triple Alliance treaty in Rome and Vienna, according to which a claim to compensation held good even in case of only temporary occupation of Serbian territory (D 594).[1]

But the very same day, even before Germany had declared war on Russia, a Cabinet Council in Rome decided not to take part in the war. France was notified of this decision with remarkable rapidity, actually on the 1st of August, so that directly mobilization was ordered she could send her troops from the south to the north-east frontier, whilst the German Ambassador was only informed of it twenty-four hours later (F 124, D 675). Owing to the attitude

[1] For text of Art. 7, vide App. I. No. 28, p. 243.

adopted by England, it is hardly likely that, even if Austria had given way sooner on the question of compensation, it would have helped matters. True, the Italian Ambassador in Vienna considered that Russia had " clearly proved " herself the aggressor by her mobilization, and the Ambassador in Berlin could not bring himself to transmit the declaration of neutrality in person (D 510, 756). But the opinion of the two diplomats did not count.

11. THE BELGIAN QUESTION.

The Belgian question has not been dealt with, in giving an account of the crisis of 1914, because it has no connection with responsibility for the outbreak of war. The German plan of campaign had been in force since the winter of 1900–1, and had not led Germany into taking advantage of the extraordinarily favourable opportunity for a war of prevention in 1905–6, or of any of the later opportunities. Nor did this plan prevent the German Government from continuing their efforts to maintain peace in July 1914, even at the price of finally abandoning the diplomatic attitude they had first adopted.

From the international point of view, the Imperial Chancellor used the only appropriate word, when he spoke of the violation of Belgium's neutrality as a wrong, on the 4th of August, 1914. The efforts made to justify it later on must be described as mistaken. What has become known, since the outbreak of war, of England's endeavours to influence Belgian neutrality, cannot be considered any justification for the German plan of operations, which was drawn up in the winter of 1900–1. Nor is a breach of international law legalized by the fact that another State contemplates a similar act. All that can be said for the German action is that it was taken for purely military reasons. Although the opinion is not so general now, the military experts, not only in Germany, but also in the other States, considered at that time, that, in a war on two fronts, the German army leaders would have no choice but to strike a decisive blow in the west with the least possible delay. But a frontal attack on the strongly fortified French front, Verdun–Belfort, would have involved considerable delay, the only way of striking the blow quickly was by going round through Luxemburg and Belgium. The question whether another plan of operations, taking the offensive in the east, and remaining on the defensive in the west, would have held out sufficient prospect of success, could only be exhaustively dealt with in a special military essay.

But the frank admission that Germany did wrong, does not give the other Powers any right to sit in judgment on her. The War Minister, Haldane, has disclosed the fact that, on hearing that Sir Edward Grey had taken over the obligations Lord Lansdowne had already incurred towards France,[1] he immediately put himself in touch with the French military attaché, with a view to selecting a place of assembly for the British Expeditionary Force opposite the Belgian frontier.[2] If the French army took the offensive directly it was completely mobilized, as provided by the General Staff's protocols of 1911, 1912, and 1913, the British army, assembled on the north flank of the French forces, in the neighbourhood of Maubeuge, could not march anywhere except on Belgium. Therefore the Anglo-French plan of campaign led, just as much as the German plan, to a violation of Belgian neutrality. The King of the Belgians told the German military attaché himself, in May 1914, that he thought the French danger the greatest, and that the espionage carried on by the French General Staff on Belgian territory was a source of anxiety to him.[3]

It is not honest indignation, but pharisaical presumption on the part of England and France to represent the German plan of campaign as an unparalleled crime. The instances of violation of neutrality by their own countries ought to be a warning to politicians and historians in London and Paris to be more careful in passing judgment.

[1] Repington, *The First World War*, 1914–18, p. 4.
[2] Haldane, loc. cit., pp. 31 and 168.
[3] For the report sent by the German military attaché in Brussels, May 7, 1914, vide Reichstag Committee of Enquiry, Part 2, p. 95.

PART V

APPENDIX I

DOCUMENTARY EVIDENCE

No. 1. On the 3rd of December, 1884, Courcel reported Bismarck's having said to him : " My wish is that the time should come when you could forgive us Sedan, as you have forgiven Waterloo," and he then continued : " If we followed that advice, perhaps one of Bismarck's successors might say to our grand-children : ' I want you to forgive us a fresh defeat, and a fresh dismemberment, as you forgave Sedan.' That shows that the levity of those who, blinded by temporary Party interests, and deceived by fallacious historical theories, have tried to justify the treaties of 1815 in the eyes of France, and to moderate the resentment felt by the French people, with regard to the painful amputations that took place at that time, was not only reprehensible, but might be fraught with disastrous consequences." On the 20th of January Courcel protested again, not only against the treaties of 1871, but also against those of 1815 (Poincaré, in *Les Origines de la Guerre*, pp. 20-23).

No. 2. Delcassé succeeded at that time in getting the alliance, which was originally only intended for the preservation of peace, extended by the addition " and maintenance of the balance of power in Europe ". It was agreed, at the same time, that the military conventions, which were originally only to have held good as long as the Triple Alliance existed, should remain in force for the same length of time as the diplomatic agreement. As to this, Delcassé wrote that it was precisely when the alliance was dissolved that the military conventions would be necessary. " What would happen if the Triple Alliance were dissolved . . . if, for instance, the Emperor Francis Joseph . . . suddenly disappeared, and if Austria were threatened with a break up, which might perhaps be favoured by others, and from which they might anyhow hope to benefit. . . .[1] What could make it more urgently

[1] The words omitted here are as follows : " *Quel sujet plus capable de compromettre la paix générale et de rompre l'équilibre entre les forces euro-péennes ?* "—[Tr.]

necessary for France and Russia not only to have a common aim, but to be prepared to achieve it ? " (French Yellow Book, *L'Alliance Franco-Russe, Nos.* 93–95).

No. 3. There was only one occasion, the 16th of May, 1888, when Waldersee thought Bismarck had at last come round to the idea of a preventive war. He writes that the Crown Prince (later on William II.) had confided to him " in strict confidence ", that the Chancellor " had now made up his mind not to shrink from war any longer " (Vol. I. p. 399). Waldersee claims to have heard this from the War Minister as well (loc. cit., p. 401). But only a month later, at the end of June, Waldersee again says that he differs from the Chancellor, who " does not wish to involve Germany in any war " (loc. cit., p. 410).

No. 4. The Italian Foreign Minister, Tittoni, had said to the Austrian Ambassador, Freiherr von Lützow : " Don't give me away, but in reality I am almost glad of your annexation ; what I fear most is a badly defined, ambiguous state of affairs ; it is a source of danger." All he asked of his Austrian colleague, on the 4th of October, was to forego the Sandjak, and Article XXIX of the Berlin treaty, and to make explicit statements as to the Straits. Aehrenthal said, on the 6th of October, that he accepted the conditions mentioned, and therefore considered the agreement between Italy, Russia, and Austria, " concluded in principle" (Friedjung, Vol. II. pp. 231–232). Directly England opposed Austria, Tittoni's attitude changed. At the beginning of December he stated in Parliament that he had not pledged himself to anything, as far as Aehrenthal was concerned. The apology he made to Lützow was that his difficulties had been increased owing to public opinion (Friedjung, Vol. II. p. 255).

No. 5. The decisive instruction to the German Ambassador in St. Petersburg, Count Pourtalès, is published in O. Hammann's *Bilder aus der Kaiserzeit*, App. V. p. 155. The text shows the fallacy of the assertion that it contained a threat of war. Germany stated that unless Russia agreed unreservedly to the annexation, she would withdraw, and " leave things to take their course ". " The ultimate responsibility would then rest with M. Isvolsky, seeing that we have made a last honest effort to help him to clear up the situation in an acceptable way." It should not be assumed that a possible general war was amongst the things it had been decided must be " left to take their course ". The reference was to an Austrian march on Serbia, against which Russia could not have taken any action at that time.

No. 6. Von Bethmann Hollweg's *Betrachtungen zum Weltkrieg,* Vol. I. p. 87. For details of the opposition made by the Russian intelligentsia, see Hammann's *Der misverstandene Bismarck,* p. 171, and Miliukov's statement in the Duma on the 15th of March, 1911. For the opposition made by Sir Edward Grey, see Siebert, pp. 202 and 243. Grey objected to the proviso of the treaty, fearing that Russia would eventually allow Germany to carry on the line from the Persian frontier to Teheran, which would have absolutely wrecked the whole policy England had pursued for six years, and he even thought of resigning (Siebert, pp. 391–392).

No. 7. Message from the Chief of the Staff of the Warsaw military district, Mobilization Department, No. 2540, dated September 30, 1912, original in the Imperial archives at Potsdam. An attempt has been made by the Entente to represent this as an order connected with manœuvres, or purely theoretical operations. That is very unlikely to have been the case, if only on account of its having been sent from the mobilization department, and also on account of its purport and date. In order to dispose of pretexts of this kind once for all, General Dobrorolsky, who was Director of the Mobilization Department in 1914, was asked how the order was to be understood. The answer given by the General, who lives in Belgrade, and has remained loyal to the Tsar, was : " The order contains instructions which were to be operative in case of a war which was expected in 1912, in connection with the declaration of war on Turkey made at that time by Serbia and Bulgaria " (letter from Dobrorolsky to the author).

No. 8, loc. cit., p. 347. It is true that, in a telegram to the French Ambassador in St. Petersburg, Poincaré maintained that he had only said " France would stand by the treaty of alliance, and would even give Russia military support, if the *casus fœderis* arose " (*Affaires Balkaniques*, Vol. I. No. 263). According to this the promise would have been limited to the case of an attack by Austria-Hungary supported by Germany. But apart from the fact that the question was not of a joint attack by the Central Powers on Russia, merely of a possible Austrian action against Serbia, it should be remembered that the French Yellow Book on Balkan Affairs was put together under Poincaré's auspices, solely with the object of defending his policy.

No. 9. Siebert, in the *Süddeutsche Monatshefte*, January 1922, p. 191. According to French sources Russia wanted to support Rumania without appearing to do so. Rumania was to keep the Bulgarians sufficiently occupied to prevent their annihilating Serbia, but without enabling the latter to score such a success that Austria would intervene and a general war might be the result. Rumania, for her part, wanted Russia to supply her with munitions, and France to lend her money. This was not considered in Paris to be compatible with the declaration of neutrality (*Affaires Balkaniques*, Vol. II. No. 368 and 369).

No. 10. This is not the view taken by Friedjung, Vol. III. p. 304, and Professor Hoetzsch, loc. cit., p. 311, both of whom consider that the Russian policy had failed. It seems to me that, like Schebeko, we must distingush between what is Slav and what is Russian. The interests of the Balkan States were only the ostensible, not the true motive which inspired Russia's policy, however. Friedjung was misled by the belief that the third Balkan war was responsible for the great armament programme, whereas General Dobrorolsky has shown that this programme was decided upon much earlier.

No. 11. (a) The German Ambassador von Tschirschky's report of March 23, 1914, on the interviews in Vienna (*Deutsche Politik*, June 11, 1920).

" His Majesty has been graciously pleased to give me the following particulars of the interviews he has had to-day with the Emperor Francis Joseph, Count Berchtold and Count Tisza, to enable me to send Your Excellency a report.

" He did not really go beyond discussing the general political position with His Majesty the Emperor Francis Joseph and Count Berchtold. Both appeared very anxious about Rumania and Russia. They thought Rumania already as good as lost to the Triple Alliance. He tried to reassure them on both points. As far as Rumania was concerned, he told them what the Crown Prince of Rumania recently said in Berlin : It was distinctly in Rumania's interest to side with the Triple Entente ; the domination of a Slav Russia, with Serbia at her back, would be intolerable for Rumania ; it was true that in consequence of the changes that had taken place in the position, during and since the second Balkan war, Rumania must now look more to Berlin to be the connecting link between her and the Triple Alliance.

" His Majesty remarked that both the Emperor Francis Joseph and Count Berchtold quite understood this, they had both accepted the fact, and expressed a hope that Berlin would do all that was possible in this direction. He then pointed out very emphatically that, although he would certainly do his very best to exert influence in Bucharest, it was also the business of Austria-Hungary to do her utmost to improve the relations between Vienna and Bucharest. Both had heartily agreed as to this.

" As regards the Russian preparations for war, he had said it could not be denied that they were extensive, and that we had every reason to keep a watchful eye on them, but that he did not think belligerent intentions against Austria or Germany were mainly responsible for them. For one thing, Russia was compelled by France to take military measures, otherwise no money would be forthcoming, and then again it was very probable that more was known in Russia about Turkey's unfortunate position than in Berlin and Vienna, and that the preparations on the west and south-west frontier were protective measures in case of eventual action against the Turks. As to this Count Berchtold, in particular, thoroughly agreed.

" His Majesty had a very interesting interview with Count Tisza, whom he thought quite a remarkable man, with a mind of his own, and lucid ideas. The Rumanian question was the first discussed. He had told Count Tisza that he was glad to hear the negotiations between him and the Rumanian authorities had not been unsatisfactory on the whole, and that he, the Minister, had been pleased with the attitude of the latter. Count Tisza had confirmed this, and then said there could be no question of the negotiations with the Rumanians breaking down. On the contrary, he had got on very well with their leaders, and in future he should take steps calculated to satisfy the Rumanians on his own initiative. He had already met them on many points, and intended to make them still further concessions with regard to Church and school, in respect of which they really had been treated with unjustifiable harshness. He even intended making the Rumanians a grant of State money for their schools. The course of the negotiations hitherto, and his firm determination to meet the Rumanians as far as possible, justified the hope that in time the not altogether unreasonable dissatisfaction now felt by the Rumanians might die out.

" His Majesty pointed out that Rumania did not ask the Hungarian Government to do anything very great for the Hungarian Rumanians, they merely thought concessions in small matters, connected with administration and schools, both imperative and desirable.

" As far as future conditions in the Balkans were concerned, Count Tisza spoke of a union between Serbia and Montenegro as the event which would probably be of most importance in this respect. He regarded the union itself as inevitable. Austria-Hungary's main interest was, now as ever, to keep Serbia, as a Russian outpost, at a distance from the Adriatic. From this point of view, although the Monarchy would not oppose the union of the greater part of Montenegro with Serbia, the intention was, in this event, to allot the Montenegrin littoral to Albania. The districts of Istip and Kotchana might be made over to Bulgaria as compensation. It would be of decisive importance to work hand in hand with Rumania in all these questions, and whenever possible to let Rumania act as mediator both in the case of Serbia and Bulgaria. Rumania must not be taken by surprise, and every effort must be made to carry out the Monarchy's policy in agreement with Rumania and with her co-operation. Count Tisza had asked him to do his best to support Austria-Hungary in this policy at Bucharest, and he had willingly given a promise to that effect.

" Count Tisza then said, speaking generally, that in view of the systematic way in which the Entente Powers worked together in the whole sphere of policy, particularly in the Balkans, where they played into one another's hands with great skill, it would be advisable for the Triple Alliance Powers also to discuss all their political plans carefully and exhaustively beforehand, and decide on the means of carrying them out. He, the Minister, had no doubt at all that the Balkans were at present the main object of the Entente Powers' political activities, and that in course of time they were to be used as a battering ram against Austria-Hungary in case of a great European war. If things became serious, the Monarchy was to be kept fully occupied by an offensive from the south-east, and in this way to be prevented from coming to the assistance of Germany, so that the latter might be left to face the attack on two sides single-handed.—VON TSCHIRSCHKY."

(*b*) Report of the Minister at the Imperial Court, von Treutler, on the visit to Miramar (*Deutsche Politik* of June 11, 1920).

" His Majesty found the Archduke and Heir to the Throne in an excellent frame of mind. To begin with, he was quite delighted when he heard that he would meet the King of Italy at the manœuvres. He did not for a moment see anything disagreeable in this news, but said at once that it would give him great pleasure to meet the King on neutral ground, and thus have an opportunity of having a good talk with him.

" When they went on to discuss questions of high policy, the Heir to the Throne said that Rumania and Greece must be a wall in the Balkans to protect the Triple Alliance against the Slavs ; and Turkey also if possible. On this occasion he spoke strongly against Count Berchtold's behaviour with regard to Bulgaria and Rumania in not negotiating with Sofia through Bucharest.

" His Majesty told him that the mistake could probably be repaired if only strict loyalty were observed towards Bucharest by Vienna ; the King and Crown Prince had repeatedly said that they would be faithful to the Triple Alliance. Above all, it was necessary that the Rumanian question should again be dealt with in Hungary as Tisza had evidently dealt with it already, and intended to continue doing, according to his own statements. His Majesty took this opportunity of telling the Heir to the Throne what a good impression Tisza had made on him, and urged him to have confidence in this true statesman. The Archduke promised to consider this advice seriously.

" The Heir to the Throne then touched upon Austria-Hungary's domestic policy quite spontaneously, and said, in some excite-ment, that the Slavs were becoming altogether too provocative and audacious, he looked upon that as a great danger. His Majesty entered into this delicate question, and told the Archduke quite frankly that he was confident that Austria ought to pursue a German policy ; all the same, advantage should be taken of the

Czech opposition and obstruction to give them a real good lesson one day. The Archduke said he was quite of that opinion ; he confessed that the German politicians were, for the most part, uncongenial to him, but he considered that questions of this vital importance must be dealt with from a higher point of view than one's feelings with regard to temporary deputies.

" Under these circumstances the visit to Miramar went off extraordinarily well. His Majesty went on board the Dreadnought *Viribus Unitis*, one of the ships forming the fleet anchored off the Castle, and the impression she made on him and the other naval members of the party was very favourable. The Heir to the Throne and the Duchess were obviously anxious to make their exalted guest's stay as pleasant as possible. The parting was accordingly of a very cordial nature.—TREUTLER."

(*c*) Report of the Minister at the Imperial Court, von Treutler, on the interviews at Konopischt (*Deutsche Politik* of May 14, 1920).

" His Majesty the Emperor had political talks with the Archduke-Heir to the Throne, both before and after dinner on the 13th of May, the second day of his stay at Konopischt. The first talk was suggested by the telegram which had come from Athens shortly before, indicating that the differences between Turkey and Greece threatened to assume a serious character. In the course of this conversation His Majesty sent for me ; in the Archduke's presence he gave me a *résumé* of what had previously been discussed, somewhat as follows :

" ' I informed the Archduke of the purport of the Athens telegram. We agreed that in view of the situation having consequently become more critical, the King of Rumania must be sounded, to ascertain what he thinks of the state of affairs, and whether, that is, what steps he will take to try to avoid, and possibly prevent, any infringement of the provisions of the Bucharest peace. The Archduke heartily agreed with what His Majesty said as to this, and asked whether there was any prospect of the King being willing to intervene. I replied that King Carol would be very likely to act in the sense we desired, as his interest in upholding the Bucharest peace was as great as ours. It was accordingly agreed that His Majesty should send corresponding instructions to the Foreign Office, and the Archduke promised to ask Count Berchtold to have similar instructions sent to the Austrian Minister in Bucharest.'

" In conclusion, both the exalted personages spoke of their mutual personal antipathy to the King of Bulgaria, and His Majesty said that, according to information that had recently reached him, the King knew of this antipathy, but intended making great efforts to conciliate his two opponents.

" The next morning His Majesty gave me the following account of the second conversation, which had taken place after dinner, with no third person present :

" Taking present questions as his starting-point, the Archduke first spoke of Italy with great disapproval. The fact that Italy had sent such a man as Aliotti to Durazzo (in Albania) and kept him there, showed her *mala fides*. The occurrences in Trieste, and their echo in Italy also showed that she made it very difficult for her ally to live in peace ; such a state of affairs could not go on permanently. In addition to that the King of Italy did not seem inclined to do anything to improve matters. He (the Emperor) had tried to pacify the Archduke. He had particularly pointed out that in the frontier provinces mistakes were probably made by subordinate officials on both sides, which had unfortunate consequences further afield. As regards the King, he too had had a feeling for years, which he had often been obliged to overcome, it was not till their last meeting in Venice that the way had been paved to more cordial relations. The King seemed to have learnt a good deal, and the new conditions brought about by the Tripolitan war had shown the Italians, and particularly the Monarch himself, that France was their real enemy, and led them to form a truer estimate of the value of the Triple Alliance. In anticipation of the meeting between the Heir to the Throne and the King, at our manœuvres, His Majesty had apparently taken great trouble to dispel the Archduke's distrust of the latter.

"The conversation then turned to Hungary, and here the Heir to the Throne seems to have expressed his antipathy still more strongly, and spoken uncommonly plainly. He described the conditions in Hungary as absolutely anachronous and mediæval, and said that Hungary was the battle-ground of individual families, and that the oligarchic form of government amounted to downright tyranny over all the non-Magyar elements, which constituted far more than 50 per cent. of the whole population. The number of Magyars had always been incorrectly given, the real number was perhaps two and a half million. The name of the man at the head of the Government was immaterial ; every Hungarian tried more or [less openly to secure advantages for Hungary at the expense of Austria, and to the prejudice of the Monarchy as a whole. He, the Archduke, knew that the Emperor had been very favourably impressed by Tisza. But perhaps he had not formed quite a correct estimate of him, for Tisza's deeds did not coincide with his words. In reality Tisza was already a dictator in Hungary, and was trying to act as one in Vienna too. ' Even now Vienna trembled when Tisza was coming, and everyone fell down before him when he arrived in Vienna.' It was particularly unsatisfactory that Tisza should have openly professed his belief in the independence of the Hungarian army as an ideal to be pursued.

" His Majesty had interrupted the Archduke, to say that of

course he disapproved of Tisza when he heard that he was insubordinate, and tried to shift the centre of gravity of the Monarchy, to the disadvantage of Austria. But he thought him such a strong and exceptional man that he could only advise his not being thrown overboard, but being kept under iron-handed control, and his valuable qualities then turned to account.

" My impression is that His Majesty's intention was to humour the Archduke without making him suspicious by abandoning his well-known high opinion of Tisza too hastily. On the other hand, the Heir to the Throne had evidently insisted, very cleverly from his point of view, that it was Tisza's fault if the interests of the Triple Alliance were badly safeguarded, for it was he who oppressed the Hungarian Rumanians, contrary to the promises he had made at Schönbrunn. Finally the Archduke went so far as to ask the Emperor whether he could not see that Tschirschky was instructed to lose no opportunity of reminding Tisza not to lose sight of the necessity for winning over the Rumanians by treating their fellow countrymen in Hungary properly. His Majesty promised to commission Tschirschky to go on perpetually saying to Tisza : ' Sir, remember the Rumanians '. The Archduke was quite satisfied with that.

" To explain this part of the conversation, I may perhaps be permitted to add that, shortly before, Colonel Bardolff had spoken to me about Tisza, and had very cautiously expressed ' the fear that existed at Konopischt ' that, owing to a Hungarian Ambassador having represented the Dual Monarchy in Berlin for so many years, we might have learnt to see the conditions through Hungarian spectacles. I pointed out, in answer, that there need be no anxiety as to that, as we received information from our own representatives as well ; I already knew that the fact of my most gracious Sovereign having spoken so frankly and favourably of Tisza was what had given rise to the fear. This was far more simple than seemed to be assumed. Tisza was such an active energetic man that it was quite natural that he should have made a great impression on the Emperor ; for that matter, if the Archduke would acquaint His Majesty with the reasons for holding a different opinion, they would certainly be given due weight.

" In connection with what the Archduke and his confidant said on this subject, it was of interest that His Imperial Highness should have informed His Majesty that he had recommended Szögyény's successor, and hoped that Prince Hohenlohe would be a most satisfactory representative.

" His Imperial Highness found the greatest fault with Czernin's behaviour at Bucharest, particularly with the celebrated interview, and spoke openly of it, although Czernin is his protégé.

" The Archduke spoke with equal frankness of Bohemia, and Prince Thun's want of success, and very fortunately laid stress on the necessity for protecting the Germans, who must constitute the ' ferment.' 'A compromise' could no longer be hoped for from the Parties, it would have to be dictated by Vienna.

"There is nothing to fear from Russia, in the Archduke's opinion ; her internal difficulties are too great to allow of her pursuing an aggressive foreign policy.—TREUTLER."

No. 12. General Dobrorolsky (Director of the Russian Mobilization Department of the Russian War Office, 1914), *Die Mobilmachung der Russischen Armee* 1914 (German translation), p. 14 (*Verlag für Politik und Geschichte*, Berlin, 1922). Dobrorolsky writes that the "inevitability" of having to strengthen the fighting forces substantially had long since been foreseen, and that the project had only been postponed till 1913 owing to various circumstances, amongst them the constant fresh appointments to the post of Chief of the General Staff.

No. 13. The first incorrect information respecting the German Army Bill appeared in *Heer und Politik* on the 15th of February. On the 17th the *Temps* announced three Army Bills, and added that the War Office was in favour of the three years' service period. Isvolsky reported as to this on the 27th of February (so-called Russian Blue Book, pp. 336–7). On the 10th of March the Three Years' Service Bill was submitted to the French Chamber, the German Army Bill was published eighteen days later, on the 18th of March.

No. 14. Buat, *L'Armée allemande pendant la guerre de* 1914–18. Buat was Director of the second section of the French General Staff during the war, and attended the Washington Conference with Briand as an expert in 1922. For Buat's statistics, with criticisms, vide Reichstag Committee of Enquiry, 1st sub-Committee, Part 2, p. 152.

No. 15. According to the records of the former Prussian War Ministry, and the reports of the French Chamber during the war, published in the *Journal Officiel*, the supplies of ammunition when war broke out were :

	Infantry Rounds.	Field Artillery Rounds.
Germany	970 million	5·2 million.
France..	1,310 million	5·68 million.

No. 16. The following facts are worth noting :

(*a*) On the 14th of January, 1914, the supplies of flour for Paris were increased, in case of traffic being blocked in the event of mobilization. The Military Governor said : "Time presses. This is quite a special year. We cannot tell what it may bring. We cannot tell whether we may not have mobilization in March or April" (*Deutsche Nation*, May 1921, p. 361).

(*b*) At the beginning of May France opened negotiations with Switzerland with a view to supplying her with food in case of war, stating that there would then be a hunger blockade against Germany (Schoen, p. 173).

(*c*) As lately as in July 1914, Germany exported wheat to the value of sixty-seven gold marks (von Schulze-Gaevernitz, *England und Deutschland*, p. 107).

No. 17. Conrad (von Hötzendorf), Vol. III. p. 669–70. Vide also the *Weltbühne* of August 31, 1922, *Die Europäischen Generalstäbe vor dem Weltkrieg*, and October 12, 1922, *Diplomatie und Generalstab*. After the conversation of May 12th, the two Chiefs of the German and Austrian General Staffs had no further talk before the outbreak of war, although Moltke was at Carlsbad from the end of June till July for a second course of waters. General von Conrad says in a letter to the Central Office of Enquiry into the causes of the war (Berlin) that statements to the contrary are untrue.

No. 18. Report sent by Von Wiesner, head of a section of the Austro-Hungarian Foreign Office. Austrian Red Book, 1919, Part I. No. 17. Unnumbered Telegram.

"SARAJEVO, *July* 13, 1914.

" All the leading circles here are confident that the Greater-Serbian propaganda carried on here by societies and other organizations emanates from Serbia, and that it is not only done with the knowledge and approval of the Serbian Government, but is promoted by them.

" The material submitted to me by civil and military authorities as a basis for this belief may be classified as follows : Material from the period before the murder contains nothing to show that the propaganda was promoted by the Serbian Government. But although there is little of it, the material is quite sufficient to show that the agitation was promoted by societies in Serbia, and tolerated by the Serbian Government.

" Judicial enquiry into the murder.

"Nothing to prove or even suggest that the Serbian Government was accessory to the murder or its preparation or to the supply of weapons. There is, on the contrary, a good deal to make this seem out of the question.

" Evidence given by the accused persons proves almost incontestably that the murder was planned in Belgrade, and that the preparations for it were aided and abetted by the Serbian Government officials, Ciganovich and Major Tankosich, both of whom supplied bombs, Browning pistols, munitions, and cyanide of potassium. No proof that Pribicevich had anything to do with it. The first reports as to this were based on regrettable misunderstandings on the part of the prosecuting police officials.

" That the bombs originally came from the Serbian arms depôt at Kragujevac is incontestably proved, but there is no evidence that they had only recently been taken from the depôt, for they might have been in the hands of the comitadjes since the war.

" Evidence of accused persons leaves scarcely any doubt that Princip, Cabrinivich, and Grabez, with bombs and weapons upon them, were secretly smuggled across the frontier to Bosnia by Serbian functionaries, at the request of Ciganovich. The arrangements were made by the frontier Captains at Schabatz and Losnica, and carried out by Customs officials. Although there is no proof that they had any knowledge of the object of the journey, still they must have agreed to keep their mission secret.

" Other information gives an insight into organization of propaganda carried on by *Narodna odbrana*. This is valuable material, which will be useful, but has not yet been sifted ; will be delivered without loss of time.

"If the intentions are the same as when I left, the following might be added to what is required of Serbia :

" (*a*) Suppression of the co-operation of Government officials in smuggling persons and goods across the frontier.

" (*b*) Dismissal of the Serbian frontier Captains at Schabatz and Losnica, and of the frontier guards implicated.

" (*c*) Prosecution of Ciganovich and Tankosich.

" I leave for Vienna this evening, arrive on Tuesday evening, and go straight to the Foreign Office.

" Verbal explanation necessary."

Only the fourth paragraph of this report was circulated by the enemy at Versailles in 1919.

No. 19. Letter from the War Minister, von Falkenhayn, to General von Moltke. (Original letter in the Imperial Archives.)

" *Personal and strictly confidential.*

" BERLIN, W. 66, *July* 5, 1914.

"YOUR EXCELLENCY,

His Majesty the Emperor-King summoned me to the Neue Palais this afternoon, to inform me that Austria-Hungary seems determined not to tolerate the plots hatched against Austria in the Balkan peninsular any longer, and to begin by marching upon Serbia if necessary ; if Russia will not tolerate this, Austria does not intend to give in.

" His Majesty gathered this from what the Austrian Ambassador said to-day when handing him a memorandum from the Vienna Government, and a letter from the Emperor Francis Joseph.

" I did not hear this conversation, and therefore cannot express any opinion upon it. On the other hand His Majesty read me both the letter and the memorandum, and as far as it was possible to form any opinion from hearing them so quickly read, they did not give me the impression that the Vienna Government had taken a definite decision. Both described the general position of the Dual Monarchy as being very black, owing to the Pan-Slav machinations. Both also said something must be done to put a stop to the intrigues with the least possible delay. But nothing is said in either as to a military solution, they point far more to an intention of taking active political steps ; for instance, reference is made to the conclusion of a treaty with Bulgaria, for which purpose they want to secure Germany's support.

"This support is to be promised, but Austria-Hungary is to be told that it would be primarily her business to take the steps required in her own interest.

" The Imperial Chancellor, who was at Potsdam too, seems not to think, any more than I do, that the Austrian Government are in earnest, although they speak with more decision than usual. At all events, he not only made no objection to the Norwegian cruise, but even advised it. In any case there is no likelihood of any decision within the next few weeks. It will be a long time before the treaty with Bulgaria is concluded. Consequently there will be no need to curtail Your Excellency's stay at Carlsbad. All the same, I thought it right to let you know that the position had become acute, although I have no instructions to do so, in order that you may not be quite unprepared for surprises, which, after all, are always possible.

" With my best wishes for the success of the cure,

" I remain, etc.,

" Your Excellency's humble servant,

" (*Signed*) VON FALKENHAYN."

No. 20. English Press opinions on the Austrian Ultimatum.

The *Westminster Gazette* wrote : " Much is said as to the attitude of Russia in the matter, but if the allegations of the Note can be substantiated, we do not imagine that the Russian Government is likely to make any very great objection to Serbia's being made to give satisfaction to Austria-Hungary."

The *Daily Chronicle* said : " The Austrian Note is drastic, yet scarcely more drastic than the reasonable self-defence of the Dual Monarchy requires it to be. . . . Austria could not tolerate this sort of thing without gravely jeopardizing not only her dignity, but her existence. . . . Serbia has a bad case, and not one in which Russia, still less the other Powers of the Triple Entente, could espouse her quarrel. The most she can wisely do is to advise Serbia to give way, at the same time pledging herself to stand guard over Austria's non-annexation assurance."

Daily News : " Austria's demands comprise nothing which would be really intolerable. Her indignation is natural, and not unjust, and the best thing Serbia could do would be to submit promptly."

The *Observer* wrote as follows : " We hope that English public opinion will be very slow to condemn the harsh determination of Austro-Hungarian policy. Let no one lift a finger or raise a voice to encourage Serbia in obstinacy, or save her from the due measure of immediate punishment she deserves. The ultimatum may be enforced even at the hazard of Russian intervention and a European war. . . . We must aid Russia to secure guarantees against the annihilation of independent Serbia, without seeking to save that culpable State from sufficient punishment."

The weekly paper, *John Bull*, was particularly unlucky in having published an article headed " To Hell with Serbia," on the 5th of August, the day after England declared war on Germany. The editor, Horatio Bottomley, subsequently became one of the most violent war agitators.

No. 21. The Prussian and Bavarian War Ministers, and the acting Chiefs of the General and Admiralty Staffs have stated most positively that no military preparations were made between the 5th and 23rd of July (Reichstag Committee of Enquiry, Part 2, pp. 63, 64, 65, 71). When Count Waldersee writes on the 17th of July, " The General Staff is ready " (D 74), it only means that the army is as ready as it is bound to be at all times. The regular annual preparations for mobilization had been completed as usual on the 31st of March, and since then no steps had been taken.

The false accusations in the French Yellow Book, with regard to premature military preparations in Germany, have all been refuted already by documentary evidence given by the German commission of four. (*Deutschland schuldig?* pp. 69-71). As regards the incorrect report sent by the French Ambassador on the 21st of July (F 15), that he had been "assured" that the preliminary notice of mobilization had been sent out to the classes in question, it has transpired in the meantime that it was merely a case of a rumour the French naval attaché had heard from his English colleague, and which neither of them had verified. (Telegram of the 22nd of July, 1914, from Bronevsky—Red Archives I. p. 164.) If the French Ambassador's telegram is correctly given, it is incomprehensible that he should have made such a definite statement on the strength of such doubtful information. The absurdity of calling up reservists on the 21st of July is apparent from the fact that some days later reservists were dismissed.

The information in D 37, that Austria was reinforcing her garrisons on the Serbian and Russian frontiers surreptitiously, has not been confirmed in any quarter. It is presumably based on the fact that the strength of the troops in Bosnia and Herzegovina had been somewhat increased for the manœuvres, which were to take place at the end of June (Austrian military report, July 28, No. 45).

No. 22. Comparison of the original minutes of the meeting held by the Prussian Cabinet on the 30th of July, with the copy in D 456, shows that a printer's mistake was made in the latter, which alters the sense. The correction is given here, with the consent of the two other editors of the documents, Herr Karl Kautsky and Professor Walter Schücking. Bethmann did not express his own opinion in saying that " the Russian could not be compared with the West European mobilization measures ". The word " *sei* " in the first line of page 177 should be struck out, and words substituted which would make the whole sentence read : " Russia's mobilization has counteracted this step ; Russia, it is true, has stated that her mobilization measures cannot be compared with the West European measures."

The Cabinet Council was probably held at midday, as the measures to safeguard the navy, which were sanctioned at the meeting, were ordered the same day—(*Deutschland schuldig ?* p. 75). On the other hand it cannot be assumed that the meeting took place on the 29th, because the Chancellor only gave details of telegrams from the Tsar and the Kaiser, for at the end of paragraph 2, page 177, it is expressly stated that the decision regarding the English and German proposals would probably be taken in Vienna " to-day ". This could not have been expected before the 30th.

No. 23. Telegram from Swerbeiev reporting his interview with Jagow on the afternoon of July 30 respecting the first Sazonov formula. (Red Archives I. p. 183.)

" As I had not received the telegram No. 2, with your proposal, up to the time named, I decided to call on the Foreign Minister to find out what impression your proposal, as communicated by Pourtalès, had made on him. The German Ambassador sums up your proposal as follows : ' Austria recognizes that her conflict with Serbia affects European interests in general, and declares herself willing to eliminate from her ultimatum those points which prejudice Serbia's sovereign rights. In this case Russia undertakes to put a stop to her military preparations.' The Foreign Minister considers the proposal unacceptable for Austria, as it would be humiliating to her, and would not lead to favourable results ; he added that owing to this, combined with the news of our mobilization against Austria, the position was worse, and it became more and more difficult to negotiate. In spite of that, the Foreign Minister went on to say that Szápáry was commissioned to continue the negotiations with Your Excellency, and that, in addition to this, Grey had made a fresh proposal, which was most probably already known in St. Petersburg. I must not omit to say that, after the bombardment of Belgrade, which, according to Serbian reports, seems to have been extremely. . . . Austria might, in my opinion, be more inclined to give way."

In the Orange Book (No. 63) the telegram was given as follows :

" I received your telegram of July 16/29, and conveyed the text of your proposal to the Secretary of State for Foreign Affairs, on whom I was calling at the time. He told me that he had received a similar telegram from the German Ambassador in St. Petersburg, and he then informed me that he considered our proposal unacceptable for Austria."

No. 24. For the rest, Moltke's warning is hardly likely to have influenced the Austrian decision. Tschirschky remarks that when he executed his last commission (about midday on the 30th— D 385 and 396), Austria had already decided to mobilize, and that Conrad would make the proposal to the Emperor in the evening (Reichstag Committee of Enquiry, Part 1, pp. 98 and 99). Not only that, but the report of Moltke's conversation with the Austrian military attaché arrived at an hour (after 10 p.m.—A III. 34) when it was well known that the Emperor Francis Joseph was not in the habit of receiving reports.

For the measures taken in Germany see Reichstag Committee of Enquiry, Part 2, pp. 9, 13, 72f. and *Deutschland schuldig ?* App. II. and III. p. 73.

No. 25. Provisions of the German mobilization scheme regarding " a state of imminent danger of war," valid in 1914.

According to the scheme of mobilization for the Germany Army, p. 45, § 20, B, the following measures were to be taken in case of imminent danger of war :

(*a*) The most important railway bridges and tunnels to be guarded in all the military districts.

(*b*) The " memorandum " to be communicated to the press containing a short summary of the military measures and activities which are not to be published.

(*c*) A state of war to be proclaimed, and publication of movements of troops and defensive measures to be prohibited.

(*d*) All men on the active list who are on leave to be recalled, in the case of all army corps.

(*e*) All troops to be recalled to their garrisons, in the case of all army corps.

(*f*) Traffic to be regulated as prescribed in App. J of the plan of mobilization (concerning suspension of private goods traffic in the frontier districts, supervision of postal communication with foreign countries).

(*g*) Measures for the protection of the frontier to be put into effect.

(*h*) The troops detailed to guard the North Sea islands to be sent to the islands, together with artillery equipment, munitions, and commissariat supplies.

Additional measures to be taken in the frontier districts:

(*a*) Railways to be guarded, important railway bridges and junctions, airship sheds and building yards, and establishments of importance for the air service and for wireless communication, to be protected against attempts to destroy them—also against attack from enemy aircraft.

(*b*) Men on the sick list, who are not expected to recover within a few weeks, to be moved from the frontier garrisons to garrisons farther back.

In case of invasion by the enemy, or of its being known that an invasion was imminent, before mobilization had been ordered, the General in command was to take all the necessary steps to call up all reservists liable for service, and men of military age fit for service, and also to remove all fit horses from the menaced districts to places farther back, and guard them. He was also to ensure, as far as possible, that the resources of his own country did not fall into the hands of the enemy, above all the food supplies stored in depôts, the State coffers, and the fuel supplies for motor vehicles. If necessary, arrangements were to be made for their destruction. He was to effect the evacuation of threatened sections of railway lines through the military railway authorities, and give them active help if required.

No. 26. The instruction to the Ambassador in Paris contained the following addition : " Secret. If the French Government declare that they will remain neutral, which is unlikely, Your Excellency will inform the French Government that, as a guarantee of neutrality, we must ask them to hand over to us the fortresses of Toul and Verdun, which we should occupy, and give back on the termination of the war with Russia. The reply to this demand must be here by four o'clock to-morrow afternoon."

The demand was made assuming that France would not remain neutral in a Russo-German war, which proved to be correct, and that even if a neutral attitude were adopted at first, it would not be maintained permanently, and an attack would be made on the unprotected west front when a favourable military opportunity occurred. If there had been a possibility of France's remaining permanently neutral, it would naturally have been advisable to offer compensation, instead of demanding guarantees. That Germany would have been satisfied with any other reliable guarantee of French neutrality, is proved by her prompt acceptance of England's offer made on the evening of August 1, which was rejected by France, and then described by England as a mis-understanding (p. 189). In view of the threatening statements Grey made on the 29th of July, Berlin could not have counted from the first on such an offer from England. For the rest, this secret supplementary instruction had no influence on the course of events, as there was no occasion to say anything about it in Paris. It was only deciphered by the " *Cabinet Noir* " in the fourth year of the war, and it was then turned to account as an effective means of carrying on an agitation against Germany.

No. 27. The fifty-six French violations of road frontiers are accurately given, as regards strength of the detachments, locality, and time, in the *Deutsche Allgemeine Zeitung* of June 25, 1919, No. 297. The original reports from which these details were collected are in the Imperial Archives at Potsdam, and a few examples of them are given here :

Altmünsterol, August 2, 10.30 a.m.—about forty shots fired—General Staff records Nos. 138, 139, 160—report of the 1st battn. of 58th Infantry Regiment, war diary, page 6 of the 2nd August, 1914—21st Army Corps, war diary app. 14.

Schluchtpass and vicinity—August 1, 8 p.m. and 11.30 p.m.—detachments of various strengths—reports of the General Staff Nos. 44, 45, 47, 58, 59, 63, 227—reports of the 4th squadron of the 14th Dragoon Regiment, war diary I of the 39th Infantry Division, and of the Head Quarters of the 15th Army Corps District, section Ia, No. 2660.

The losses were given as being, on the German side, two dragoons belonging to the 5th squadron of the 22nd Dragoon Regiment killed, on the French side one officer taken prisoner, and two men killed.

No. 28. Article 7 of the Triple Alliance Treaty.

As Austria-Hungary and Italy have no object in view but the maintenance, as far as possible, of the territorial *status quo* in the east, they undertake to exert their influence to prevent any territorial change that might be prejudicial to one or other of the Powers signing the present treaty. For this purpose they will put one another in possession of all information calculated to enlighten one another as to their own intentions and those of other Powers. Nevertheless, in the event of circumstances making it impossible to maintain the *status quo* in the Balkans or the Ottoman coasts and islands in the Adriatic and the Ægean Sea, and of Austria-Hungary or Italy finding themselves under the necessity of altering this *status* for their part, by a temporary or permanent occupation, whether in consequence of the action of a third Power, or for any other reason, this occupation shall only take place after previous agreement between the two Powers ; this agreement shall be based on mutual compensation for every territorial or other advantage each Power would obtain beyond the present *status quo*, and shall do full justice to the interests and well-founded claims of both parties.

APPENDIX II

LIST OF THE PERSONS MENTIONED IN PARTS III AND IV

BERLIN.

William II., German Emperor and King of Prussia.

Bethmann Hollweg, Dr. Th. von, Imperial Chancellor, Prussian Prime Minister and Minister for Foreign Affairs.

Jagow, Gottlieb von, Secretary of State for Foreign Affairs.

Zimmermann, Under-Secretary of State for Foreign Affairs.

Stumm, Wilhelm von, Director of the Political Department of the Foreign Office.

Moltke, von, Chief of the General Staff of the Army.

Bertrab, von, *Oberquartiermeister* of the Great General Staff and Director of the Survey Department.

Waldersee, Count, *Oberquartiermeister I* of the Great General Staff.

Falkenhayn, von, Prussian War minister.

Tirpitz, von, Secretary of State for Naval Affairs.

Capelle, von, Under-Secretary of State in the Admiralty, acting Secretary of State in the absence of the latter on leave.

Pohl, von, Chief of the Admiralty Staff.

Behncke, Paul, head of a section of the Admiralty Staff, acting Chief of the Staff in the absence of von Pohl on leave.

Szögyény-Marich, L. Count, Austro-Hungarian Ambassador.

Goschen, Sir E., British Ambassador.

Cambon, Jules, French Ambassador.

Swerbeiev, S. N., Russian Ambassador.

Tatischev, von, Russian Military Plenipotentiary.

Bollati, R., Italian Ambassador.

Yovanovitch, Dr. M., Serbian Chargé d'Affaires.

Beyens, Baron, Belgian Minister.

Lerchenfeld, Count Hugo von, Bavarian Minister.

Schoen, Hans von, Bavarian Councillor of Legation.

VIENNA.

Francis Joseph I., Emperor of Austria, King of Bohemia, etc., Apostolic King of Hungary.

Berchtold, Leopold, Count, Minister of the Imperial and Royal Household, and Foreign Minister.

Macchio, Freiherr K. von, 1st head of a section of the Foreign Office.

Forgach, Dr. J. Count, head of a section of the Foreign Office.

Hoyos, Alexander Count, Councillor of Legation, and the Foreign Minister's *Chef de Cabinet*.

Tisza, Count, Hungarian Prime Minister.

Conrad von Hötzendorf, Freiherr, Chief of the Staff of the Austro-Hungarian Army.

Tschirschky und Bögendorf, Heinrich von, German Ambassador.

Kageneck, Count, Military Attaché at the German Embassy.

Bunsen, Sir Maurice de, British Ambassador.

Dumaine, A. Chilhaud, French Ambassador.

Schebeko, de, Russian Ambassador.

Avarna, Duke, Italian Ambassador.

LONDON.

George V., King of Great Britain and Ireland.

Asquith, H. H., Prime Minister.

Grey, Sir E., Secretary of State for Foreign Affairs.

Lichnowsky, Karl Max Prince, German Ambassador.

Mensdorff-Pouilly-Dietrichstein, A. Count, Austrian Ambassador.

Cambon, Paul, French Ambassador.

Benckendorff, A. Count, Russian Ambassador.

Etter, N. de, Russian Councillor of Embassy.

PARIS.

Poincaré, Raymond, President of the Republic.

Viviani, René, Premier and Foreign Minister.

Ferry, Under-Secretary of State for Foreign Affairs.

Margerie, J. de, The Foreign Minister's *Chef de Cabinet*, and Director of the Political Department.

Berthelot, Acting Political Director of the Foreign Office.

Bienvenu-Martin, Minister of Justice, and (from July 16 to 29) acting Premier and Foreign Minister.

Messimy, War Minister.

Joffre, Chief of the General Staff and, in case of war, Commander-in-Chief of the French Army.

Schoen, W. Freiherr von, German Ambassador.

Szécsen, Count von Temerin-, Austro-Hungarian Ambassador.

Bertie, Sir F. L., British Ambassador.

Isvolsky, A. P., Russian Ambassador.

Sevastopulo, E., Russian Councillor of Embassy.

ST. PETERSBURG.

Nicholas II., Emperor of Russia.

Sazonov, S. D., Foreign Minister.

Suchomlinov, W. A., War Minister.

Januschkevitch, Chief of the General Staff.

Dobrorolsky, S., Director of the Mobilization Department of the War Office.

Pourtalès, Friedrich Count, German Ambassador.

    Chelius, von, German Military Plenipotentiary at the Russian Court.

    Eggeling, von, Military Attaché at the German Embassy.

Szápáry, Count, Austro-Hungarian Ambassador.

Buchanan, Sir G., British Ambassador.

Paléologue, Maurice, French Ambassador.

    Laguiche, Marquis de, Military Attaché at the French Embassy.

LIST OF THE PRINCIPAL SOURCES OF INFORMATION QUOTED AND OF THE ABBREVIATIONS USED

Abbreviations.	*Exact Title of Work.*
A	Austrian Red Book, 1919, *Diplomatische Aktenstücke zur Vorgeschichte des Krieges, 1914*, 3 Vols. English translation (Allen and Unwin).
Affaires Balkaniques	Ministère des Affaires Etrangères, Documents Diplomatiques—Les Affaires Balkaniques, 1912–1914, 3 Vols.
Belgian Diplomatic Documents	*Belgian Diplomatic Documents* 1905–1914. Reports from the Belgian representatives in Berlin, London, and Paris to the Foreign Minister in Brussels. Published by the German Foreign Office, 1917 edition.
Bethmann Hollweg	Th. v. Bethmann Hollweg, *Betrachtungen zum Weltkrieg*, 2 Vols. English translation, *Reflections on the World War*. (Thornton Butterworth).
Bismarck	Otto, Prince Bismarck, *Gedanken und Errinnerungen*, 3 Vols. English translation, *Bismarck, His Reflections and Reminiscences* (Smith Elder & Co.).
Bogitshevich	Dr. M. Bogitshevich (former Serbian Chargé d'Affaires in Berlin), *Kriegsursachen*. English translation, *Causes of the War* (Allen & Unwin).
Conrad	Field-Marshal (Freiherr) Conrad von Hötzendorf, *Aus Meiner Dienstzeit*, 3 Vols.
Corbett	*History of the Great War based on Official Documents. Naval Operations*, Sir J. Corbett. Admiralty Staff Publication, 3 Vols.

D	*Die Deutschen Dokumente zum Kriegsausbruch* (German White Book of December 1919). Edited jointly with Karl Kautsky by Count Max Montgelas and Professor Walter Schücking.
Demartial	G. Demartial, *Comment on mobilisa les Consciences*.
Deutschland schuldig ?	German White Book of June 1919, *Deutschland schuldig ?*
Dobrorolsky	General Sergei Dobrorolsky (Colonel and Director of the Mobilization Department of the Russian War Office), *Die Mobilmachung der Russischen Armée* 1914, German edition.
E	English Blue Book on the 1914 Crisis (*Collected Diplomatic Documents relating to the Outbreak of the European War*, published by the Foreign Office).
F	French Yellow Book on the 1914 Crisis. English translation. *Collected Diplomatic Documents relating to the Outbreak of the European War*, published by the Foreign Office.
Friedjung	Heinrich Friedjung, *Das Zeitalter des Imperialismus* 1884–1914, Vols. II. and III.
Gooss	Dr. Roderich Gooss, *Das Wiener Kabinett und die Entstehung des Weltkrieges*.
Grosse Politik	*Die Grosse Politik der Europäischen Kabinette* 1871–1914, a collection of German Foreign Office Records.
Haldane	Viscount Haldane, *Before the War*.
Hansard	Hansard's Parliamentary Debates.
Imperial Archives	Documentary information from the Imperial Archives at Potsdam.
Livre Noir	*Un Livre Noir, Diplomatie d'Avant Guerre d'après les Documents des Archives Russes*, Vols. I. and II.
Messimy	The French War Minister's Recollections of July 1914, published in the *Revue de France*, Aug. 1, 1921.
Moltke	General Helmuth von Moltke, *Errinnerungen, Briefe, Dokumente*.
Oman	C. Oman (Professor at Oxford University), *The Outbreak of the War of* 1914–1918.

Paléologue	Paléologue's Recollections, published in the *Revue des deux Mondes* of January 15, 1921. See also *La Russie des Tsars pendant la Grande Guerre*, Maurice Paléologue. English translation, *An Ambassador's Memoirs* (Hutchinson & Co.).
Poincaré	*Les Origines de la Guerre.* Six lectures delivered by M. Poincaré at the *Société des Conférences* in 1921, and first published in the *Revue de la Semaine* February 11, 18, and 25, and March 4, 11, and 18, 1921. English translation, *The Origins of the War* (Cassell.)
Pokrovsky	Professor M. Pokrovsky (keeper of the Soviet Government Archives), *Drei Konferenzen.*
Pribram	Dr. A. F. Pribram *Die Politischen Geheimverträge Oesterreich-Ungarns* 1879–1914. English translation, *The Secret Treaties of Austria-Hungary* 1879–1914, edited by C. A. Coolidge.
R	Russian Orange Book on the 1914 Crisis. English translation. *Collected Diplomatic Documents relating to the Outbreak of the European War*, published by the Foreign Office.
Red Archives	*Krasny Archiv* (a collection of Russian Official Documents).
Reichstag Committee of Enquiry	*Veröffentlichungen des 1. Unterausschusses des Parlamentarischen Untersuchungsausschusses*, Parts I. and II. Translated under the supervision of the Carnegie Endowment for International Peace (Division of International Law), and published under the title *Official German Documents relating to the World War.* The pages are differently numbered in the various German editions.
Romberg	Freiherr G. von Romberg, *Die Fälschungen des Russischen Orangebuches.* English translation, *The Falsifications of the Russian Orange Book* (Allen & Unwin).
Russian Blue Book	A collection of secret documents from the archives of the former Ministry of Foreign Affairs, dealing with the Franco-Russian relations between 1910 and 1914. (Published by the National Commissariat of Foreign Affairs.) Russ. Moscow, 1922.

Schoen   Freiherr von Schoen (former German Foreign Secretary and Ambassador), *Erlebtes*. English translation, *Memoirs of an Ambassador* (Allen & Unwin).

Siebert   B. de Siebert (Secretary of the Russian Embassy in London till the outbreak of war), *Diplomatische Aktenstücke zur Geschichte der Ententepolitik der Vorkriegsjahre.* English translation, *Entente Diplomacy and the World* (Allen & Unwin).

Tirpitz   Admiral Alfred von Tirpitz, *Errinnerungen*, new edition 1920. English translation, *My Memoirs* (Hurst & Blackett).

Zur Europäischen Politik   *Zur Europäischen Politik*, 1897–1914. Edited under the supervision of Bernhard Schwertfeger, 5 Vols.

SUPPLEMENTS

1. A MEMORANDUM ON THE MEETING AT REVAL IN JUNE 1908 BY THE RUSSIAN FOREIGN MINISTER, ISVOLSKY.

AT the Reval meeting, the British Under-Secretary, Sir Charles Hardinge, said that Russia would be " arbiter of the situation " in 1915–16, and expressed the English Government's wish that Russia should be as strong as possible for this reason. On account of the importance of these conversations, and in order to supplement the statement on page 31 (Part II. sect. 3), Isvolsky's memorandum regarding the meeting is given in full below (Siebert, pp. 777–9) :

The general impression which this meeting has left is extremely favourable from a political point of view. King Edward openly expressed his satisfaction, and sees in the meeting a confirmation and consolidation of the agreement reached between Russia and England, as well as a pledge for the further solidarity of both the Governments. His Majesty emphasized with particular satisfaction the hopeful turn of affairs in our domestic politics, and the approval which the activity of Secretary of State, Stolypin, has met with in serious English circles.

Summarizing Hardinge's various declarations, I must, above all, state emphatically that no attempt was made on his side to depart from the standpoint of concrete agreements, existing as well as prospective, or to draw us into general political combinations. Sir Charles confirmed the fact that the London Cabinet is entirely of our opinion that the *entrevue* at Reval need occasion no anxiety to the other States ; as to what may specially concern Germany, the British Government sincerely desires to maintain the very best relations with her, and does not believe that these relations will be strained for any reason in the immediate future.

" In spite of this," Sir Charles remarked to me, " one cannot close one's eyes to the fact that, if Germany should continue to increase her naval armaments at the same accelerated pace, a most alarming and strained situation might arise in Europe in seven or eight years' time. Then, without doubt, Russia would be the arbiter of the situation ; it is for this reason that we, in the interest of peace and the preservation of the balance of power, desire that Russia be as strong as possible on land and on sea."

Sir Charles reiterated this idea more than once, whereby he apparently wished it to be understood that he was expressing, not his own personal opinion, but the decided conviction of the London Cabinet.

Proceeding to individual questions of interest to Russia and England, Sir Charles spoke warmly of the hopeful results of the

Agreement signed last year, thanks to which not a single one of the questions which had recently arisen between Russia and England had taken a dangerous or acute character. According to him, it is only due to the Convention, and the absolute sincerity with which Russia fulfilled her obligations, that the incident on the Afghan frontier did not lead to the advance of Indian troops into Afghanistan; the London Cabinet appreciates our attitude all the more since, regarded from the purely formal side, the Convention concerning Afghanistan, which has so far not been recognized by the Ameer, has not yet come into force; the way in which Russia has acted has made it possible for the English Central Government to damp the ardour of the Anglo-Indian authorities; the London Cabinet is now quite sure that the incidents on the Afghan frontier will not lead to an advance upon Afghanistan. In a few weeks' time he hopes to receive the Ameer's formal consent, and to be able to inform us accordingly.

As far as Persia is concerned, Sir Charles again assured me that his Government are firmly resolved to act in full agreement with us. Our frontier incident does not cause the London Cabinet any anxiety, and they fully recognize the expediency of our actions.

The question of reforms in Macedonia was specially carefully considered. The animated discussions led to a result which seems a very near approach to a final solution. By this means, England's original proposals have been modified to an extent which, it is to be hoped, will be acceded to by the other Powers, and jointly communicated to the Porte. Now that an agreement with England has been reached, the St. Petersburg Cabinet will work out a detailed scheme of reforms, which should then be discussed by all the States, and made the starting point for a joint step by the Ambassadors in Constantinople.

2. A Russo-Japanese Secret Treaty of July 1912.

Whilst Russian diplomacy in Europe was forming the Balkan League, directed against both Turkey and Austria, it was also intent upon making the Russian troops in the Far East available for the great war, and securing Japan's neutrality. As mentioned on page 140 of the German White Book, *Deutschland schuldig?* a Russo-Japanese secret treaty was concluded on the 8th of July, 1912, which provided that, in case of being involved in a European war, Russia would withdraw her troops from Siberia and Manchuria, leaving only two Army Corps, and that in that event Japan would take over the protection of Russian interests in China. Japan further undertook not to occupy any Russian territory, particularly Vladivostok, while Russia was engaged in a European war. In return, Russia declared that she would not object to Japan's occupying the German colony of Kiau-chau, in case of war.

There can hardly be any doubt that the consent of the London Cabinet to this treaty had been obtained.

INDEX

PRINTED BY UNWIN BROTHERS, LIMITED, LONDON AND WOKING, GREAT BRITAIN